汉语作为外语教学丛书

汉语口语教学

Teaching Chinese as a Second Language: Speaking Acquisition and Instruction

柯传仁 KE Chuanren　黄懿慈 HUANG Yi-Tzu　朱嘉 ZHU Jia　著

图书在版编目(CIP)数据

汉语口语教学 / 柯传仁, 黄懿慈, 朱嘉著. —北京: 北京大学出版社, 2012.10
(汉语作为外语教学丛书)
ISBN 978-7-301-21299-8

Ⅰ. 汉⋯　Ⅱ. ①柯⋯ ②黄⋯ ③朱⋯　Ⅲ. 汉语 – 口语 – 对外汉语教学 – 教学研究
Ⅳ. H195.3

中国版本图书馆CIP数据核字(2012)第227514号

书　　　名:	汉语口语教学
著作责任者:	柯传仁　黄懿慈　朱　嘉　著
责任编辑:	沈　岚
标准书号:	ISBN 978-7-301-21299-8/H·3146
出版发行:	北京大学出版社
地　　　址:	北京市海淀区成府路205号　100871
网　　　址:	http://www.pup.cn
电　　　话:	邮购部 62752015　发行部 62750672　编辑部 62767349　出版部 62754962
电子信箱:	zpup@pup.pku.edu.cn
印　刷　者:	三河市博文印刷厂
经　销　者:	新华书店
	730毫米×980毫米　16开本　15.25印张　250千字
	2012年10月第1版　2012年10月第1次印刷
定　　　价:	80.00元(含2张DVD)

未经许可, 不得以任何方式复制或抄袭本书之部分或全部内容。
版权所有, 侵权必究　举报电话: 010-62752024
电子邮箱: fd@pup.pku.edu.cn

Contents
目 录

Introduction ·· 1
引 言 ··· 3

Chapter One   The University of Iowa Chinese Spoken Language Instruction Model
第一章 爱荷华大学汉语口语教学模式 ·································· 1
  1.1 Chinese SLA Theory and Research
     汉语二语习得理论和研究 ·· 1
  1.2 Cognitive Psychology, SLA, and Psychology of SLA
     认知心理学、第二语言习得和第二语言习得心理学 ············· 5
  1.3 Context, Motivation, and Meaning Making
     语境、学习动机和意义建构 ·· 19
  1.4 Assessment
     评估 ·· 21

Chapter Two   Linguistic Perspective of Speech Acquisition and L2 Chinese Speech Acquisition Studies
第二章 从语言学角度探析汉语二语口语习得 ······················ 24
  2. Mandarin Chinese Prosody
     汉语韵律 ·· 25
  2.1 Lexical Tones
     词汇声调 ·· 25
  2.2 Global Prosodic Phenomena
     总体韵律现象 ·· 28
  2.3 L2 Chinese Pronunciation Acquisition Studies
     汉语二语发音习得研究 ··· 31

Chapter Three Cognitive Psychological Theory and Research
第三章 认知心理学理论与研究 ··· 45
3.1 Processing Approaches
加工理论 ··· 46
3.2 Emergentist/Constructivist Approaches
自然发生论（建构主义理论）····································· 62
3.3 TAP Theory
适当迁移加工理论 ·· 66
3.4 Chaos/Complexity Theory
混沌/复杂理论 ·· 69
3.5 Learner Variables
学习者因素 ··· 74

Chapter Four Language Socialization Theory and Research
第四章 语言社会化理论与研究 ····································· 83
4.1 The Social Turn in the Language Learning Field
语言学习领域的社会化趋势 ······································ 83
4.2 Interface of Theory and Practice on L2 Instruction: TBLI
二语教学理论与实践的交集：任务型语言教学模式 (TBLI) ········ 97

Chapter Five SLA Theory and Research
第五章 第二语言习得理论与研究 ································· 102
5.1 SLA Theory: An Overview
二语习得理论：概论 ·· 102
5.2 Communicative Competence
交际能力 ··· 109
5.3 Classroom-Based Research on L2 Speaking
二语口语的有关课堂研究 ······································ 111

Chapter Six Pedagogical Theories and Research
第六章 教学法理论与研究 ··· 116
6.1 Grammar-Translation Method
语法翻译教学法 ·· 116

6.2 Direct Method
　　直接教学法⋯⋯⋯⋯⋯⋯⋯⋯⋯⋯⋯⋯⋯⋯⋯⋯⋯⋯⋯⋯⋯⋯⋯ 120
6.3 Audiolingual Method
　　听说教学法⋯⋯⋯⋯⋯⋯⋯⋯⋯⋯⋯⋯⋯⋯⋯⋯⋯⋯⋯⋯⋯⋯⋯ 122
6.4 Total Physical Response
　　全身反应法(TPR)⋯⋯⋯⋯⋯⋯⋯⋯⋯⋯⋯⋯⋯⋯⋯⋯⋯⋯⋯⋯ 128
6.5 Communicative Language Teaching
　　交际语言教学法⋯⋯⋯⋯⋯⋯⋯⋯⋯⋯⋯⋯⋯⋯⋯⋯⋯⋯⋯⋯⋯ 133
6.6 Content-Based Instruction
　　内容教学法⋯⋯⋯⋯⋯⋯⋯⋯⋯⋯⋯⋯⋯⋯⋯⋯⋯⋯⋯⋯⋯⋯⋯ 139
6.7 Task-Based Instruction
　　任务教学法⋯⋯⋯⋯⋯⋯⋯⋯⋯⋯⋯⋯⋯⋯⋯⋯⋯⋯⋯⋯⋯⋯⋯ 143

Chapter Seven　CALL Theory and Research
第七章　电脑辅助语言教学理论与研究 ⋯⋯⋯⋯⋯⋯⋯⋯⋯⋯⋯ 148

7.1 The Connections between CALL and SLA
　　电脑辅助语言教学与第二语言习得的相关性 ⋯⋯⋯⋯⋯⋯⋯⋯ 149
7.2 CALL in Pedagogical Application
　　电脑辅助语言教学之教学应用 ⋯⋯⋯⋯⋯⋯⋯⋯⋯⋯⋯⋯⋯⋯ 155
7.3 CALL in Speaking Acquisition
　　CALL 在口语习得上的应用 ⋯⋯⋯⋯⋯⋯⋯⋯⋯⋯⋯⋯⋯⋯⋯ 162

Chapter Eight　ACTFL Speaking Guidelines and National Foreign Language Standards
第八章　全美外语教学委员会口语标准和全美外语教学国家标准 ⋯⋯⋯⋯⋯⋯ 168

8.1 Introduction of ACTFL Speaking Guidelines
　　全美外语教学委员会口语标准介绍 ⋯⋯⋯⋯⋯⋯⋯⋯⋯⋯⋯⋯ 169
8.2 Introduction of National Standards
　　全美外语学习国家标准 ⋯⋯⋯⋯⋯⋯⋯⋯⋯⋯⋯⋯⋯⋯⋯⋯⋯ 180
8.3 Applications to L2 Speaking Teaching and Learning
　　在二语口语教学中的应用 ⋯⋯⋯⋯⋯⋯⋯⋯⋯⋯⋯⋯⋯⋯⋯⋯ 186

Chapter Nine　Common European Framework of Reference for Languages
第九章　欧洲共同语言参考框架 ·················· 189

9.1 Background
背景 ·················· 190

9.2 Common Reference Levels
共同语言能力量表 ·················· 192

9.3 Common Reference Levels: Qualitative Aspects of Spoken Language Use
共同语言量表：口语使用的定性特征 ·················· 199

9.4 Application: How to Use Scales of Descriptors of Language Proficiency
应用：如何使用语言能力量表 ·················· 204

9.5 Application: Language Instruction and Learning
应用：语言教学与学习 ·················· 206

Chapter Ten　Task-Based Language Instruction: Chinese Speaking Class Sample Lessons
第十章　任务型语言教学：汉语口语课堂教学方案 ·················· 211

References　参考文献 ·················· 217

Introduction

Speaking is one of our most complex cognitive, linguistic, motor, and social skills (Levelt, 1989; Bygate, 2009). Many disciplines have contributed theoretical insights and empirical findings on this multifaceted skill. They include linguistics, psycholinguistics, conversational analysis, discourse semantics, pragmatics, phonetics, phonology, vocabulary, syntax, speech communication, and education. Second language (L2) speaking has additional layers of complexity contributed from the speaker's previous linguistic system (L1) and interaction of his/her L1 and L2 at different interlanguage stages as well as other factors, such as age, learning environment, cognitive, and non-cognitive factors (Archibald, 1998; Lantolf, 2000; Doughty & Long, 2003; Mitchell & Myles, 2004; Hinkel, 2005; Robinson & Ellis, 2008; Dőrnyei, 2009; Long & Doughty, 2009).

This book reveals the multifaceted nature of the development of L2 speaking skills. Chapter 1 presents the Iowa Instructional Model of spoken language development, an integrated model that takes into consideration the nonlinear and multifaceted nature of L2 Chinese spoken language development. This chapter also provides theories and research that have direct implications on the formation of the framework of our model development. Chapters 2—9 introduce theories and models that present our curriculum and classroom instruction in a general manner. Specifically, Chapter 2 focuses on the linguistics perspective of speech acquisition and L2 Chinese speech acquisition studies, detailing the unique characteristics of Chinese speech patterns as a tonal language and the trajectories of L2 Chinese speech development. Chapters 3—5 present L2 speaking developments from three complementary perspectives: cognitive psychology, language socialization, and second language acquisition (SLA). From these three chapters, one can get an impression that as language is complex, L2 speaking skill development cannot be totally accounted for by only one perspective, cognitive psychology or socioculture. L2 speaking development is the result of the interaction of multiple systems working on multiple timescales and levels (Larsen-Freeman & Cameron, 2008). While Chapters 3—5 focus on the acquisition perspective, Chapters 6 and 7 address the instructional effects of L2 spoken language development, taking into consideration how different approaches of classroom intervention, either face-to-face or computer-mediated communication instruction, contribute to L2 spoken language development. Chapters 8 and 9 present two theory-based assessment models: the Common European Framework (CEF) and the ACTFL language proficiency and Foreign Language Standards. While our current linguistic, psycholinguistic, and sociolinguistic theories do not provide us with an integrated theory on the construct of spoken language, assessment models such as ACTFL and CEF, while being developed from the perspectives of instructors, can shed light on our understanding of the variables that can influence spoken language performance (Bygate, 2009). Chapter 10 presents two concrete examples exhibiting the implementation of our instructional model in two classes of different instructional levels. The respective teaching DVD and guide for the two classes are provided to present how the instructor from each of the class constructed the lesson based on our instructional model outlined in Chapter 1 of this book.

引 言

口语是人类最复杂的社会认知技能之一。(Levelt, 1989; Bygate, 2009)二语口语,因为说话者的母语语言系统与二语在不同语言发展时期的相互作用以及说话者的年龄、语言学习环境、认知和非认知因素等的共同影响,而呈现出多层面的复杂性。(Archibald, 1998; Lantolf, 2000; Doughty & Long, 2003; Mitchell & Myles, 2004; Hinkel, 2005; Robinson & Ellis, 2008; Dőrnyei, 2009; Long & Doughty, 2009)

这本书第一章概述了美国爱荷华大学汉语口语教学模式。这个模式整合了汉语作为第二语言口语能力发展的非线性和多元性的特点。第一章也综合介绍了对爱荷华大学口语教学模式的设计有直接影响的相关理论和研究。第二章到第九章介绍了对口语课程设置和课堂教学有直接影响的相关理论和框架。具体而言,第二章主要着眼于口语习得的语言学的层面以及汉语二语口语习得的相关研究,并阐述了汉语作为一门声调语言在口语习得上的特殊性以及汉语二语口语的发展轨迹。第三、四、五章从认知心理学、语言社会学和第二语言习得等三个相辅相成的方面具体阐述二语的口语发展轨迹。综合这三章的内容,我们可以看出语言的复杂性,当然二语口语的发展也不能从认知心理学或是社会文化理论的任何一个方面单独解释。二语口语能力的发展是多个系统在不同时期和多个层面长期作用的结果(Larsen-Freeman & Cameron, 2008)。第六章和第七章从前面几章的习得层面过渡到实际的教学影响,阐述了不同课堂教学模式对口语发展的影响,包括传统的面对面模式和电脑辅助的交际教学模式。第八章和第九章介绍了两个以理论为依托的测试模式:欧洲共同语言参考框架(以下简称 CEF)和全美外语教学委员会(以下简称 ACTFL)的语言水平纲领和全美外语学习国家标准。尽管目前语言学、心理语言学和社会语言学的相关理论仍不能提供一个能综合解释口语发展的理论框架,这两个框架都是从教师的角度发展而成的(Bygate, 2009), CEF 和 ACTFL 的评估模式仍有助于我们进一步了解口语能力发展的各个变量。第十章展示了在爱荷华口语教学模式指导下的两个不同年级的教学实例。本书附有具体的教学DVD和教学方案。必须说明的是,这两堂课并非口语课堂教学的标准示范,根据不同的理论指导,口语课堂教学可以有不同的实践方向。这两堂课因课文内容、学生水平以及口语训练目标的差异而有所不同。我们的目的在于通过真实课堂情景的展现,给读者提供讨论的实例,并希望对汉语口语教学的理论与实践有所启发。

Chapter One 第一章
The University of Iowa Chinese Spoken Language Instruction Model
爱荷华大学汉语口语教学模式

The University of Iowa Chinese spoken language instruction model is based on Chinese second language acquisition (SLA) empirical research and draws on work in pedagogy, assessment, and Chinese pedagogical grammar. Some of these theories have more direct influences on our curriculum, while others influence our classroom methodology. The overarching principle of our curriculum and methodology is meaningful practice with consideration of combining a focus on form with the task syllabus, in task-based language teaching. In this chapter, we will present our model within the framework of theories and research in applied linguistics and SLA, which have direct influences on our instructional model. The theories, models, and research that our model has drawn on in a more general way will be introduced and described in Chapters 2-9.

　　爱荷华大学汉语口语教学模式整合了汉语作为第二语言习得的研究发现以及在教学、测试和汉语教学语法方面的相关研究成果。这些理论对我们的课程设置有直接的影响,有些则对具体的课堂教学方法有所指导。我们总的教学原则是有意义的课堂操练,即以语法为中心的课堂教学与任务型语言教学相结合的模式。在本章中,我们将逐一阐述应用语言学和第二语言习得的理论研究如何直接影响我们的教学模式。其他相关的理论、模式和研究会在接下来的章节中介绍和讨论。

1.1 Chinese SLA Theory and Research 汉语二语习得理论和研究

At the curriculum level, our model is based on second language (L2) Chinese empirical studies. Two comprehensive studies are particularly relevant to the development of our speaking model: Ke & Read (1995) and Ke (2005). Ke and Read (1995) investigated the nature of progress that CFL learners made in an intensive program of over 5 years with students from across the U.S.A. The subjects were 222 students from four instructional levels. The Chinese language ability was measured using Oral Proficiency Interview (OPI) and the Chinese Proficiency Test (CPT), a test developed by the Center for Applied Linguistics that measures the skills of listening comprehension, grammar, vocabulary, and reading. The students took the two exams both at the beginning and end of the 9-week intensive study period. One of the major findings of this study was that students from a particular instructional level had different achievements in their Chinese language proficiency. In addition, there were different kinds of profiles within and between different modalities among the learners.

在课程设置方面，我们的口语教学模式主要根据汉语作为第二语言的实证研究。其中两个对我们口语教学模式有决定性影响的综合研究是Ke & Read (1995) 和 Ke (2005)。Ke & Read在1995年的研究中调查了美国一个语言强化项目里的汉语二语学习者五年内的语言发展情况。受试者为来自四个不同汉语水平的222名学生。他们的汉语水平的评估标准为全美外语教学委员会口语能力面试评估（以下简称OPI）和汉语水平考试（以下简称CPT）。CPT考试由美国应用语言学中心研发，主要用于测量学生在听力理解、语法、词汇和阅读方面的能力。学生在为期九周的强化学习中各参加了两次这两种评估测试，一次是在强化项目开始时，一次是在强化项目结束时。这项研究的一个主要发现是某一特定教学水平的学生在汉语语言水平的发展上并不一致。除此以外，学习者本身也呈现出很多不同之处。

The second study (Ke, 2005) that aided in the development of our Chinese spoken language instructional model investigated the patterns manifested by CFL learners in their acquisition of Chinese grammatical features at different stages of study. The subjects were 64 CFL learners at four instructional levels in an intensive program. The Chinese Speaking Test (CST), a tape-mediated standardized oral proficiency test modeling the OPI developed by the Center for Applied Linguistics, was used as the instrument. Nineteen Chinese linguistic features identified from a variety of Chinese grammar books and textbooks used in the U.S.A. were selected for examination in the study. The subjects were sampled twice during the intensive program: once at the beginning of the program and once at the end of the program. Three general patterns were found: 1) A linear progressive pattern suggesting that the mastery of certain linguistic features correlates to the improvement of the subjects' proficiency; 2) A U-shaped pattern showing that the subjects' performance on certain linguistic features decreases after their initial successful learning and increases again as they become more proficient with the language; and 3) A plateau pattern indicating that the learning of certain linguistic features becomes stabilized at a fairly advanced stage of the subjects' interlanguage development.

对我们的教学模式有决定性影响的第二项综合研究(Ke, 2005)调查了以汉语作为外语的学习者在不同学习阶段里汉语语法特点的发展模式。被试者为某一个汉语暑期强化课程中四个不同水平的64名学生。测试工具采用了由美国应用语言学中心以OPI为蓝本研发的录音标准化口语能力测试:汉语口语考试(CST)。研究者从全美当时所使用的语法和教科书中抽取了19项汉语语言点作为测试中考察的依据。被试者在该强化课程中接受两次测试:一次是在课程开始时,一次是在课程结束时。研究发现三个基本的模式:1)一些特定语言点的掌握和学生语言水平的发展存在线性的关联性;2)一些受试者在某些语言点的表现上呈现U型发展模式,意味着学习者从最初的正确表现、历经错误出现与表现的回落,到随着语言水平提高后表现回升的发展模式;3)一些受试者在某些语言点的学习上呈现高原型的发展趋势,体现出他们在语言发展的中介语阶段的相对稳定性的特征。

Taking these two studies together as a whole, one could hypothesize that CFL interlanguage development is not linear and that there are many paths to its development. Learners differ in cognitive and experiential maturity, learning styles, learning aptitudes, and motivation, and are exposed to different learning resources and pedagogical interventions. Interaction between learners' internal factors and learning conditions generates different learning profiles at any time. These two studies support an emergentist perspective of SLA. From an emergentist perspective, the emergence of complexity, fluency, and accuracy can be seen, not as the unfolding of some prearranged plan, but rather as the system adapting to a changing context, in which the language resources of each individual are uniquely transformed through use (Larsen-Freeman & Cameron, 2008; Larsen-Freeman, 2006).

  这两项综合研究的结果显示出汉语作为外语语言发展非线性的假设和其发展多途径化的特点。同时,学习者在认知成熟度、学习风格、学习潜能、学习动机和所接受的学习资源和教学介入上都有不同。这些来自于学习者的内在因素与外在的学习条件相互作用,呈现各个时刻都有所不同的学习特征。这两项研究为二语习得的发展学说理论提供了依据。根据发展学说理论,在习得的过程中我们可以窥见语言发展的复杂性、流畅性与准确性。然而,这些特色的呈现并非依循事先规划的发展轨道,而是通过一个不断适应环境变化的系统,在这个系统中个人的语言资源通过语言的使用得以转化(Larsen-Freeman & Cameron 2008; Larsen-Freeman, 2006)。

These two studies (Ke & Read, 1995; Ke, 2005) have direct implications to our spoken language development model. As different participants follow different routes to Chinese SLA and the rate of changes fluctuate for different participants at different times, our curriculum covers instructional materials in an iterative and spiraling process, revisiting the same topic again and again as well as paying attention to how our learners acquire their L2 Chinese knowledge and develop their L2 Chinese speaking skills as a result of influences between the learner and the learning environment.

  这两项研究(Ke & Read, 1995; Ke, 2005)对我们口语教学模式的设置有直接的影响。因为研究中的学习者依循不同的汉语二语习得轨迹,在不同时期体现出学习的波动变化;而我们的教学模式在教学材料上采用了循环和螺旋式的安排,在不同时期回顾温习相同的话题,并且注重学习者和学习环境之间的相互影响,以及学习者汉语语言知识的掌握与口语技能的提高。

1.2 Cognitive Psychology, SLA, and Psychology of SLA
认知心理学、第二语言习得和第二语言习得心理学

While our spoken language instructional model draws on theories and research on cognitive psychology, SLA, and psychology of SLA in a principled way, some of the theoretical insights from those disciplines are more discerning and carry more weights than the others in our model. A number of theories on language learning are particularly relevant to the development of our speaking model: implicit and explicit learning as well as timing in foreign language instruction.

我们的口语教学模式以认知心理学、第二语言习得和第二语言习得心理学等理论研究成果为依托，而在这些跨学科的理论框架中，有一些对我们的模式也有决定性的影响。本节仅列举两个与我们的教学模式有紧密联系的语言学习理论：隐性和显性学习以及外语教学中的时序性。

1.2.1. Explicit and Implicit Learning
外显和内隐学习

"Explicit" has something to do with consciousness, while "implicit" is associated with unconscious, automatic, or indirect processes. The explicit-implicit contrast has been explained in three different concepts: learning, knowledge, and memory. Explicit knowledge is acquired through explicit learning and is stored in explicit memory, while implicit knowledge is acquired through implicit learning and is stored in implicit memory. In other words, implicit knowledge is knowledge that is not explicit. The outcomes of explicit learning is the construction of explicit, verbalizable, metalinguistic knowledge in the form of symbols (concepts) and rules, specifying relationships between the concepts (Hulstijn, 2002). Instructional treatment is explicit if rule explanation forms a part of the instruction (deduction) or if learners are asked to attend to particular forms and try to find the rules themselves (induction). Conversely, when neither rule presentation nor directions to attend to particular forms are a part of a treatment, then that treatment is considered implicit (DeKeyser, 2003; Norris & Ortega, 2000).

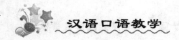

"显性"与意识有关,反之"隐性"则与潜意识、自动性和间接过程有关。有关学者从三方面解释了显性与隐性学习之间的对比:学习、知识和记忆。通过显性学习、认知储存于浅层记忆的知识被称为显性知识。通过隐性学习、认知储存于深层记忆的知识则是隐性知识。换句话说,隐性知识是非显性的知识。通过显性学习,我们创建显性的、可阐述的、以概念和法则形式呈现的语言知识,显性学习也强化了概念之间的关系(Hulstijin, 2002)。如果在教学过程中对语法规则的解释沿用了自上而下的引述性教学,或要求学习者特别关注某些具体的语言形式,并归纳出相关规律的自下而上学习模式,这一类的教学方式归结为显性的教学介入。反之,当自上而下的引介规则或者是自下而上的总结规则在教学过程中并未出现时,我们称其为隐性学习 (DyKeyser, 2003; Norris & Ortega, 2000)。

Much of the discussion on SLA and L2 pedagogy have focused on the place of form-focused instruction in L2 teaching and learning. Most of the SLA researchers agree with what most of the teachers have always believed: There is a role for instruction in L2 learning. However, researchers differ quite substantially on the implementation details of procedures of curriculum design and classroom methodology. That is, they may agree that instruction "works", but they have different views about how it leads to changes in learners' language knowledge and use. The simplest characterization of this is discussed in terms of whether there is an "interface" between what is explicitly taught/learned and changes or development in the interlanguage of the learner. Three positions have been distinguished: 1) No interface; 2) Strong interface; and 3) Weak interface.

许多与二语习得和二语教学相关的讨论都集中在二语教学过程中语言形式的教学。大多数二语习得学者和教师都同意:教学在第二语言学习中发挥一定的作用。然而学者在如何设计课程和课堂教学方法的细节存在很大的分歧。在承认教学的作用的同时,他们可能对教学如何改变和影响语言知识的发展与应用有非常不同的理解。其中的一个分歧在于讨论学习者的中介语发展是否存在一个过渡期。关于这个讨论,学者提出三种不同的立场:1) 没有接合;2) 弱接合;3) 强接合。

No interface: The no interface position claims that acquired knowledge and learned knowledge are stored separately and have separate functions, and that the results of explicit learning can never lead to implicit (acquired) knowledge. According to the no interface position, while instruction can give the learners the impression that their interlanguage has changed, it actually provides the learners with the information that they can use to monitor their language production, leading to changes in observable behavior, but only under certain conditions of attention to form (Krashen, 1985, 1994, 1999). However, even those who hold to the no interface position recognize that some individuals are very skilled at monitoring their behavior very efficiently, giving the impression that the underlying interlanguage structure has changed.

没有接合：持有这一立场的人认为习得的知识和学习的知识分别储存在不同地方，而且功能各不相同。在显性的学习下，隐性知识是不可能生成的。根据这个观点，尽管教学会给学习者一种他们的中介语确有改变的印象，但教学的实际作用仅仅在于告知学习者他们可以掌控自己输出的语言信息，造成行为上语言形式的改变(Krashen, 1985, 1994, 1999)。但持有这个观点的人也承认，某些个别的学习者在掌控他们的语言行为上非常娴熟有效，以至于让人以为其语言背后的中介语的结构确实发生了改变。

Weak interface: R. Ellis (1997), disagreeing with strong interface position (that proposes that explicit knowledge of L2 items can be fully converted into automatized procedural knowledge through practice) and non-interface position (that proposes that learned explicit knowledge can never become implicit procedural knowledge), suggested a weak interface position. Explicit knowledge of L2 items may develop into implicit knowledge of L2 items if learners are developmentally ready to accommodate the new knowledge into their interlanguage systems. Formal practice or natural communication can help to develop explicit knowledge of L2 items into automatized implicit knowledge in communication. This means that instruction can only create conditions that give learners easier access to the patterns that are present in the language, helping them to "notice" information that can help to alter their interlanguage if they are ready-developmentally and motivationally to make that change.

  弱接合：强接合观点的支持者认为显性的二语知识可以通过练习转化为自动化的内隐性知识；没有接合的支持者强调，学习的显性知识永远不可能转换成隐性的内化知识。不同于上述两方的立场，R.Ellis(1997)提出他的弱接合说。根据他的观点，如果学习者已经准备好将新知识融入中介语系统，第二语言的显性知识还是有可能发展成为隐性的二语知识。正规训练或者日常交流都有助于这个转换的过程。这意味着教学只能在一定程度上协助学习者摄取语言中已经存在的规则，帮助他们在发展阶段和学习动机都有所准备的前提下注意到这些信息，并进一步促成知识的转化与改变。

Strong interface: The strong interface position claims that explicit knowledge plays a significant role in developing L2 knowledge and can gradually become implicit through practice. According to Bialystok (1979), explicit knowledge can be transformed into implicit knowledge by "formal practicing", which is either conscious study of the target language or attempts to automatize already-learned explicit knowledge. It is the role of practice to gradually bridge the gap between explicit knowledge and use. Some authors (DeKeyser, 1998; Hulstijin, 1995; McLaughlin, 1978, 1990; Schmidt, 1995) argue that the information provided in form-focused instruction can lead directly to changes in learners' internal representations of the target language. This "strong interface" position is compatible with much of the foreign and L2 teaching that organizes lessons around a particular language feature that is targeted for presentation and practice in mechanical and/or meaningful drills, or in activities that create opportunities to use the feature in highly controlled contexts. Research support for this view includes work under the framework of skill acquisition theory (DeKeyser, 2007a).

  强接合：这一观点的支持者认为显性知识在二语发展的过程中起到了举足轻重的作用，并最终通过练习转化成隐性知识。根据Bialystok(1979)，通过"正式训练"，无论是有意识地学习目的语，或者是不断强化并自动生成已经习得的显性知识，最终将转换为隐性知识。练习弥补了显性知识和语言使用之间的差距。还有一些研究者认为，通过语言形式教学而生成的信息可直接改变学习者内部的目的语表现形式(DeKeyser, 1998; Hulstijin, 1995; McLaughlin, 1978, 1990; Schmidt, 1995)。"强接合"的观点与我们在语言课堂中,设计一个高度控制的情境,通过各种机械性或有意义的操练强化相关语言点有相通之处。与此观点相关的一些研究包括技能习得理论(DeKeyser, 2007a)。

Other researchers discussed the role of instruction with respect to rules of various levels of difficulty within the framework of explicit vs. Implicit learning. DeKeyser (2003) hypothesized that if rules are perceived to be very easy, their instruction would neither be useful nor necessary: For easy rules, instruction may speed up explicit learning process; for moderately difficult rules, instruction may stretch ultimate attainment; for difficult rules, instruction may enhance later implicit acquisition by increasing the chances of noticing; and for very difficult rules, instruction may not be useful and effective. Norris and Ortega (2000), in their review of studies, which investigated the effectiveness of implicit vs.explicit approaches with respect to L2 instruction, showed that explicit grammar explanations, coupled with more communicative activities, are consistently more effective in the instructed L2 setting than solely inductive approaches in which the learners is given no explicit explanation. In general, SLA researchers who adopt a cognitive linguistic perspective tend to emphasize on the benefits of explicit teaching. Learning general linguistic patterns explicitly compensates for the rich input that an L2 learner lacks, by guiding the learners to accurate generalizations (Hudson, 2008; Robinson & Ellis, 2008).

在显性和隐性学习的框架下,许多研究者通过各个角度就教学的作用展开讨论。DeKeyser (2003) 提出,如果规则是明显且容易观察的,教学所能起到的作用微乎其微,甚至没有必要;对于容易的规则,教学可以加速显性学习的过程;对于中等难度的规则,教学可以促进和增加最终的可获取性;对于难度较大的规则,教学可以通过提升学习者的注意力来提升后续的内化习得过程;而对于难度极高的规则,教学不一定有效。Norris & Ortega (2000)在研究中探讨第二语言教学中直接教学和间接教学的有效性,他们发现,结合交际的活动,直接解释语法比间接的教学方式更有效。

总而言之，从认知语言学观点出发的二语习得研究者比较强调直接学习的优势。学习者直接学习语言规则，不但可以弥补二语学习者所缺乏的二语语言输入，而且可以引导学习者准确地归纳相关规则。(Hudson, 2008; Robinson & Ellis, 2008)

Cognitive theories on explicit vs. implicit learning approaches have implications in our CFL spoken language development curriculum. Our speaking curriculum provides learners with plentiful opportunities for L2 exposure in which learners "learn by doing". Our curriculum practices a systematic and balanced concern for accuracy, fluency, and complexity, with consideration of information processing theory. In our practice of combining task-based activities with structural practice, specific procedures on the adoption of explicit, implicit, deductive, or inductive approaches as well as on the length of input and output phase for implementation details of our communicative activities are dictated by the level of complexity of the targeted linguistic items and tasks. For instance, cognitively and semantically more loaded linguistic features and tasks require more sub-steps in the explicit intervention of the input phase, whereas universal or cognitively and semantically less loaded ones can be treated inductively and with shorter input phase. Other factors that influence adjustments of specific procedures of our instructional activities include learners' interlanguage stages, students' learning styles, and individual differences in language learning aptitude.

　　认知理论中关于外显和内隐学习策略的讨论对我们的对外汉语口语发展教学模式深具启发的作用。在提供二语学习者充分接触二语的前提下，我们爱荷华大学中文部的口语教学模式本着让学生在"做中学"的原则，系统地综合考虑了语言准确度、流利度和复杂度之间的平衡。在结合任务型教学活动和有组织地练习过程中，我们也根据目标句型及任务的复杂程度适当地采纳外显型、内隐型，自上而下，自下而上的学习模式，并兼顾交际活动的输出和输入的时间长短。例如，在认知和语义上较为复杂的语言点和任务，我们在语言输入的阶段会要求更多的外显介入；至于那些通用的或者说从认知和语义上都相对简单的例子，应该可以通过自下而上的学习方式处理，同时输入阶段的耗时相对也较短。其他对我们教学模式产生影响的因素包括学生的中介语阶段、学生的学习风格,以及学生语言学习能力的个体差异。

1.2.2. Timing in Foreign Language Instruction
外语教学中的时序性

Timing in foreign language instruction includes both developmental and pedagogical timing. Developmental timing involves the concepts of sequence and processes in language learning. Interlanguage development is systematic, and not random. For many sub-areas of interlanguage development, learners go through several stages motivated by the complex interaction of multiple forces. Those forces include the evidence available or absent in the input and knowledge or interference of previous linguistic system (L1) as well as the interaction between L1 and L2 at different levels of the linguistic system, such as speech, syntax, semantics, and discourse. Other factors that influence interlanguage development include cognitive processing influences (Skehan, 1998; Skehan & Foster, 2001), frequency of exposure (Ellis, 2002), communicative pressures, and social incentives that learners experience as they use the language to make meaning. Ortega (2009) provided a review of studies on sequences of SLA on a number of target languages.

　　外语教学中的时序性既包括语言发展的时序性,也包括教学的时序性。语言发展的时序性涉及语言学习中有关次序性和过程的相关概念。中介语的发展是非常系统的,并非随机无规则的。在中介语的发展中,学习者会经历多种因素相互作用的几个阶段。这些影响的因素包括母语缺乏的知识,也包括在不同阶段母语和二语在句法、口语、语义、话语等语言系统上的相互作用。其他影响中介语发展的因素还包括认知过程的影响(Skehan, 1998; Skehan & Foster, 2001)、语言接触的频率(Ellis, 2002)、交际压力,以及学习者在使用语言创造意义的学习过程中所经历的社交动机。读者可参照Ortega (2009)以了解一系列目的语二语习得过程的研究。

Pedagogical timing involves the sequence of classroom activities. Ortega (2009) proposed five generalizations about the relationship between interlanguage development and instruction, with implications of developmental sequences for L2 and foreign language teaching: 1) Instruction cannot affect the route of L2 development in any fundamental way; 2) Instruction can have some effect on processing, fostering some and inhibiting others; 3) Instruction can be ineffective and even counterproductive when it ignores developmental readiness; 4) Not all sequences present equal challenges for instruction; and 5) Instruction has a major positive effect on the rate of development and level of ultimate attainment.

教学时序性涵盖了课堂活动的各个层面。Ortega (2009)提出了五条准则,探讨中介语发展和第二语言和外语教学的关联性,以及不同教学阶段的启示:1)教学本身并不能从根本上影响第二语言发展的轨迹;2)教学对内化过程有一定影响,促进与阻碍并存;3)忽略发展适时性的教学是无效甚至是有滞后作用的;4)每一个发展过程对教学的要求是不一样的;5)教学对语言发展速度和最终的成果有正面的影响。

A number of SLA researchers (Lightbown, 1993; Ortega, 2009) recommend that we should not plan our L2 curriculum according to known sequences and processes of L2 development, owing to a number of reasons. First, learners are at different levels of L2 proficiency and very few developmental sequences are elaborated in SLA studies. We do not have sufficient descriptions of all the aspects of the grammar of any target language to plan our curriculum according to known developmental sequences. In addition, our knowledge on how different sequences relate to each other in the grammar of individual learners is limited. Second, complexity of language input may contribute to learning. Using known sequences of SLA studies to plan our curriculum may tempt our language teachers to teach language as a collection of discrete items. It must be noted that language learning amounts to much more than the learning of vocabulary, grammar, pragmatics, phonology, etc. Learning an L2 calls for a much more encompassing approach than focusing on bits and pieces of language. Finally, when learners are taught what is "too advanced", they may still benefit from it, acquiring what is developmentally "next", rather than what is directly taught. Given the multifaceted nature of language learning, it would be a challenge to integrate all the knowledge of SLA and L2 pedagogy for the purpose of instructional material development and curriculum development.

很多二语习得研究者(Lightbown, 1993; Ortega, 2009)建议我们不应该依照已知的二语发展过程和程序来设计和规划二语课程。首先,学习者处于二语发展的不同阶段,目前二语习得领域关于语言发展顺序的研究寥寥可数。仅仅依托于已有的发展顺序不足以保证我们能清晰全面地了解任何目的语的语法,甚至进而指导我们的课程设置。除此以外,我们对个别学习者语法的发展顺序了解甚少。其次,语言输入的复杂性可能有助于学习。若单凭二语习得研究得出的已知语言发展顺序来规划课程,语言教师将倾向把语言作为一个个分散的语言点来进行教学。然而,语言的学习远不止于学习语音、词汇、语法、语用等个别方面。学习一门外语需要一个更兼容并包的策略,而不只是专注在语言的单一方面进行孤立式的学习。最后,在传授给学习者所谓的"过于高深"的知识时,学习者仍能从中受益,从而进一步习得比直接教学内容更高一层的知识结构。基于语言学习的多元性,若寄希望于融合二语习得和二语教学领域的所有知识来设计相关的教学材料和课程设置是不现实的。

Discussion of pedagogical timing has been centered on whether form-focused instruction should be integrated within communicative interaction (use language, intervening to instruct or correct within the context of interaction) or be provided in separate lessons (teach first, then practice; or use language, then teach lesson based on observed problems) (for a review on this issue), see Long (2009).

对教学时序性的相关讨论主要集中在:"以语言形式教学为中心的教学模式应该融入交际的互动过程(使用语言、教学介入或者在交流过程中的纠错)",或者是"应该以单独的课型出现(先教,再练习;或者先使用语言交际,再根据所观察到的问题进行相关教学)"(Long, 2009)。

The role of instruction is related to the discussion of pedagogical timing. All theoreticians and practitioners agree that there is a role for instruction. However, they disagree on the nature of the role. What is the role of classroom learning? In addition to the discussion on the interface between explicit and implicit learning, at least two other roles have been identified: to prepare learners to continue learning outside the classroom and to provide learning opportunities that are not available outside the classroom. How does the classroom provide what is not available outside? Communicative interaction? Form-focused instruction? Both? If both, should they be separate? Or, integrated?

教学的作用与教学的时序性息息相关。所有的理论者和实践家都同意教学有其作用。然而,对于教学作用的本质却各执一词。课堂学习的作用到底是什么?除了先前对外显学习和内隐学习阶段的讨论外,目前至少已提出了两个教学的作用:为学生在课外的后续学习做好准备,以及提供课堂外没有的学习机会。那紧接着的一个问题就是"课堂如何提供学习者课外没有的学习机会呢"?是互动性的交流,还是对语法形式的教学呢?也或者是二者兼而有之?如果是后者的话,那它们应该分开还是综合呢?

Whether one hypothesizes a weak interface or a strong interface between what is explicitly taught/learned and the changes or development in the interlanguage of the learner, one must still answer the question of whether form-focused instruction is best provided in lessons or activities that are separate from communicative interaction or in pedagogical behaviors that are integrated within the ongoing communicative activities. One opinion is that form-focused instruction and communicative interaction should be separate in classroom instruction. One researcher who emphasized on the value of separating form focus from ongoing communicative language is VanPatten (2004). He demonstrated that learners have difficulty attending to form and meaning at the same time, and that students cannot pay attention to everything at once. VanPatten posited that instruction is most effective when the demands of ongoing communication are taken away and the learner is not only able, but is required, to focus on one feature and its related meaning at a time. VanPatten developed an approach that he called "processing instruction" for teaching certain language features that learners seem unable to acquire without very pointedly separate instruction.[1]

　　无论教学是否直接影响语言学习者中介语的发展，我们不得不面对的问题是：以语法为中心的教学模式应单独呈现，还是该融入以交际互动为中心的教学过程？其中一派观点认为，语法与交际互动在课堂教学中应该分开进行。这一派观点最具代表性的研究者是 VanPatten (2004)。他指出学习者很难同时兼顾形式和意义，而在教学过程中学生也不可能同时关注形义。VanPatten 提出，在除去交际压力的情况下，针对某个特定的语法形式所进行的教学是最有效的。VanPatten 根据这个观点提出了"输入处理教学"的教学模式，此模式强调对学习者无法轻松习得的一些语言点进行个别的强化教学。

Other researchers and theorists also support separation of form and ongoing communication. Stern (1992) stated that "...communicative activities are an essential component of a language curriculum but there is still a place for a separate analytic language syllabus." Similarly, Higgs and Clifford (1982) posited that "...the premature immersion of a student into an unstructured or 'free' conversational setting **before** certain fundamental linguistic structures are more or less in place is not done without cost."

　　其他研究者和理论家也支持这种形式和交际活动分离的观点。Stern

---

[1]. One of the main principles of processing instruction is to focus on one thing at a time, very deliberately taking the feature out of a communicative setting, so that learners cannot understand the meaning from the context, but are forced to pay attention to the language form itself. Furthermore, processing instruction requires the learner only to understand and not to produce the language feature (in a context that makes guessing a poor strategy). It should be emphasized that VanPatten did not claim that processing instruction is necessary or desirable for teaching all language features, and in recent writings (for a review, see VanPatten (2004)), he has provided guidelines for determining the features that are good candidates for this type of instruction. Furthermore, it is in the context of these guidelines that we could observe that language form, while isolated from the demands of communicative interaction, is not separated from the meaning that they convey. Indeed, processing instruction is proposed only for those features that can be presented in terms of how they influence the meaning.

输入处理教学的主要原则之一就是有一说一，即一次只专注于一个语言点，同时将其在交际语境中的特点完全剥离，这样学习者就不能通过语境来了解语义，而不得不从语言形式本身着手。除此以外，输入处理教学只要求学习者理解而不需要生成相关语言点(在此情景中用猜测的策略是毫无成效的)。需要指出的是，VanPatten 并没有声称输入处理教学是教授所有语言点的一种必不可少或者理想的模式。在他最近的文章中(for a review, see VanPatten (2004))，VanPatten 提出了辨别那些适用输入处理教学模式的语言点的评判标准。由此，我们通过这些评判标准可以观察到那些从交际活动的需求中孤立出来的语言形式并没有与它们所传达的意义相分裂。这也说明，输入处理教学的这种模式仅仅适用于那些与其所传达意义息息相关的语言形式的教学。

(1992)表示,"虽然交际活动是语言课程的根本,但是针对语言点进行特定的强化教学仍有它存在的必要。"同样地,Higgs & Clifford (1982) 提出,"在学生尚未掌握基本语言结构之前,即融入无结构的、或者所谓自由的对话式的教学,必须付出一定程度的代价。"

There are a number of reasons for separation of form and ongoing communicative activities. First, it is consistent with the traditional presentation-and-then- practice pedagogy. It is also in line with the information processing theory that stipulates that humans are limited capacity processors. In addition, there is also a motivational aspect of it, given the perception that there would be no interruption of communicative interaction once the forms have been singled out for treatment first.

此外,基于以下几个原因,这些学者也支持将形式与交际活动分开。第一,这个观点与传统的"先介绍规则,再进行演练"的教学方式相吻合。它也支持信息加工处理理论关于人类只能处理有限信息的假设。当然,这个观点还有一定的心理促进作用,尤其是建立在"只要排除了语言形式上的困难,实际的交际互动就会畅通无阻"的假设前提下。

A different opinion posits that form-focused instruction should be integrated into communicative interaction. Long has perhaps been most explicit in arguing that focus on language form should be fully integrated into ongoing communicative interaction (for a review of Long's argument on this), see Long (2009). The classic example of Long's focus on form is a situation in which students are engaged in completing a task in small groups. As the teacher circulates, she notices that students in several groups are making a particular error. She claps her hands and directs students' attention to the problem in a brief intervention, in which they are told (or reminded) about the correct way of doing what they are currently doing incorrectly. Then, the students return to the task at hand, better equipped with the language that they need to complete the task successfully, using correct language forms.¹

不过,另外一派学者提出了不同的观点,强调以形式为中心的教学应该与交际活动相结合。Long就是持有这种观点的学者中最具代表性的一个(Long, 2009)。而结合形式与交际互动的一个经典范例就是学生在小组中共同完成一项任务的过程。在学生进行小组活动中,教师在巡视时发现某些小组都犯了个具体的错误。她拍手示意大家注意并简单提醒学生正确的形式。接下来,学生继续进行中断的小组活动,使用刚由老师纠正过的正确语言成功完成任务。

In addition to Long's focus on form position stipulated within his interaction hypothesis, there is a new insight from cognitive psychology that also lends theoretical support to the integration position. This is the transfer appropriate processing (TAP) theory. TAP may offer some explanation regarding why integrated form focus might be effective. Research by cognitive psychologists has shown that we are more likely to recall something if we are placed back in the contexts in which we learned it in the first place. This suggests that if we learn something in an isolated lesson on a ba construction, we are most likely to recall it when we take a test, isolating this feature. If we experience learning in a context where the form has relevant meaning in an ongoing communicative interaction, triggered, perhaps, by the co-occurrence of particular words yesterday, last night, etc., then when these contexts (linguistic or situational) occur again, our ability to retrieve the appropriate forms may be enhanced (more explanation on TAP is presented in Chapter 3).

---

1. In some of his writings, Long goes so far as to argue that teachers should provide focus only on those language features that arise naturally in the course of a task or activity in which students are using the second language in meaningful interaction. He distinguished between focus on form and focus on formS-the latter being a pedagogical intervention in which the teacher presents a particular language feature and creates activities in which students can practice using it. Focus on formS is characterized by the isolation of a single language feature outside ongoing activity or the choice of activities for the purpose of practicing particular features.
Long在一些文章中,甚至提出教师应该只关注那些在一项任务或活动过程中自然出现的语言点,学生在此任务或活动过程中用第二语言进行着有意义的交流。他区分了焦点式语言教育和强调以形式为中心的语言教育。后者就是大家所熟悉的一种教学干预,即教师介绍一个特别的语言点并创造不同活动使学生得以练习使用该语言点。这种聚焦于形式的语言教育的特点就是把一个语言点从大的语境中抽离出来或者说是为了练习特定的语言点而挑选特定的活动。

除了 Long 在他的交流/互动假说中强调交际与形式结合观点以外，认知心理学领域也从另一角度对结合说提供了理论支持。其中最著名的就是适当迁移加工理论(TAP)。适当迁移加工理论也为结合式观点的成效提供了解释。根据认知心理学家的研究证明，若我们能重现学习的情境，我们更有可能回想起所学的知识。换而言之，若我们在某一篇课文中学到了"把"字句结构，我们有可能在考试中针对这一结构的题目回忆起这个结构。如果我们是在进行的交流互动中学习某种语言形式，当这些情景（语言的或者是情境的）再度出现，我们重现这个语言形式的能力将大大增加。本书第三章对适当迁移加工理论有较详尽的讨论。

Both the separation and integration positions are plausible in explaining certain processing patterns for certain linguistic phenomena. It is important to note that not all components of a linguistic system are created equally. Some features may be treated separately, while others integrally. It would be more efficient to treat cognitively, syntactically, and semantically heavily loaded linguistic and pragmatic features separately to remove multiple demands on attention, before providing comprehensible input and meaningful interaction. Features included in this category are those that are rare or absent in classroom interaction, those that are difficult to perceive in normal speech (and even in normal text), or similar to L1 patterns; therefore, errors may be confirmed in peer-peer interaction. Pronunciation practice, such as tone, combination of tones, rhythm, and intonation is another item of separation, because separation would provide explicit guidance for articulation, phrasing, and intonation.

当然无论是分离说还是结合说都在某个程度上解释了部分的语言加工模式。我们必须留意，语言系统中的各个成分的重要性并不相同。有些语言要点可以单独处理，但另一些就需要综合考虑。举例而言，把一些在认知、句法和语义上都很复杂的语言或语用点适合分开处理，以求在提供可理解性输入和有意义的互动之前解除注意力的负担。这些语言点涵盖了那些在课堂互动中几乎不会出现，或是在正常话语中很难关注到，或者是和母语形式接近，因而在学生彼此交流时普遍出错的语言点。语音练习中的声调、声调结合、韵律和语调也可作为另一个适合分离学习的例子。

因为单独加强学习可以直接而有效地对发音、分段以及语调造成影响。

Integration may be most valuable for consolidating knowledge (knowing how to use a feature in context), finding relationships among features (dealing with complexity; e.g., aspect markers, zero pronouns, etc., within a discourse context), and developing fluency/automaticity.

　　反之,结合形式与交际在整合知识层面(例如:如何在语境中使用某一语言点)、发现语言点间的关系(针对语言的复杂性,比如:时态助词、零冠词等等以及语言点在谈话语境中的关系和作用),以及语言发展的流利度和自动性方面都非常有效。

1.3 Context, Motivation, and Meaning Making　语境、学习动机和意义建构

Humans are social beings and, therefore, no learning is independent of environmental influences. Language acquisition cannot be separated from the social arena in which it takes place (Ellis & Larsen-Freeman, 2006). Dynamic systems theory takes a socially grounded approach in which neither the internal development of the organism nor the impact of the environment is given priority in explaining behavior and its change. According to Larsen-Freeman and Cameron (2008), context is a part of the system and its complexity, which means that the internal faculties of the agent (i.e., learner) and the various aspects of the environment are all contributors to the complex system of forces that make up the lifespan of SLA. This dynamic perspective allows us to simultaneously consider the ongoing multiple influences between environmental and learner factors as well as the emerging changes in both the learner and the environment as a result of development. Our Chinese program pays attention to emotions, interests, and L2 proficiency of our learners because these factors have been shown to have a powerful impact on learning behavior and outcomes.

　　人类是社会性的动物,因此学习并非孤立于环境影响而单独存在的。语言习得当然更不能脱离其发生的社会范畴。基于社会学的观点,动态系统理论认为在解释生物的行为和变化上,内在发展或者是外在环境的影响

并没有先后之分(Ellis & Larsen-Freeman, 2006)。根据 Larsen-Freeman & Cameron (2008)的最新理论,语境是系统的一部分,无论是身处其中的施事者(即:学习者)还是环境本身的各个方面,都是这个复杂系统中的一部分,共同建构了二语习得的过程。这个动态的观念使我们得以同时考虑环境和学习者之间的相互影响以及在发展过程中的一连串改变。爱荷华大学中文部非常强调学习者的情绪、学习兴趣和他们的二语水平,因为这些因素对整个语言学习的行为与效果造成极大的影响。

Our program promotes the development of functional language ability through learner participation in communicative events. In consideration of language proficiency development and learners' need, our program has used the ACTFL (American Council on the Teaching of Foreign Languages) Proficiency Guidelines (1999) as the curriculum organizing principle. By making the curriculum relevant to the learners, we are more likely to foster optimum motivational conditions for continued engagement in language learning (Ushioda, 1997; Dőrnyei, 2001).

根据爱荷华的口语教学模式,学习者通过积极参与交际活动,从而提升他们运用语言的能力。在考虑学习者具体需要和语言能力发展的情况下,爱荷华的口语教学模式采用了美国外语教育协会(ACTFL)的语言水平纲领(1999)作为我们的课程设置准则。我们希望将课程大纲与学生的具体需要紧密结合,从而在最优质的语言学习环境中激励学生继续学习汉语(Ushioda, 1997; Dőrnyei, 2001)。

Meaningful interactive practice is a major characteristic in our efforts to engage our learners in communication to allow them to develop their communicative competence. Ortega (2007) argued that interactive practice among peers should play an important role in formal L2 instruction. She claimed that "...optimal L2 practice in the foreign language classroom should be interactive, truly meaningful, and with a built-in focus on selective aspects of the language code that are integral to the very nature of that practice." Interactive practice in pair or group allows students to talk more and negotiate for meaning more often, and affords better opportunities for the expression of a wider variety of meanings and functions (Robinson, 2001). Meaningful practice is also optimal for motivation because students are more willing to invest in the task and take risks (Dőrnyei, 2001). Detailed information about language socialization theory and research is presented in Chapter 4 of this book.

通过有意义的互动练习,我们吸引学习者参与语言交际活动,从而提高他们的交际能力。Ortega (2007) 认为,学习者间的互动练习在正规的二语教学中起重要作用。她指出,"在外语课堂上的优化二语练习应该是互动的、有意义的,同时练习本身应该与所练习的语法点紧密相连。"两人一组或以小组形式进行的互动练习让学生有更多交际和投入语义协商的机会,也使学生能在不同的情境下广泛地使用某个特定的语言表达形式 (Robinson, 2001)。有意义的练习同时也能成为学生学习的动力,在学生更愿意投入任务的同时,他们也更愿意冒险尝试 (Dőrnyei, 2001)。关于语言社会化的相关理论和研究将在本书第四章作更深入的探讨。

1.4 Assessment 评估

Assessment plays a number of important roles in L2 instruction. At the theoretical level, assessment models could complement our lack of understanding on spoken language development (Bygate, 2009). We have limited knowledge on how learners develop their L2 spoken language. In other words, we have limited knowledge on what L2 speaking involves, how less proficient speakers become more proficient, or what learning tasks are relevant for developing learners' proficiency. Assessment models, such as the Common European Framework of Reference (CEFR) and the ACTFL OPI[1], could be used to organize the language curriculum. While our spoken language curriculum is content-based and

---

1. Both the Common European Framework of Reference and the American Council on the Teaching of Foreign Languages Oral Proficiency Interview were developed by testers, and are elaborated through teachers or teacher-tester informants. While some criticize these scales for lack of validity, others argue that despite all their inadequacies, the scales do seem to resonate with and contribute to teachers' intuitions about the nature of language development (see Bygate (2009) for a discussion on this).
欧洲共同语言参考框架和全美外语教学委员会口语能力面试评估两项评估框架都是由测试者创建,并由教师和教师测试者详细阐述。虽然仍有人批评这些框架量表缺乏效度,但其他人则指出尽管它们还存在不足之处,但这些框架中的量表确实是反映了语言发展的本质,同时也促进了各教师院校语言教学的发展。

culture-integral, in the areas of accuracy, fluency, complexity, and text types, we have used the ACTFL Proficiency Guidelines as our organizing principles for the development of our curriculum objectives. Details of the descriptors of the ACTFL proficiency scales are provided in Chapter 8 of this book.

评估在二语教学中举足轻重。理论上,评估框架可以补充我们口语发展的知识的不足(Bygate, 2009)。换言之,我们对于学习者的二语口语习得发展了解非常有限。相关的评估框架,像是欧洲共同语言参考框架(CEFR)和全美外语教学委员会口语能力面试评估(OPI),都可以用于语言课程的组织规划。从语言的准确度、流利度、复杂度,以及文本类型各个方面,爱荷华大学的口语教学模式以内容为基础并融合文化的特点,同时采用ACTFL的语言水平纲领作为设计课程目标的指导准则。本书第八章将更详细介绍ACTFL的相关水平条例。

At the curriculum level, assessment could be used to evaluate whether the students have achieved the learning goals as stipulated in the curriculum objectives. In our Chinese program, formative and summative assessments are integrated (Ke, 2006). Formative assessment is essentially feedback, both to the teacher and the learners about the learners' present understanding and skill development to determine the way forward. Summative assessment describes learning achieved at a certain time for the purpose of reporting to stake holders, such as parents and administrators in summative form. At Iowa, our formative assessment tests tend to be criterion-referenced, and are designed to assess how much of the content of the course or program is being learned, and thereby provide links to the course objectives and program goals (Ke, 2006). Other features of our formative language testing include: 1) Componential and analytic scoring; 2) Skills integration; and 3) Derivation from classroom activities (Ke, 2006).

在课程设置上,评估框架可以用于评估学生是否已经达到课程设置中的学习目标。爱荷华大学的中文部交替使用形成性评估和总结性评估(Ke, 2006)。与教师和学习者都有直接的联系,形成性评估主要体现在反馈上,通过对学生当前学习水平和技能发展的评估引导教学的下一步。总结性评估则是描述学习者在一定时期内的综合学习成果,以求向父母或相关行政人员等利益群体汇报。在爱荷华大学,我们的形成性评估测试倾向于参照标准测试,也就是我们的评估标准侧重于中文部开设课程中的内容,在相关课程目标与中文部的总体发展目标间建立联系(Ke, 2006)。其他形成性语言测试的特点包括:1) 成分与分析测试;2) 技能整合;3) 从课堂活动衍生(Ke, 2006)。

Chapter Two　第二章
Linguistic Perspective of Speech Acquisition and
L2 Chinese Speech Acquisition Studies
从语言学角度探析汉语二语口语习得

Focusing on the linguistics perspective of speech acquisition, this chapter discusses the major L2 Chinese speech acquisition studies by detailing the unique characteristics of Chinese speech patterns as a tonal language and the trajectories of second language (L2) Chinese speech development.

　　本章将从语言学的角度出发，进一步探讨与对外汉语口语习得相关的主要研究，特别是就汉语作为一个声调语言的特色，以及对外汉语口语发展的轨迹进行讨论。

The phonology of Mandarin Chinese consists of both segmental and suprasegmental features. The segmental part includes both initials and finals. As the overwhelming majority of L2 Chinese pronunciation studies are on the suprasegmentals (Ke & Li, 2011), we will not cover the linguistic characteristics of Mandarin initials and finals in this book. Readers who are interested in those features, can refer to the works of Norman (1998) and Duanmu (2000).

　　汉语的语音学包括了音段音位和超音段音位(传统上称"节律")的特征。音段音位包括元音与辅音。超音段音位是除元音、辅音等音色特征以外，包括音高、音强、音长和其相互关系的一切特征。它在语音学中以声调、语调、重音等形式呈现。超切分音位在交际活动中可发生不同形式的变化，使话语呈现不同的韵律特征。由于大多数的汉语二语语音研究都是与超音段音位有关(Ke & Li, 2011)，我们在本书中将不探讨汉语元音和辅音的语言学特征，相关讨论请参考 Norman (1998) 和 Duanmu (2000)。

2. Mandarin Chinese Prosody　汉语韵律

Perhaps, the most challenging feature of learning to speak Chinese as a second language at the speech level is the mastery of its prosodic patterns. At the local or lexical level, Chinese prosodic pattern is realized by tones; and at the non-lexical or global level, it is realized by intonation or rhythm.

　　对于汉语二语学习者而言，口语习得最大的难点也许就在掌握汉语的韵律结构。在最基础的词汇阶段，汉语的韵律结构是以声调来体现；而在词汇以外，在句子和段落的层次，汉语的韵律结构通过语调和节奏体现。

2.1 Lexical Tones　词汇声调

2.1.1. Lexically specified Tones
　　　声调：认字辨意

Chinese is a tonal language. Three terms are used when one discusses a tonal language: fundamental frequency (F0), pitch, and tone. F0 is a phonetic or acoustic term referring to the signal itself: How many pulses per second does the signal contain. Pitch is a perceptual term referring to the hearer's perception of that signal: Is it heard as high in pitch or low in pitch? Tone is a linguistic term referring to a phonological category that is linguistically significant. In modern Chinese, tone contributes to the formation of phonemes at the syllable level. This means that the pitch contour associated with a syllable can distinguish lexical meaning. Mandarin Chinese has four phonemically contrasted lexical tones, which are often referred to as Tone 1 through Tone 4. The Chinese language's use of tone is complex. The four tonal shapes can be described to be distributed across 1-5 registers, with "1" being the lowest pitch value and "5" being the highest value (Chao, 1969). Figure 2.1 provides a visual description of the distribution of the four tones on the five registers. These registers are not fixed according to F0, but vary according to the normal voice range of individual speakers. While the tone of a morpheme in isolation can be constant, the actual manifestation of tones in context varies according to the tones that precede and follow them as well as the syntax, semantics, and pragmatics at the phrase or sentence levels (Liberman & Pierrehumbert, 1984; Peng, et al., 2005).

汉语的最突出的一个特色就在于声调。讨论声调语言,会提到声音的基本音频(F0)、音高以及声调。基本音频(基频,F0)是一个语音标志,表示每一秒钟的振动频率,决定语音音调的高低。音高与知觉相关,强调听者对这个语音信息的感知:这个语音的音高是高,还是低?声调则是一个语言学名词,表示在语音上的某一个重要类别。在现代汉语中,声调表示一个音节发音高低升降的变化,并具有区别意义的作用。汉语普通话有四个基本声调,分别称为第一声、第二声、第三声和第四声。然而,汉语声调的使用十分复杂,根据赵元任在1969年发表的"五度标记法",通过一条竖线划分的四格五度来表示音调的相对音高,一是最低,而五是最高的音高。并在竖线的左侧画一条短线或一点,表示音高升降变化的形式。这些调值并非以基本音频为基础而固定不变的。这些调值会根据个别说话者正常音域范围的不同而有所差异。

虽然某语素的声调在单独发音时是固定不变的,但是在不同的语境中,声调会随着前后语音、或是词组与子层次的句法、语义和语用有所不同(Liberman & Pierrehumbert, 1984; Peng, et al., 2005)。

Figure 2.1: Tone distribution on the five registers
图 2.1 五度标记法

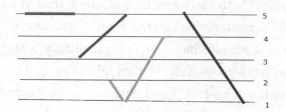

2.1.2. Tone Sandhi
变调

Tone sandhi is another important feature in Mandarin Chinese lexical tone realization. For instance, Tone 3 can be realized in three different F0 contours according to its adjacent tone. When it precedes another Tone 3, it is realized as

Tone 2 ("23"). When Tone 3 precedes Tone 1, Tone 2, and Tone 4, it is realized as a low-falling tone ("21"). Furthermore, when it is at the final position of a prosodic unit, it is realized in its citation tone (Tone 3) value, namely low-dipping shape ("214").

发音时每个音节的声调相互影响,或多或少发生变化,而不能保持原来的调值,称为变调。变调是汉语通过声调辨析词汇的另一个重要特色。例如,根据相邻语音的不同,第三声可以呈现出三种不同的基频曲线。当两个三声连读时,前面的三声的发音转为二声型("23")。当第三声与一声、二声或是四声连读时,发音为半三声("21"),只读原来第三声的前一半降调。而当三声位于词语、句子的末尾时,则读为原调("214")。

2.1.3. Neutral Tone
轻声

Neutral tone is another characteristic of Mandarin Chinese prosody. A number of particles, such as the perfective aspect marker le and bound morphemes such as zi in zhuozi (table), are unspecified for tone and become "neutral tone". Distributions of neutral tones are primarily from two linguistic considerations: syntax and word formation. Examples of syntactic consideration include the following:

轻声是汉语音律的另一个特色,在词语或句子中,有的字会失去原有的声调而被读得又轻又短,这种必须在词语和句子中体现而不能独立存在的语音现象,就是轻声。许多语助词,包括完成体标记"了"以及黏着语素"桌子"的"子",都没有被标上声调而读成"轻声"。轻声的出现基于两个语言学上的考量:句法以及构词。因句法上的考量而读成轻声的例子如下:

- Verb duplications indicating trial: 试试、尝尝、看看、走走
- Directional complements: 进来、出去、上来、下去
- Post-position indicating location: 桌上、楼下、屋里、窗外
- Resultative complements: 气坏、吃掉、听到
- Pluralization suffix: 同学们
- Sentence-final particles: 多美啊、出事了、对的、行吗、回家吧

- Adjectival or adverbial markers: 鲜红的（玫瑰）、认真地（研究）、高兴地（跳起来）
- Aspect markers: 躺着（看书）、吃了（午饭）、去过（那里）
- 动词重叠以表示尝试：试试、尝尝、看看、走走
- 趋向补语：进来、出去、上来、下去
- 表示位置的后位字：桌上、楼下、屋里、窗外
- 结果补语：气坏、吃掉、听到
- 复数后缀词：同学们
- 句尾语气助词：多美啊、出事了、对的、行吗、回家吧
- 形容词或副词标志：鲜红的（玫瑰）、认真地（研究）、高兴地（跳起来）
- 时态标志：躺着（看书）、吃了（午饭）、去过（那里）

Examples of word formation for the distribution of neutral tones include the following:
因构词而形成的轻声，包括以下几个例子：

- Duplication: 妈妈、叔叔、哥哥、星星、宝宝、猩猩
- Second syllable in bound disyllabic words: 玻璃、萝卜、玫瑰、牡丹、琵琶、葫芦
- Second syllable of certain commonly used disyllabic words: 明白、事情、工夫、告诉、姑娘、耳朵
- Noun suffix: 桌子、盖子、石头、尾巴
- 叠字：妈妈、叔叔、哥哥、星星、宝宝、猩猩
- 黏着双音节词中的第二个音节：玻璃、萝卜、玫瑰、牡丹、琵琶、葫芦
- 某些常用双音节词的第二个音节：明白、事情、工夫、告诉、姑娘、耳朵
- 名词或代词后缀：桌子、盖子、石头、尾巴、什么

2.2 Global Prosodic Phenomena　总体韵律现象

2.2.1. Word/Phrase/Sentence-level Stress
字/词/句层次的重音

In Mandarin Chinese, at the word level, stress can be realized in the contrast between full-loaded morphemes (syllables) and neutral-toned morphemes. That is, a full-loaded syllable receives stress, while the neutral-tone syllable does not. At the word level, combination of stressed and unstressed syllables forms a part of the rhythm pattern of Mandarin (Ke, 1992). It is very common for the second syllable in a lexicalized disyllabic word to become unstressed in Beijing Mandarin Chinese (Chao, 1969). In addition, whether the second syllable is stressed or unstressed can be linguistically significant for certain disyllabic words, such as dōngxi (thing) and dōngxī (east-west). Word/phrase-level tone and intonation variations could also be the outcomes of interface between phonology, syntax, and pragmatics (Ford & Thompson, 1996；冯胜利, 1997).

汉语在字的层次，重音可以通过完全语素(音节)与轻声音节的对比来体现。即完全音节在发音上发重音，而非轻声的音节。在字的层次，重音音节与非重音音节结合，构成了汉语音韵规律的一部分(Ke, 1992)。在北京话里，双音节的字词里第二个音节不发重音是十分常见的(Chao, 1969)。此外，第二音节是否发重音对某些双音节的词而言十分重要。例如，东西的"西"读轻声时表示一个物件，而在发一声时则代表了方位词中的西方。在字词层次，声调与语调上抑扬顿挫的变化都有可能是语音、句法以及语用相互作用所产生的结果(Ford & Thompson, 1996; 冯胜利, 1997)。

At the phrase or sentence levels, certain syllables, such as particles de (的、地、得), zhe (着) and le (了), post-position words de shihou (的时候) and limian (里面), and conjunction he (和) are unstressed. Similar to English, unstressed syllables in Beijing Mandarin are produced with reduced duration. Furthermore, similar to the combination of stressed and unstressed syllables in disyllabic words in Beijing Mandarin, the intermediate unstressed syllables inserted between neighboring stressed syllables in a phrase or sentence creates a rhythmic pattern in Beijing Mandarin Chinese (王洪君, 2008).

在词组或是句子的层次，某些音节，像动态助词"的、地、得、着、了"，以及位于后位的附加词"的时候"、"里面"，与连词"和"均非重音。如同英语，汉语中的双音节词不加重音的音节都比较短。就像北京话里重音与非

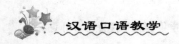

重音音节组成的双音节词,非重音的音节被插入词组或句子中,与发重音的音节相邻,进而形成了汉语声韵的规律。(王洪君,2008)

2.2.2. Declination and Final Lowering at the Sentence Level
　　句子层次的弱化与句末降调

Declination refers to the phenomenon in which the F0 range in a phrase or sentence becomes lower at the end than at the beginning. In Beijing Mandarin, the rate of declination is faster at the beginning and slows down as the sentence continues. The overall declination and final lowering of the global pitch range throughout the utterance in Beijing Mandarin, however, does not involve substantial changes in the lexically determined pitch contours within an utterance. In other words, the pitch variations that realize the lexical tones are preserved under the overall sentential F0 declination (沈炯, 1985).

　　弱化指在一个句子中基本音频的范围在句末变得比句首低的现象。在北京话中,句子开始时弱化的速度较快,而随着句子的延续,弱化的速度变慢了。全句弱化以及句末音高下降在北京话中十分明显,不过,并不包含在话语中受词汇影响而在音高升降曲线上的转变。换句话说,在全句音频弱化之下,仍然保留了通过音高的不同来体现词汇的声调(沈炯,1985)。

2.2.3. Pitch Range of Statements Verse Questions
　　陈述句与疑问句的音高范围

While there is an overall declination and final lowering of F0 pitch range in a Beijing Mandarin utterance, questions and statements could be distinguished by the global pitch range throughout the utterance. For instance, yes/no questions are produced in an overall higher pitch range than statements (Shen, 1990). Other researchers also found that the pitch range becomes narrower in questions than in statement, because the base line in questions is also raised (沈炯, 1985).

　　虽然在北京话中,呈现全句弱化以及句末音高下降的现象,但是仍可通过话语中整体音高的范围了解疑问句和陈述句的区别。例如,是非疑问句的音高高于陈述句(Shen, 1990)。在其他的研究中也发现,由于疑问句的音高调值上升的关系,疑问句的音高范围比陈述句窄(沈炯,1985)。

Overall, the rhythmic structure of Mandarin Chinese includes three layers: prosodic word, prosodic phrase, and intonation phrase. Each of them is characterized by an interaction between physiological and linguistic influences. Rhythm, duration, and intonation are universal phenomenathat commonly exist in different languages, but their manifestation is language specific (Cao, 2003).

大体而言,汉语韵律结构包含了三个层次:字的韵律、词组韵律以及词组语调。每一个层次均受到语言学与生理学的交互影响。韵律、音长以及音调在不同语言中普遍存在,然而在不同语言里呈现的方式却有所不同(Cao, 2003)。

2.3 L2 Chinese Pronunciation Acquisition Studies[1]　汉语二语发音习得研究

2.3.1. L2 Chinese Tonal Acquisition Studies
汉语二语声调习得研究

Learning to perceive and produce tones of Chinese is difficult for L2 learners, particularly for those of a non-tonal language background. According to McGinnis (1997), "There is nothing secondary about tone in Chinese, yet to most learners of Chinese as a second language, the suprasegmental feature of lexical tone is so far removed from their native language experience as to render the mastery of tones problematic, neglected, or both" (p. 228).

汉语的声调是二语学习者的一大难点。对于那些母语非声调语言的学习者来说,分辨声调的不同以及准确发音简直难如登天。McGinnis(1997)曾提到,"在汉语里没有比声调更重要的了,对大多数汉语二语学习者而言,汉语词汇声调的超音段音位特征并无法从母语中习得,因此他们多半认为汉语的声调是无法有效掌握的难点,甚至可略之不顾。"(p. 228)

---

1. A major part of this section is from Ke & Li (2011).

The first published study related to CFL tonal acquisition was carried out by Chen (1974). The purpose of this study was to investigate the overall pitch range of English speakers when speaking their native language and when speaking Chinese as a second language, and of Chinese speakers when speaking Chinese. In this study, four Midwestern Americans read two versions of a conversation, one in English and one in Chinese. Four native Chinese speakers read the same conversation text in Chinese, and the acoustical range of each speaker was analyzed and the Hertz ranges were normalized to find comparable measures of pitch range. Chen found that the pitch range of a native Chinese speaker speaking Chinese was 154% wider than that of a native Midwestern English speaker speaking English. The Americans were observed to widen their normal pitch range by 62% when speaking Chinese, but they had to widen this range by 55% again to match a native Chinese speaker's pitch range.

陈广才于1974年发表第一个与汉语二语声调习得相关的研究。这个研究旨在探究英语为母语的学习者在说英语以及说汉语时音高的调值,并与汉语为母语者在说汉语时的音高调值做比较。研究中,四个来自美国中西部的被试者分别朗读中文与英文版本的一篇对话。另外四个母语为汉语的被试者则读同一篇中文版的对话。陈广才分析每一个被试者的声学测距,并通过常态化他们的赫兹听觉范围来寻找相应的音高范围计量单位。陈广才发现,中文为母语者的音高范围比美国中西部英语为母语的被试者宽,差距高达154%。这些美国的被试者在说中文的时候,他们的音高范围比说英语时宽了62%。不过,若要达到与汉语为母语者相等的音高范围,他们仍需再拓展55%的音高。

Subsequent studies on tonal acquisition focused on tonal perception and tonal production. Miracle (1989) investigated tone production of 10 American students who had studied Chinese for at least 1year. In contrast to Chen's (1974) findings, Miracle found the students' overall pitch range to be comparable with native Chinese speakers who read the same sentences. Of the 408 possible tokens, the learners made 175 errors, with an error rate of 42.9%. The distribution of errors among the tones was not significant. Most of the errors within each tone were equally register and contour errors.

之后声调习得的研究将重心放在声调的感知以及输出。Miracle (1989)以十名学习汉语至少一年的美国学生为对象,研究他们的声调发音表现。不同于陈广才(Chen, 1974)的研究,Miracle发现,当汉语为母语者读相同句子时,这些美国学生的整体音高范围与汉语为母语者十分相近。在408个标记中,这些学生犯了175个错误,失误率达42.9%。多数声调的错误和调域以及调型曲线有关。

Shen (1990) studied the tonal production errors of eight Americans, each with 4 month's experience studying Chinese. The learners read a familiar lesson from a textbook, written in pinyin. In contrast to Miracle's (1989) results, Shen found that most of the errors that these learners made were related to tonal register, rather than tonal contour. Of the 360 errors, 320 were related to register. Shen also observed that the students fell into two significantly different ability levels regarding tone production. For the higher ability group, there was no significant difference in the error rate between the four tones; however, the lower ability group made significantly more errors on Tones 4 (56%) and 1 (17%) than on the other tones (9% of errors for Tones 2 and 3 as well as the neutral tone). All the errors related to Tones 1 and 4 were errors of register, while all those related to Tone 3 were contour errors. Furthermore, most of the errors related to Tone 2 were errors of register. Shen theorized that this confusion results from the interference from the use of stressed syllables in English language.

沈晓楠在1990年发表的研究中分析八名美国学生的声调输出错误,每个学生学习汉语的时间为四个月。这些学生被要求读一篇熟悉的课文,而课文是以拼音的方式呈现。不同于Miracle (1989)的研究,沈晓楠根据其研究结果,指出学生犯的声调错误,大多数与声调调域而非声调调型曲线有关。在360个错误中,320个和调域有关。沈晓楠更发现学生在声调输出上,可依照他们的能力分为两类。能力较佳的一组,在四个声调的出错率上没有显著的差异。不过,能力较差的一组,在四声(56%)和一声(17%)上的出错率明显高过其他声调(二声、三声和轻声的出错率皆为9%)。所有与一声和四声相关的错误均和调域错误有关,与三声有关的错误则是起

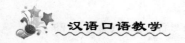

因于调型。至于和二声有关的错误也是与调域有关。沈晓楠把这个结果归因于英语当中重音音节发音的干扰。

McGinnis (1997) investigated students' errors in tonal perception. The learner's tonal perception was tested for single Chinese syllables, two-syllable groups, and three-syllable groups. The results showed that in perceiving tones, American students at the beginner's stage of learning Chinese most often got confused with Tones 2 and 4 as well as Tones 1 and 2.

　　McGinnis (1997)研究学生在声调感知上所犯的错误,测试学生在单音节、双音节以及三音节词汇的声调感知能力。结果显示在声调的感知上,初级的美国中文学习者多半无法正确分辨二声与四声、一声与二声的区别。

McGinnis (1997) also investigated the relative learning effects of the use of two often-used romanization systems, gwoyeuromatzyh (GR) and hanyu pinyin (PY). The results of the study showed that while the GR students had tonal error rates of about 14% at the midpoints of both their first and second semesters of the Chinese study, the students who had learned the PY romanization system improved from 13% errors to 12% from the first to second semester of the study. There was a significant difference observed between the two second-semester errors rates. While McGinnis was careful to state that the teaching technique is a more significant factor in student's success than romanization system, he suggested that if the complexity of GR, when compared with PY, is greater, then the effort and time required for students to learn it will be more, and the lack of learning improvement the use of GR engenders makes PY the better choice of romanization system.

　　McGinnis (1997)更分析使用国语罗马字(GR)以及汉语拼音(PY)等两种常用罗马字系统的学习效果。研究结果显示,使用国语罗马字(GR)的学生在学汉语的第一个与第二个学期中的声调出错率皆为14%,而使用汉语拼音的学生第一个学期到第二个学期之间,他们的声调出错率则从13%降为12%。两组学生在第二学期里的声调出错率呈现显著差异。虽然

McGinnis 很谨慎地表示，教学技巧比罗马字系统来得重要，但他同时也建议，因国语罗马字比汉语拼音更为复杂，学生必须花费更多的时间与心力来学习这套系统。因使用国语罗马字的学习进步幅度有限，更显得拼音是一个比较好的选择。

Chen (1997) investigated both students' tonal perception and production. All the six participants in his investigation had studied Chinese at the university level for more than 1 year, and had varying levels of informal Chinese language experience. In a test of tonal perception, the students tended to confuse Tones 2 and 3 as well as Tones 1 and 4. In a test of tonal production based on natural speech samples, Chen and another rater agreed on 35 tonal errors. According to Chen's analysis, only 12 of these errors were recognizable as other Chinese tones mistakenly used; the other two-third of the production errors were mid-range level tones, which do not exist in Chinese. Subsequently, Chen analyzed the speech samples on the basis of meaningful phrases of four or five syllables, rather than single syllables. At this level of analysis, the tonal patterns that the students produced were recognizable as patterns of English phrase-level intonation, in which various mid-range level tones are employed. Finally, although the tonal patterns in all the students' speech samples at some point reached the two extreme pitch levels in the scale used to depict the normal pitch range of the Chinese speakers, the students' tendency to use English intonation patterns (mid-range level tones) significantly reduced their opportunity to extend their range to a full five registers.

陈青海(1997)针对学生的声调感知和声调输出进行研究。实验被试为六名在大学中学习中文超过一年的学生，他们在学校的中文课以外还有一些课外的学习经验。在声调感知的测试中，这些学生对二声、三声，以及一声、四声感到混淆。在声调输出的测试里，陈青海和另一位评分者挑出了35个声调错误。根据分析，其中只有12个错误为和其他声调混用；其他三分之二的输出错误均为在汉语中不存在的中度平声声调。陈青海根据有意义的四个或五个音节词组分析这些口语范例，而非针对单音节分析。从这个分析中可看出，学生输出的声调模式十分类似英语短句层次的音调，使用各种中音高、平声的声调。最后，虽然所有学生口语范例中的声调模式在某个程度上达到了汉语母语者正常音高范围内的两个极高点,但这些学生仍倾向使用英语的音调模式(中音高、平声),而降低了他们达到五个全音域的机会。

In addition to Chen's (1997) study, there is another study that had focused on CFL pronunciation at the prosodic level. Viger (2007) investigated the differences between the English and Mandarin utterance-level prosodic contours produced by native and non-native speakers. A particular focus of this study was on global pitch setting and pitch contours at sentence boundaries. One of the major findings of this study is that previous linguistic system (L1) English speakers imported a final-syllable rise on the final syllable in Mandarin questions, and that there was no sign of global pitch setting transfer from English to Mandarin. Viger (2007) offered a number of explanations for the absence of long-range intonation planning or transfer: 1) Limited online processing resources; that is, the global prosody is sacrificed for the sake of local prosody; 2) Insufficient evidence in the L2 input for the global prosody, when compared with the local prosodic phenomena; 3) Lack of explicit instruction, because no CFL textbooks provides any information on global prosody; 4) Slow speech rate; and 5) Although L2 speakers produced both local and global prosody, they confined their productions to syllable-length windows of time, without the long-range intonational planning.

在陈青海(Chen, 1997)的研究之外,另有在韵律层次分析汉语二语发音的研究。Viger (2007)的研究探讨母语者与非母语者在英语和汉语的韵律曲线上的差异。这项研究特别侧重总体音高以及句子之间的音高曲线。这项研究的其中一个重要发现在于母语为英语者在汉语疑问句的最后一个音节有音高升高现象,但并没有任何证据显示这个总体音高的表现是由英语迁移至汉语的。Viger (2007)提出了一些解释:第一,由于信息处理的资源有限,总体的韵律因细部的韵律做了某些调整;第二,相较于细部的韵律现象,并没有足够的证据证明第二语言对总体韵律的影响;第三,缺少明确的指示:没有一本对外汉语教学的课本提出任何与总体韵律有关的信息;第四,较慢的语速;第五,虽然二语使用者的口语输出包含了细部与总体的韵律,他们的口语仍限于音节长度,而缺少大范围的音调变化。

A recent study by Winke (2007) investigated CFL learners' production in relation to memory and the target language proficiency. The investigator analyzed tonal production errors made by 52 university-level CFL learners, who were native speakers of English, heritage learners, and native speakers of Asian languages other than Chinese. The data indicate a positive relationship between correct tonal production and reading proficiency. In addition, rote and working memory as well as L1 transfer were not significant factors in tonal production.

Winke (2007) 研究汉语二语学习者的口语表现与记忆容量和汉语能力的关系。这项研究分析52名在大学里学中文的学生的声调输出错误。这些被试者包括了母语为英语的学生、华裔学生以及母语为亚洲其他语言的学生。研究指出声调输出是否正确与阅读能力有正相关的关系。此外,死记硬背、工作记忆以及母语的迁移在声调输出上并不是十分重要的因素。

2.3.2. Auditory Training Studies on Chinese Tone Acquisition
汉语声调习得之听觉训练研究

While most of the studies on tonal acquisition have used CFL learners at different levels of proficiency during their CFL learning career, particularly, during their first or second years of CFL learning, two studies have investigated the effects of auditory training on subjects who have never been exposed to Chinese. Wang et al. (1999) investigated whether auditory (perceptual) training can be applied to the acquisition of non-native suprasegmental contrasts. The experimental design included a pretest, a training phase, and a posttest. Both the control and experimental groups (N=8 for each group) were employed. Four tones were trained pair-wise with a systemic increase in difficulty of tone contrasts. The order of tone pair presentation was from easy to most difficult, in accordance with the error analysis obtained from the trainees' pretest. The trainees' identification accuracy revealed an average of 21% increase from the pretest to the posttest. Their findings also show that Tone 1 and Tone 4 are most resistant to improvement. Accordingly, Wang et al. (1999) suggested that non-natives' perception of L2 sounds does not remain constant and that language-specific perceptual patterns are modifiable to some extent.

  大部分声调习得的研究都是分析不同程度的对外汉语学习者,特别是学了一年或是两年的学生在学习汉语过程中的声调感知与输出,有两个研究是针对从未学过汉语的被试,分析他们在听觉训练下的效果。在Wang et al. (1999)的研究中,探析听觉(感知)训练是否能有效帮助非母语者习得超音段音位。实验设计包括了一个前测、一个训练阶段以及一个后测。实验采取控制组与实验组两组,每组各有八名被试。四个声调,两个两个一组,声调对比的难度随实验的进行递增。实验难度的递增与受试前测的失误分析结果一致。比较被试在前测与后测的成绩之后发现,被试的准确率提高了21%。研究结果更显示了被试在一声和四声上最难有所进展,而非母语者在对二语声音的感知上并非保持一致不变,语言特有的感知模式在某个程度上是可更改的。

Following the investigation of the effects of auditory training on Chinese tonal perception, Wang et al. (2003) examined the Chinese tonal productions before and after perceptual training. The primary question that they addressed was whether perceptual training can affect production, such that training efforts could result in positive transfer from one modality to the other. The subjects in their study went through the same auditory training on Chinese tonal perception similar to that in the study by Wang et al (1999). The trainees' posttest tone productions improved by 18%, when compared with their pretest productions, indicating significant tone production improvement after perceptual training. In addition, it was found that pitch height and pitch contour are not mastered in parallel, with the former being more resistant to improvement than the latter. Overall, the two above-mentioned studies have shown that perceptual training has facilitative effect on the production domain; however, the nature of the relationship between perception and production is still not clear.

  上述研究(Wang et al., 1999)探究了汉语声调感知听觉训练的效度,而之后另一个研究(Wang et al., 2003)则比较知觉训练前后汉语声调输出的表现。这个研究主要是探讨感知训练是否对声调输出的表现造成影响,训练是否造成某些特征的正迁移。在这个研究里,被试也接受与(Wang et al., 1999)研究一样的听觉训练。研究发现被试的后测成绩比前测成绩进步了18%,这意味着知觉训练有助于声调输出的表现。此外,音高以及音高升降曲线(调型)无法同时兼顾,前者比后者更困难。总体而言,这两项研究皆证明感知训练对声调输出的正面效果,但感知与输出在本质上的关联性仍有待进一步的研究。

2.3.3. CFL Segmental Study
对外汉语音段研究

There has been only one study investigating CFL segmental acquisition. Shi and Wen (2009) reported a dissertation study of Wen (2008), which focused on English vowel production by Chinese students and Chinese vowel production by American students. Four Chinese speakers and four American speakers participated in this study. The participants loudly read out seven Chinese characters representing seven Chinese vowels and ten English words representing five English vowels. Acoustic analyses were conducted focusing on the first formant (F1) and the second formant (F2) on the resonant frequencies of the vowels in questions. The study found transfer effects on vowels that appear similar in both Chinese and English during the production of Chinese vowels by American students. The study also found idiosyncratic and unstable articulation patterns for the Chinese vowels that do not have similar categories in English.

截止目前为止,只有一个探讨对外汉语音段习得的研究。石锋和温宝莹在2009年的研究中,根据温宝莹于2008年发表的博士论文进行讨论,探究中国学生的英语元音发音和美国学生的汉语元音发音。实验对象为四名中国学生和四名美国学生,这些被试按正常语速朗读七个含有汉语基础元音的单音节字以及含有五个英语基础元音的单词。在语音分析中,元音的音质取决于第一共振峰(F1)与第二共振峰(F2)的元音共振频率。研究发现美国学生遇到汉语元音和英语十分相似时,母语的迁移现象十分明显。

这项研究也发现，对于英语中不存在的元音，英语为母语的学习者会与母语混淆，并造成此类元音发音的不稳定。

2.3.4. Direction for Future CFL Pronunciation Studies
   未来汉语二语语音研究的方向

While CFL pronunciation acquisition studies have provided valuable data for our understanding of certain learning tasks, there are many fundamental issues that researchers need to consider for future studies. First, most of the researches conducted have been focused on the perception and production of individual lexical tones without consideration of the overall context at the phrasal or intonation level. There seems to be a consensus in the field that most of the CFL learners, at some point during their interlanguage development, tend to develop good control on both segmental and super-segmental features at the syllable or local level, but their control at the phrasal or intonation level appears to be quite problematic or "洋腔洋调" and remains so for the rest of their CFL learning career. Given the complicated relationship between tones and intonations in Chinese,[1] CFL intonation acquisition is much harder than tonal acquisition. This is particularly true for learners of non-tonal language background. Future CFL pronunciation acquisition studies should move from focusing on both segmental

---

1. There have been several assumptions on the interplay between tone and intonation in Chinese. According to Fry (1968), lexical tones are likely to be modified by, but never completely subordinated to, intonation. Abe (1955, 1971, 1980) asserted that intonation cannot affect the basic shape of tone because tone is solid enough to resist perturbation generated by intonation. Shen (1990) argued that in Mandarin, intonation-tone interaction involves a change in both the tonal shape and pitch scale of a given tonal pattern. Nevertheless, the basic features of tones remain intact.Cao (2009) suggested that in the context, tonal variation related to pitch contour of a syllable is relatively limited, but the variation of pitch register in quite free.Therefore, in context, the relative stability of pitch contour ensures the lexical distinction, while the variability of the register forms the basis of the simultaneous superposition between local tones and global intonation.In this sense, the variability of the syllable register is the key point to understand the relationship between tone and intonation, including accent and rhythm.
学者就汉语中声调与语调的相互作用提出了几种不同的说法。Fry(1968)指出，词汇声调有可能因语调影响而改变，但并不完全附属于语调。Abe(1955, 1971, 1980)主张语调不能影响声调的基本结构，因为声调本身十分坚固，足以抵挡语调引起的一些影响与变化。Shen(1990)主张，在汉语中语调与声调的交互作用涉及一个既定声调模式在声调结构以及语调高低范围上的变化。尽管如此，声调的基本架构仍旧是完好无损的。Cao(2009)指出，在语境中，一个音节与音高调值相关的声调变化相对来说较有限，但在音高调域上的变化则是相当自由的。因此，在语境中，当音高调值的变化形成了细部声调以及总体语调同时重合的基础，音高调型的相对稳定就确保我们能够有效地辨析词汇。从这个意义上讲，音节调值的变化是理解声调和包含口音及韵律在内的语调之间的关系的重要关键。

and super-segmental features at the syllable level to the prosodic level, such as rhythm, co-articulated tones, and timing and coordination between tone and intonation. In addition, as learners of different native language backgrounds may manifest different prosodic patterns for CFL pronunciation learning, in our focus on conducting CFL speech learning at the phrasal level, it is important to understand the speech patterns of the learners' native language and their interactional effects between the L1 and L2 at various L2 proficiency stages and in different learning settings.[1]

  虽然汉语二语语音习得研究已经为这个领域贡献了不少宝贵的研究成果,展望未来,我们仍有许多值得继续探究的课题。首先,多数的研究侧重个别词汇声调的感知与输出,并未将词句或是音调层次的语境因素纳入考虑。这个研究领域的学者似乎已有共识,认为大多数的汉语二语学习者在中介语的发展过程中会逐渐在音节或是细部层次有效掌握音段音位以及超音段音位的特色,但在短句或是音调层次却会发生问题,在其学习汉语的时间里仍无法完全消除所谓的"洋腔洋调"。基于汉语声调与语调之间的复杂关系,对外汉语的语调习得比声调习得更加困难,对于母语为非声调语言的学习者尤是。未来的对外汉语发音习得研究应该从侧重音节层次的音段音位以及超音段音位的特色,走向韵律层次,分析韵律节奏、声调的发音、时机以及声调与语调的连结。此外,由于学习者母语背景的不同,他们在发音学习的过程中也会显现出不同的韵律模式。当我们将重心放在短句层次的汉语二语口语习得时,我们必须了解学习者母语的口语模式以及在不同二语能力阶段里,和不同的学习环境中母语与二语之间的交互影响[1]。

It is also important to note that most of the CFL speech acquisition studies have employed relatively small sample sizes with exclusive use of cross-sectional design. With increased CFL enrollments, it is no longer a

---

1. For instance, English is a word-stress language with polysyllabic shortening. Its phrase duration decreases as the number of syllables in the phrase increases. It is also found that English has a global pitch declination, with longer durations occurring at the edges of a phrase (Turk & Shattuck-Hufnagel, 2000).
  例如,英语就是一个有多音节省略现象的重音语言。当词语中音节的数量增加时,词语的长度会随之缩短。我们也得知英语在较长语句的末端有整体音高下倾的现象 (Turk & Shattuck-Hufnagel, 2000)。

challenge to address the issue of sample size. Given the universal and individual nature of speech learning, it is important that our studies include both cross-sectional and longitudinal designs for the purpose of triangulating data. Keeping track of the same group of learners for a number of years, from in-state programs to study-abroad programs as well as from different curriculum schemes, can generate data on the learners' pronunciation profile at different stages of proficiency, as well as onthe effects of instruction and learning setting on CFL pronunciation acquisition.

  我们也必须留意,大多数的对外汉语口语习得研究的实验样本数量较小,采取横断实验设计。随着对外汉语学习者人数的增加,样本数的大小将不再是个难以克服的问题。由于口语习得不仅是普遍的也是个人的一个研究课题,若能同时纳入横断以及纵向的实验设计,将有助于进一步交叉、检视、整合数据。在几年内持续观察同一组学习者,从国内的项目到海外留学项目,从不同的课程设置,都可以收集分析学习者在不同学习阶段的语音概况以及不同教学与学习情境对汉语二语语音习得的影响。

Future research should also identify effective instructional methods on the acquisition of Chinese pronunciation. Ultimately, one has to address a central pedagogical question—What are the pedagogically sound methods that can effectively increase a student's awareness of the pitch range and contours as well as the intonation patterns? —and transfer those perceptions into accurate production. While the relationship between perception and production with respect to L2 speech learning is not well understood,[1] the popular thinking is that perception precedes production. In other words, training in tonal and prosodic production would be effective only after one has a high level of awareness regarding their phonological and phonetic features. Empirical studies are needed

---

1. Dinnsen (1983) reported a number of studies in which speakers produce sounds according to systematic linguistic rules, while they cannot reliably perceive the different results of the rules. In addition, several researchers found that the native speakers of Japanese learning English actually produce the "r/l" distinction better than what they perceive (Archibald, 1998).

  Dinnsen (1983) 表示,许多研究指出说话者根据有系统的语言规则来发音,即使他们无法完全可靠地理解这些规则的不同。此外,一些研究者发现日文为母语的英语学生在辨别"r/l"上,口语的输出优于听觉的感知(Archibald, 1998)。

to provide conclusive evidence on the perception and production relationship, and the best pedagogical practice for the acquisition of CFL speech needs to be identified. Finally, CFL speech learning research should also be guided by a better theory. It is theoretically expected that there are many interactive factors involved in one's L2 speech learning. A particular target language sound system has its own acquisition order based on its linguistic features' learn ability. The L1 features interact with a number of L2 speech learning factors, such as L1 transfer, maturational and developmental factors, and learning setting. It is important to note that major L2 speech learning theories are for segmental learning.[1] They do not predict patterns of suprasegmental learning. It is time for the CFL researchers to collaborate on a model of CFL speech learning and start the dialectic process of verifying or rejecting hypotheses, to define and modify the model further.

未来也应该将汉语语音习得的教学法纳入研究的范畴。最终,我们仍需回到最核心的教学问题上:最能有效提升学生对音高、音高曲折和音调的意识,并将感知转移为准确输出的教学法是什么。虽然在二语口语习得

---

[1] For a review on a biologically based argument, see Lenneberg's (1967) Critical Period Hypothesis. According to Lenneburg's Critical Period Hypothesis, during child development, there is a period during which language can be acquired more easily than at any other time. For a review on a phonological account and interaction between L1 and L2, see Eckman's (1977) Markedness Differential Hypothesis, Major's (1986, 2001) Ontogeny Model, and Flege's (1995) Speech Learning Model. Those theories make certain predictions.For instance, establishing new phonetic categories after a learner has passed the critical period or sensitive periods is a real challenge. Learners of L2 may fail to discern the phonetic differences between pairs of sounds in the L2, or between L2 and L2 sounds, either because phonetically distinct sounds in the L2 are "assimilated" to a single category, because the L1 phonology filters out features (or properties) of L2 sounds, which are important phonetically, but not phonologically, or both.In addition, phonetic learning for similar sounds does not progress much along with L2 experience, whereas new sounds benefit from learning. Likewise, learners are more likely to perceive or produce new, rather than similar, L2 phones authentically. Finally, at early stages, universal factors (termed as Universal Grammar or UG) will not play a major role because the influence of transfer is strong and that of developmental factors is minimal.However, at later stages of acquisition, the role of UG will increase because of the decrease in transfer and developmental factors.
回顾以生物学为基础的论点,可以参考 Lenneberg's (1967)的语言习得关键期假说。根据这个假说,在儿童发展的过程中有一个语言发展最容易的关键期。根据 Eckman's (1977)的标记差异假说、Major's (1986, 2001) 的个体发生模型以及 Flege (1995)的口语习得模型,当中的文献综述回顾了语音分析以及母语和二语的相互作用。这些理论提出了一些预测。例如,当一个学习者已经错过语言习得的关键期,发展建立一个新的语音类别就会是一个艰巨的挑战。由于语音学上相异的语音在二语中可能被同化而归入同一个类别,或由于母语语音滤除了二语语音上十分重要的一些特征,使得二语学习者无法正确辨别二语中的不同语音。除此之外,尽管仍可通过学习习得新的语音,但二语近似音的习得进展十分有限。同样的,学习者在针对新的二语语音的感知以及输出上,比近似音来得容易。最后,在语音习得的早期阶段,由于母语迁移的强烈影响以及发展性因素的作用极小,普遍因素(称"普遍语法"或 UG)并不会扮演主要的角色。不过,在语言习得的后期,因语言迁移的影响下降,普遍语法的重要性随之升高。

上,我们还无法完全掌握感知与输出之间的关联性,最为人接受的看法是感知先于输出。换句话说,声调与韵律输出的训练只有在对语音音位与音型的特征有高度意识的情况下才能显出功效。当我们在对外汉语口语习得上寻求最有效的教学法时,我们需要实证研究来提供感知与输出关联性的决定性证据。最后,对外汉语口语研究必须有坚强的理论作指导。在理论中,在二语口语学习的发展过程里,许多因素交互影响。根据其语言特征的可习得度,每个语言的语音体系都有独特的习得顺序。母语的特征与母语迁移、发展成熟度以及学习环境等二语口语习得的因素互相影响。值得注意的是关于二语口语习得的主要理论着重于语音的习得,而这些理论本身并不预测具体学习的模式。现在是对外汉语界研究者群策群力提出汉语二语口语习得模型、辩证假说以及进行修正的难得时机。

Chapter Three 第三章
Cognitive Psychological Theory and Research

认知心理学理论与研究

Similar to linguistic theories, cognitive psychology has significantly influenced research on speech acquisition and the development of Iowa spoken language Instructional model. In this chapter, we focus on second language (L2) speaking development from the perspective of cognitive psychology. We start with the general applications of cognitive approaches in second language acquisition (SLA) and then discuss in detail the processing approaches, connectionism, transfer appropriate processing (TAP) theory, and chaos/complexity theory. Finally, we describe how learner variables would have an impact on L2 speaking acquisition.

  跟语言学理论一样,认知心理学对汉语口语习得研究的影响也不容小觑。认知心理学理论同时也对爱荷华大学汉语口语教学模式的形成与发展影响巨大。在本章,我们将从认知心理学的角度剖析第二语言的口语发展。我们将先介绍二语习得认知理论的特点,再讨论信息加工论,连结理论,适当迁移加工理论以及混沌/复杂理论。最后,我们将探究与学习者个人相关的各种因素如何影响汉语二语的口语习得。

In contrast to linguistic theories, which focus on language components of SLA, cognitive approaches put more emphasis on the learning process (Mitchell & Myles, 2004). From this perspective, acquiring L2 is similar to learning other skills. As a result, cognitivists claim that knowing how human brain processes and learns new information allows us to better understand L2 acquisition process. Furthermore, cognitivists primarily view the learner as an individual and not as a social being, because they are more interested in the internal processes of the mind, and how an individual interacts with social contexts is not their primary concern. One of the common criticisms towards cognitive approaches is the ignorance of social factors and their clinical way of treating language learning. According to Mitchell and Myles (2004), cognitive theories come into two different camps—processing theorists and emergentists (constructivists). In the following sections, we will go through the main arguments of these two camps.

不同于侧重研究语言成分的语言学理论,认知理论的重心在于学习的过程(Mitchell & Myles, 2004)。从认知心理学的角度,学习一个新的语言和学习其他技能并无不同。因此,认知心理学家提出,知道人脑如何加工处理新的信息能让我们更了解第二语言习得的过程。

认知心理学家认为学习者是一个独立的个体,而不是一个社会存在。由于他们较关注内在思维的过程,人与外在社会环境的互动并不是他们关心的重点。因此,认知理论一直被攻击忽略社会因素以及用一种类似临床病理学的的角度剖析语言。Mitchell & Myles (2004)指出,认知理论可以分为两大阵营:加工理论以及自然发生论(建构主义理论)。在下面的章节,我们将逐一讨论这两大理论。

3.1 Processing Approaches 加工理论

Processing theorists claim that language skills have special features that are different from other skills. Therefore, it is necessary to develop processing theories that complement property theories of language, such as Universal Grammar. As processing approaches are concerned with the operation of cognitive mechanisms in the context of L2 learning, they investigate how L2 learners process linguistic information and how their ability to process L2 develops overtime (Gass & Selinker, 2008).

加工理论学家指出,语言知识的特征使其有别于其他的技能。因此,我们有必要发展加工理论,使其填补包括普遍语法(Universal Grammar)在内等研究语言本质的理论的不足。由于加工理论关注在二语学习的环境下认知机制的运作,它们研究二语学习者如何处理语言信息以及二语加工能力发展的过程(Gass & Selinker, 2008)。

3.1.1. Memory
记忆

A great number of information processing approaches have focused on how information is detected, recognized, and entered into memory storage. Cognitive psychologists have divided the memory system into three levels: sensory, short-term, and long-term memory (Kellogg, 2007). Sensory memory refers to the brief perception of stimuli prior to being perceived, recognized, and entered into short-term memory. There are two primary types of sensory memory. Visual sensory memory is called iconic memory, and has a large capacity, but a brief duration of about 250 milliseconds (Sprling, 1960). Auditory sensory memory is called echoic memory (Neisser, 1967). Its duration is also brief, but aural stimuli such as speech are stored for longer periods of time than visual stimuli in short-term memory (Kellogg, 2007).

大部分的信息加工理论者重在信息被察觉、辨识以及输入记忆贮存的过程。认知心理学家将记忆体系分成三层：感官(Sensory)、短程(Short-term)以及长程记忆(Long-term) (Kellogg, 2007)。感官记忆指对外在刺激的感知，刺激首先必须通过感觉器官才能被察觉、辨识以及进入短程记忆。感官记忆主要分成两种：视觉感官记忆与听觉感官记忆。视觉感官记忆又称图像记忆，它有较大的容量，但持续的时间很短，仅有250毫秒(Sprling, 1960)。听觉感官记忆又称回声记忆，它的持续时间也很短暂，但相较于视觉刺激，在短程记忆中听觉刺激可以储存较久(Kellogg, 2007)。

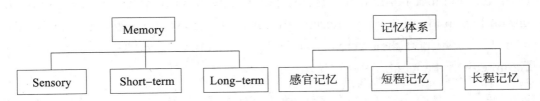

Figure 3.1　Threee-level memory systems　　图3.1　三层记忆体系

Short-term memory, also called working memory, is easy to access and has a limited capacity. Working memory, similar to the Random Access Memory (RAM) in a computer, provides a mental space to hold information for further processing. The earliest and the most influential multi-component model of working memory was proposed by Baddeley (1986, 2001). In Baddeley's system, there are three components of working memory. These are a phonological loop, avisual-spatial sketch pad, and an episodic buffer.

短程记忆,又称工作记忆,容易存取但容量有限。工作记忆就像电脑的内存,为之后信息的处理加工过程提供一个储存信息的心理空间。Baddeley(1986,2001)提出的工作记忆多重成分模型是最早也最具影响力的。根据Baddeley的模型,工作记忆包含了三个成分:语音环、视觉空间模版以及情节缓冲器。

Figure3.2　working memory systems　　　　图3.2　工作记忆体系

The phonological loop is a short-term store for the transient retention of verbal information. It comprises two parts: a phonological store that holds information in a phonological form and a rehearsal process that repeats a series of speech elements on a loop to prevent them from decaying. The phonological loop plays an important role in vocabulary acquisition and L2 learning (Baddeley, Gathercole & Papagno, 1998). With regard to language acquisition, the phonological loop is not used to remember familiar words. Instead, it aims to provide temporary storage of unfamiliar phonological materials because there is no existing knowledge available to support their verbal learning (Gathercole & Baddeley, 1993; Baddeley, Gathercole & Papagno, 1998).

语音环主要负责短暂储存语音信息,它包含两部分:语音储存装置以及发音复述装置。语音储存装置保留了语音形式的信息,由于保留的时间十分短暂,大约在两秒之内就会衰退,必须通过发音复述装置进行复述才能继续保持这些信息。语音环在词汇习得以及第二语言学习上十分重要(Baddeley, Gathercole & Papagno, 1998)。对于语言习得,语音环并非用于记忆熟悉的词,由于并没有现存的知识来帮助词语学习,因此语音环用于提供一个暂时的空间储存不熟悉的语音材料(Gathercole & Baddeley, 1993; Baddeley, Gathercole & Papapgno, 1998)。

There have been a number of claims about phonological loop. First, researchers have verified the effect of phonological similarity, which means words that sound similar are more difficult to remember than those that sound different. On the contrary, semantic similarity has comparatively little effect, which supports the assumption that verbal information is mostly coded phonologically in working memory (Conrad, 1964; Baddeley, 1966). Second, researchers have found an articulatory suppression effect. When people are asked to say something irrelevant aloud, the articulatory rehearsal process is blocked and the memory traces in the phonological loop decay.

先前的研究提出了一些与语音环有关的观点。首先,研究证明"语音相似效应",表示相似的语音比相异的语音记忆的难度更高。相对来说,语义的相似效应影响力较有限,这也证实了工作记忆里大部分的语言信息是以语音形式编码的假设(Conrad, 1964; Baddeley, 1966)。其次,研究也发现"发音抑制效应"。当人们被要求大声说出与表达内容不相关的词语时,发音复述的过程受到阻碍而语音环中的记忆痕迹消退。

The visual-spatial sketch padis assumed to hold information about what we see and provides a transient space for visual and spatial representations, such as shapes, colors, or the location of objects. It permits one to rehearse information by visualizing it. Baddeley (2000) added an "episodic buffer" to his model of working memory, which is dedicated to linking information across domains and storing integrated events. The episodic buffer is assumed to have access to long-term memory, allowing the retrieval of phonological, visual, and spatial information or data from long-term memory.

视觉空间模版提供一个暂时的空间保存以视觉或空间形式呈现的信息,像形状、颜色或物体的地点。视觉空间模版容许我们通过视觉化的过程复述信息。在2000年的研究中,Baddeley在他的工作记忆模型里加入

"情节缓冲器"。情节缓冲器用于连结不同领域的信息并将之储存整合的事件。情节缓冲器也被认为拥有进入长程记忆的途径,提取长程记忆中语音、视觉以及空间的信息。

For L2 acquisition, as claimed by Ortega (2009), we need working memory to store information as well as integrate new information with that already encoded in long-term memory. As described by Ellis (2005), working memory "provides a place for us to develop, apply, and hone our metalinguistic insights into an L2" (p.337).

在习得第二语言上,Ortega (2009)指出,我们通过工作记忆储存信息,并将新的信息与在长程记忆中编码的信息作整合。Ellis (2005)表示,工作记忆"为我们提供一个空间用以形成、应用和磨炼我们二语元语言的洞察力"。(p. 337)

Working memory has been extensively discussed in SLA since the mid-1990s and individual differences in working memory capacity have received much attention. It is assumed that a greater working memory capacity leads to more efficient L2 learning. We will discuss about this issue in Section 3.5—learner variables.

从90年代中期起,工作记忆在二语习得研究上受到广泛的讨论,而工作记忆容量的个体差异则受到极高的重视。人们认为较大的工作记忆容量可以带来更有成效的二语学习。我们将在第五小节讨论学习者的个人因素。

With regard to L2 working memory capacity, there are two observations. First, researchers have found that the working memory capacity of L2 is smaller than that of the previous linguistic system (L1) (Harrington & Sawyer, 1992; Towell & Dewaele, 2005). Although there are many explanations to account for this L2-L1 lag, there have been very few studies carried out to further investigate this observation. Second, it has been suggested that as L2 proficiency develops, the L2-L1 lag in working memory should become smaller. However, this assumption lacks strong empirical evidence from SLA research.

至于第二语言的工作记忆容量,有两个主要的观察与发现。第一,研究发现第二语言的工作记忆容量比母语小(Harrington & Sawyer, 1992; Towell & Dewaele, 2005)。虽然有许多关于二语与母语差异(L2-L1 lag)的解释,相关的研究仍十分有限。其次,人们一般认为随着二语能力的发展,二语与母语在工作记忆上的差异应该会随之缩小。然而,这个假说在二语习得研究中缺乏有力的事实基础。

Long-term memory focuses on representation and has unlimited capacity (Ortega, 2009). There are primarily two types of long-term memory: explicit-declarative memory and implicit-procedural memory. According to Tulving (2002), explicit-declarative long-term memory stores knowledge of events, facts, and concepts. It also refers to the understanding of what the world presents to us. We are consciously aware of these kinds of mental representations. As shown in Figure 3.3, explicit-declarative memory consists of two components. Semantic memory stores knowledge of concepts and facts, while episodic memory involves knowledge of events in which people are personally involved. Semantic memory includes knowledge of historical events, memories of laws and organizational rules, and concepts such as intelligence, sympathy and imagination. Episodic memory refers to memories from childhood to adulthood, including both funny and sad incidents.

长程记忆注重记忆的呈现,它的储存容量是无限的(Ortega, 2009)。长程记忆主要有两种:外显陈述性记忆以及内隐程序性记忆。根据Tulving (2002)的研究,外显陈述性长程记忆储存与时间、事实以及观念相关的知识,它也代表我们对外在世界的理解。如图表3.3所示,外显-陈述性记忆包含了两个部分:语义记忆(semantic memory)以及事件记忆(episodic memory)。语义记忆储存与观念与事实有关的知识,而事件记忆所储存的只是则和人们亲身经历的事件有关。语义知识包括了历史事件的知识、法则和组织规则以及像智力、同情心以及想象力等观念。事件记忆则涉及我们从小到大的回忆,不论悲喜都包括在内。

Implicit-procedural long-term memory stores things that we know without being aware of the fact that we know. It also includes two components, motor skills and conditional responses, which reflect our knowledge of how to respond to the world (Kellogg, 2007).

内隐程序性长程记忆储存我们拥有但却没有意识到的知识。内隐程序性记忆有两个类别:动作技能以及条件式反应,呈现我们用来回应外在世界的知识(Kellogg, 2007)。

Figure 3.3　Long-term memory systems　　　　　图 3.3　长程记忆体系

When looking at language acquisition, it is important to understand the close relation between memory and language instruction. At the elementary level, semantic knowledge about the target language is accumulated when students are provided with a variety of background knowledge about the target language, such as vocabulary and grammar rules related to daily situations. As language proficiency levels advance, students can apply the knowledge in semantic memory to different kinds of events stored in episodic memory.

在语言习得上,我们必须了解记忆与语言教学的密切关系。在基础阶段,通过学习与日常生活有关的词汇与语法等目的语的背景知识,学习者快速积累语义知识。随着他们语言程度的提高,学习者逐渐可以用词汇记忆中的知识描述储存在事件记忆里的各种事件。

3.1.2. Automatization and Restructuring
自动化以及重整

Many information-processing models, developed by cognitive psychologists, have been applied to research on language acquisition. The focus of information processing models in SLA is to investigate how different memory stores deal with new L2 information and how this information is automatized and restructured through repeated activation.

许多认知心理学家提出的信息加工模型被应用在语言习得的研究上。二语习得的信息加工模型探究不同的记忆储存空间如何处理新的二语信息,以及信息如何通过重复激活达到自动化和重整。

According to McLaughlin (1987, 1990), the process of L2 learning involves acquiring a complex cognitive skill. To achieve higher accuracy and better fluency, intensive practice is required. When learners gain more control over the acquired skill, they simplify, unify, and restructure the knowledge. Learning is a cognitive process, which involves internal representations and knowledge restructuring. As claimed by McLaughlin (1987), automatization and restructuring are essential factors in cognitive theory. Shiffrin and Schneider (1977) argued that the way we process information may either be controlled or automatic. Learning allows us to shift from controlled to automatic processing via repeated practice.

根据McLaughlin (1987, 1990)的模型,二语学习的过程涉及了复杂认知技能的习得。为了达到更高的准确性和更佳的流利度,高密度的练习是必要的。当学习者更能掌握所习得的技能时,他会简化、整合和重组他的知识。学习是一个认知的过程,涉及内在的呈现及知识重建。McLaughlin (1987)强调,自动化以及知识重整是认知理论的重要因素。Shiffrin & Schneider (1977)指出,信息处理的方式有两种:控制加工以及自动加工。通过重复的练习,学习能让我们从控制加工转移到自动加工。

Figure3.4　Controlled processing vs. Automatic processing

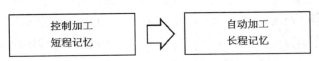

图3.3　控制加工与自动加工

In acquiring new L2 information, learners first depend on controlled processing. This requires a lot of attention control on the part of the learner and is constrained by the limitations of short-term memory. For example, a beginner wanting to introduce himself in Chinese will probably frame the following sentence: 你好, 我叫王大明。Initially, the learner selects and puts together these words and memorizes them in a chunk. Through repeated activation, the word sequences become automatic. In contrast to controlled processing, which takes a lot of cognitive resources and runs serially, automatic processing takes less efforts and few cognitive resources. Hence, many automatic processing tasks can run in parallel (Ortega, 2009).

在习得新的二语信息的过程中,学习者首先依赖控制加工,但在学习中需要大量的注意力,也受短程记忆的限制。例如,初学者学习用汉语做自我介绍时会用到"你好,我叫王大明"这几个词。最初,初学者选择、组织这几个词的顺序,并将这几个词以一个整体区块的形式记起来。通过反复激活,这几个词的顺序达到了自动化。不同于需要大量认知资源以及按一定顺序运作的控制加工,自动加工利用的认知资源较少,也不太费精力。因此,我们可以同时进行多样自动化加工的任务(Ortega, 2009)。

McLaughlin (1987, 1990) used his information processing model to explain the issue of fossilization, which refers to the fact that L2 learners keep their non-native-like structures and are unable to achieve native-like stages. In McLaughlin's model, fossilization is the result of a premature automatic processing. Automatic processing is difficult to modify because it is outside the attention control of the subject. As a result, erroneous constructions are likely to remain in the learner's interlanguage (McLaughlin, 1990).

McLaughlin (1987, 1990) 用他提出的信息加工模型解释语言习得的固化问题。固化现象指二语学习者一直保持他们不标准的语言结构,语言程度也无法达到像母语者一样的阶段。在 McLaughlin 的模型里,固化是自动化加工未成熟的结果。一旦一个技能达到自动化,意味着这项技能的执行已经不需要额外的注意力就可完成,若要对已达自动化的技能进行修正是十分困难的。因此,错误的结构会一直留在学习者的中介语当中

(McLaughlin, 1990)。

3.1.3. U-shaped Learning
U 型学习曲线

In the process of knowledge restructuring, U-shaped patterns may occur and reflect the destabilization of linguistic use. As shown in Figure 3.5, at the earliest stage of learning, students are only presented with one kind of target-like form. Therefore, they are able to produce error-free utterances. However, when students are introduced new forms, they have to compare their stored knowledge with new information. In the process of restructuring knowledge, students encounter a certain period of confusion. As a result, at the second stage, a learner appears to lose what he/she knew at the earlier stage and his/her linguistic behavior deviates from the target language norms (Gass & Selinker, 2008). It takes some time for the students to eventually restructure their L2 knowledge, but at the third stage, they are able to use both the new form and the old form in target-like ways.

在知识重整的过程中，U型学习曲线有可能会出现，反映学习者在语言使用上的不稳定现象。如图3.5所示，在学习的初步阶段，学习者只会学到一种标准的表现形式，因此，他们可以说出毫无错误的句子。然而，当他们接触到其他新的形式时，他们必须在新的信息以及已习得的知识之间做比较。在重整知识的过程中，学习者会经历一段混乱期。因此，在第二个阶段，学习者似乎失去了他们在前一阶段习得的知识，他们的语言表现也偏离了标准(Gass & Selinker, 2008)。学习者需要一些时间重整他们的二语知识，在第三阶段，他们可以正确辨别、使用新旧两种表现形式。

For example, when beginners learn interrogative sentences in Chinese, they start by learning to initiate a "yes or no" question by adding "吗" at the end of a declarative sentence. However, after other forms of interrogative sentences are introduced, the learners will encounter a period of confusion. It is common to see a learner put two question forms in one sentence, such as "你喜欢不喜欢中国饭吗？" After the learners restructure their knowledge, they then know the difference between the two interrogative sentence forms and are able to use the target form accurately.

例如，当初学者学汉语的疑问句句型时，他们会先学到在陈述句句末加上"吗"的是非疑问句。但是，但他们接触其他疑问句的句型时，他们会产生一个迷惑期。学习者将两种疑问句型混用、组成一个错句"你喜欢不喜欢中国饭吗？"的情况十分常见。在学习者重整知识之后，他们知道这两个疑问句式的差别，也能正确使用这两个句型。

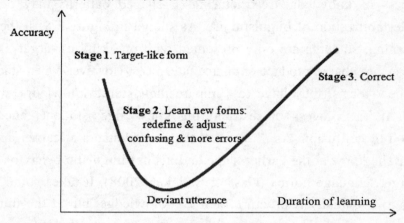

Figure3.5　Schema of U-shaped behavior Source: (Gass & Selinker, 2008)

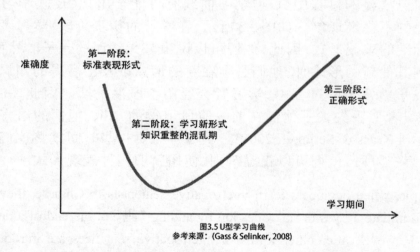

图3.5　U型学习曲线参考来源：(Gass & Selinker, 2008)

3.1.4. Knowledge Type
知识的种类

3.1.4.1. Declarative Knowledge and Procedural Knowledge
陈述性知识与程序性知识

Anderson (1983, 1985) proposed the Adaptive Control of Thought theory (ACT model), in which practice leading to automatization is the main concept. Anderson's model has influenced the development of skill acquisition theory. Skill acquisition theory defines learning as a transformative process, allowing automatic processes to take over controlled processes as the learner becomes more proficient. This process has been called proceduralization or automatization. It enables declarative knowledge to become procedural knowledge. Declarative knowledge refers to knowing about something, which is accessible to conscious awareness. Procedural knowledge is inaccessible to conscious awareness and relates to motor or cognitive skills that involve sequencing information (Gass & Selinker, 2008).

在 Anderson (1983, 1985)提出的思维适应性控制理论(adaptive control of thought theory，ACT model)中，"练习可以促进自动化的完成"是理论的主轴。Anderson 的模型影响了技能习得理论(skill acquisition theory)的形成与发展。技能习得理论认为学习是一个转变的过程，随着学习者熟练度的提高，让自动化加工取代控制加工。这个过程也可称为知识的程序化或是自动化。它使得陈述性的知识转变为程序性的知识。陈述性的知识泛指有意识地知道某件事情。程序性知识与动作或是认知技能有关，但我们无法有意识地察觉程序性知识的存在 (Gass & Selinker, 2008)。

Use of language is considered to involve procedural knowledge. With regard to L2 speaking acquisition, both L2 learners and teachers know that understanding a rule does not mean being able to apply it in speaking. Let us consider an example of the use of a measure word in Chinese. In contrast to English, it is necessary to add a measure word after a number when describing an item in Chinese. For example, to describe a desk, a beginner might initially know that he/she needs to add a measure word between the number "一" and the noun "书桌". However, he/she may not be able to consistently produce the measure word "张" in real conversations. This is because this particular learner has declarative knowledge of the rule, but it has not yet been proceduralized. With intensive practice, this knowledge can eventually become automatic.

语言的使用被认为和程序性知识有关。我们谈到第二语言的口语习得,学习者和教师双方都明白,知道一个规则并不代表有能力将这个规则实际应用在口语中。我们可以举汉语量词的使用为例。不同于英语,在用汉语描述一个物件时,我们必须在该物件的数目后面加上一个适合的量词。例如,为了要描述一张书桌,初学者刚开始可能知道他必须在数目"一"和名词"书桌"中间放入一个量词。但是,在实际对话中他可能无法每次都记得要使用量词"张"。这是因为他虽然拥有量词规则的陈述性知识,却还没有达到程序化。在密集的练习之下,这个知识就可能达到自动化。

According to Anderson, there are three stages, moving from declarative to procedural knowledge (Anderson, 1985).

Anderson指出,从陈述性知识到程序性知识有三个阶段:认知阶段、连结阶段以及自动化阶段(Anderson, 1985)。

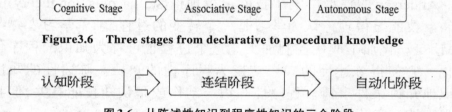

Figure 3.6　Three stages from declarative to procedural knowledge

图3.6　从陈述性知识到程序性知识的三个阶段

At the cognitive stage, the learner initially acquires knowledge. In the Chinese measure word example, the learner is told that a measure word must be inserted between the number and the noun. At the associative stage, the learner learns to associate an action to a declarative knowledge. He/she learns how to add a measure word when the context requires it. At the autonomous stage, as the learner's actions become more automatic, he/she might not explain or even be conscious of what he/she is doing (Mitchell & Myles, 2004). When the knowledge becomes proceduralized, it is accessed automatically.

在认知阶段,学习者先习得知识。在上述与汉语量词有关的例子中,学生被告知必须把一个量词放入数目词和名词之间。在连结阶段,学生学习将行为与陈述性知识连结起来。他会学到在情境需要下如何使用量词。在自动化阶段,学生的行为变得越来越自动,他可能不需要解释,甚或没有意识到他自然而然的行为(Mitchell & Myles, 2004)。当知识程序化之后,可以自动地被取得。

3.1.4.2. Implicit Knowledge vs. Explicit Knowledge
内隐性知识与外显性知识

Implicit and explicit knowledge are concerned with the distinction between declarative knowledge and procedural knowledge, discussed in the previous section. As pointed out by Gass and Selinker (2008), declarative knowledge forms the basis of explicit knowledge, and procedural knowledge underlies implicit knowledge (p.243).

内隐性知识与外显性知识和上一小节中讨论的陈述性知识与程序性知识的差别有关。Gass & Selinker (2008)指出,陈述性知识构成了外显知识的基础,而程序性知识则构成了内隐知识的基本成分 (p. 243)。

Awareness makes implicit knowledge distinct from explicit knowledge. When it comes to learning, implicit learning takes place simply, naturally, and unconsciously. On the other hand, explicit learning refers to a more conscious acquisition process (Ellis, 1994). Let us take language acquisition as an example. The acquisition of L1 grammar is implicit. We are naturally exposed to linguistic input and extract regularities without explicit instruction. In contrast, adult acquisition of L2 is different. In his Input Hypothesis, Krashen (1982) proposed that SLA is similar to first language acquisition. It comes naturally as a result of implicit processes occurring while learners are exposed to comprehensible L2 input. However, what L2 learners can acquire implicitly from communicative contexts is quite limited, when compared with the native speakers. To enhance accuracy, L2 adult learners need additional resources of explicit learning (Ellis,

2008). Explicit learning in SLA can be achieved in various ways, such as attending to language forms, noticing negative evidence, and actively guided practice that aims to develop automatized skills.

内隐知识与外显知识因意识的有无而不同。学习时内隐性学习是自然而然地、无意识地发生的。相对的,外显性学习则是通过一个更有意识的习得过程(Ellis, 1994)。我们以语言习得为例,母语语法的习得是内隐的,我们自然地接触语言的输入以及在没有明示教学的情境下提取规则。不过,成人的二语习得与母语习得不同。根据Krashen(1982)的输入假说,第二语言习得和第一语言习得类似。当学习者在自然的情境中接触可理解的二语输入,二语就会像母语一样通过内隐式的学习习得。然而,相较于母语者,二语学习者在交际语境中所能自然习得的仍十分有限。为了提高准确度,二语的成人学习者需要额外的显性学习资源(Ellis, 2008)。二语习得的显性学习有许多不同的方式,例如将注意力放在某些语言形式、特别留心负面证据以及通过针对培养自动化技能的引导式练习。

3.1.5. Processability Theory
可加工式理论

A number of SLA researchers have attempted to investigate the factors controlling the way in which L2 learners process linguistic input. They have examined the processing demands made by various aspects of L2, and the implication in learn ability and teach ability of L2 structures. Pienemann (1998, 2003) proposed that we can better understand SLA with a theory of grammar and a processing theory. Pienemann's process ability theory is aimed at clarifying how learners acquire the computational mechanisms to comprehend and produce L2 forms. As Pienemann claimed that language acquisition is the gradual acquisition of computational mechanisms, understanding how these mechanisms work allows us to predict an L2 learner's developmental path. Within this theory, there is a progression hierarchy, in which one procedure is a prerequisite for the next. Learners are unable to access hypotheses about L2, which they cannot process. The following six levels are presented in the progression hierarchy:

若干二语习得研究者企图探究控制影响二语学习者处理语言输入的因素。他们检视了第二语言不同层面的加工处理需求，以及第二语言结构的可学性和可教性。Pienemann (1998, 2003) 提出，借由语法理论和加工理论，我们能更了解第二语言的习得。Pienemann 的可加工式理论旨在阐明学习者如何习得机械计算装置，并用之来理解以及输出二语形式。由于 Pienemann 主张语言习得是一个习得机械计算装置的渐进过程，理解这个机制的运作能让我们预测二语学习者的发展轨迹。根据这个理论，有一个习得的先后程序，在这个结构中第一个步骤的完成是第二个步骤的先决条件。学习者不能跨越到他们无法加工处理的二语阶段。在发展层次中有六个不同的阶段：

- Level 1. No procedure: Single word utterances
- Level 2. Category procedure: Lexical morphemes
- Level 3. Phrasal procedure: Phrasal morphemes
- Level 4. Verb phrase procedure: Movement of elements within a verb phrase
- Level 5. Sentence procedure: Subject-verb agreement
- Level 6. Subordinate clause procedure: Use of a particular tense based on something in the main clause

- 阶段一：无程序：单字表达
- 阶段二：语类程序：实义语素
- 阶段三：名词短语程序
- 阶段四：动词短语程序
- 阶段五：句子程序
- 阶段六：从句程序

Pienemann (1998) used this theory to provide a better understanding of the acquisition of morphology and syntax of L2. Using data collected in a variety of languages, including English, German, and Swedish, he identified developmental paths for these languages. Pienemann reported that the beginning and end of stimuli are easier to remember and manipulate due to perceptual saliency. This means that students will initially learn how to move elements from inside to outside; that is, to sentence-initial or sentence-final positions. Then, they will develop the ability to move elements from outside to inside before being able to move elements within sentences.

　　Pienemann (1998)通过这个理论为二语形态学及句法学的习得提供了一个更好的注解。在包括英语、德语和瑞典语等他所收集的众多语言数据中, Pienemann发现了这些语言的发展轨迹。他指出由于知觉的显著性特点, 刺激的首尾部分更容易记忆和操控。这意味学生会先学如何把要素从句里移到句外, 也就是句首或句末的位置。之后他们将在能把要素在句内移动之前, 发展把要素从句外移入句内的能力。

In addition, Pienemann developed a Teaching Hypothesis (Pienemann, 1998). He argued that L2 learners follow a rigid path to acquire certain grammatical structures. Stages of acquisition cannot be skipped through formal instruction. Only when the previous stages have been successfully completed, the grammatical structures in the next stage could be learned. Therefore, instruction will be most effective if an instructor focuses on "the next stage" of the acquisition route (Pienemann, 1998:250).

　　此外, Pienemann提出了教学假说(Pienemann, 1998)。他主张第二语言学习者依照一套固定的轨迹习得某些语法结构, 而学习者无法通过正规教学跳过习得的阶段。唯有之前的阶段都已经成功地完成之后, 才能习得下一个阶段的语法结构。因此, 若是教师能把重点放在习得轨迹的"下一个阶段", 教学才会更有成效 (Pienemann, 1998:250)。

3.2 Emergentist/Constructivist Approaches　自然发生论(建构主义理论)

Emergentists claim that language development is driven by communicative needs and acquired through usage. Learners extract regularities from language input and build associations in their brains. Constructions are basic units of language presentations, which are developed through form-meaning mappings, integrating into a speech community and knowledge internalization. High-frequency constructions are more readily accessed than low-frequency units, because a learner's perceptual system is more likely to expect the occurrence of high-frequency units in the language input (Ellis, 2007).

  自然发生论主张语言的发展源于交际需求的驱动,并通过使用而习得。学习者从语言输入中提取规律并在他们的大脑中建立连结。作为语言呈现的基本单元,结构的发展是通过形式与意义的连结,整合语言社群以及知识的内化。由于学习者的感知体系在中介语输入中更期待高频率结构的出现,因此高频率的结构比低频率的结构更容易习得(Ellis, 2007)。

Within an emergentist or constructivist framework, there are a number of approaches including emergentism, connectionism or associationism, constructivism, cognitivism, functionalism, Competition Model, etc. (MacWhinney, 1999). According to Ellis (2006), there are three important principles of emergentist approaches. These are associative learning, probabilistic learning, and rational contingency. Associative learning refers to creating connections between personal experiences and learning targets. Our brains are neurobiologically programmed to be sensitive to the statistical properties of the input; when the frequency of occurrence is higher, the connections become stronger (Ortega, 2009). Learning occurs when a learner's personal experience and a learning target are closely connected. Emergentists also claim that learning is not categorical. Instead, learning is a kind of probabilistic calculation, which is guided by rational contingency. Our brains automatically calculate the possible outcomes based on accumulated experience, recent relevant evidence, and clues in the context (Ellis, 2006, 2007).

  在自然发生论或建构主义的框架下,有许多不同的理论,包括自然衍生论、连结主义或联想主义、建构主义、认知主义功能主义、竞争模型等等(MacWhinney, 1999)。Ellis (2006)归纳出自然发生论的三个原则:联想式学习、概率学习以及理性关联学习。首先,联想式学习是指在学习目标和个人经验当中建立连结。在先天的设计上,我们的大脑对输入的统计特征十分敏感,当事件的发生频率较高时,连结也会较强(Ortega, 2009)。当一个学习者的个人经验与学习目的产生密切的连结时,让学习发生的充分条件已经完备。自然生成论者也主张学习并非绝对的、分类的,反而,学习是一种在理性权变引导下的概率计算。根据过去积累的经验、最近相关的证据以及情境中的线索,我们的大脑自动计算可能的结果 (Ellis, 2006, 2007)。

In the following paragraphs, we briefly introduce the connectionist perspective, which is one of the main emergentist approaches. Subsequently, we investigate how SLA research is conducted with the connectionist framework.

在之后的段落里,我们将简短介绍自然发生论学派中主要的一支——连结主义的观点。然后,我们会探讨如何在连结主义的架构下进行二语习得的研究。

The connectionist approach is also known as the associationist approach. With the development of the computer technology since the mid-1980s, the use of connectionist approaches have also been applied to the study of memory and learning. Over the past decade, the connectionist framework has been used in SLA. Unlike the processing approaches discussed in the previous sections, the connectionist approach emphasizes that learning occurs through associative processes. According to Ellis & Schmidt (1997), connectionism attempts to develop a computationally parallel distributed processing (PDP) model, which stresses that learning does not occur in sequential stages, but in a parallel way. In other words, learning is not rule-governed, but is driven by the construction of associative patterns (Mitchell & Myles, 2004).

连结主义亦称为联想主义。随着电脑科技在80年代中期快速地发展,连结主义也应用在记忆与学习的相关研究。在过去的十年中,连结主义的架构也应用在二语习得的研究上。不同于在前面章节讨论的加工论,连结主义强调学习是通过连结的过程而产生的。Ellis & Schmidt (1997)指出,连结主义试图发展一套平行分布处理模型,强调学习并非在不同的阶段里依序产生,而是以平行的形式。换言之,学习并非受规则制约支配的,学习时受到连结模式的建构所驱动(Mitchell & Myles, 2004)。

Figure 3.7 is a visual representation of a computationally PDP model. Connectionist models are based on associations among neurons; learning takes place as the strength of association between nodes increases and the associative patterns are repeated over time (Mitchell & Myles, 2004).

图3.7将平行分布处理模型视觉化。连结主义模型以神经元(节点)之间的连结为基础;当节点之间的连结强度增加,而连结模式随着时间的推移而重复,学习因此而产生(Mitchell & Myles, 2004)。

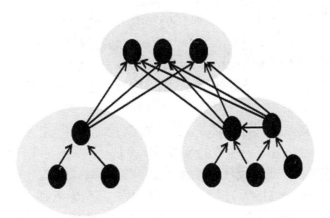

Figure3.7　a complex network consisting of several modules. The arrows indicate the direction of flow of excitation or inhibition. Source: (Eleman et al, 1996)

图3.7　包含数个模组的复杂网络。箭头表示刺激或是抑制的方向。参考来源:Elman et al, 1996

Although there have been a few SLA studies carried out with the connectionist models, a number of researchers have attempted to apply connectionist approaches to their studies (Sokolik, 1990; Soklik and Smith, 1992; Ellis & Schmidt, 1998; Kempe & Mac Whinney, 1998; MacWhinney, 1999, 2001; Ellis, 2003). N. C. Ellis and Schmidt (1997) used an artificial language to investigate adult acquisition of plural morphology using a connectionist model. Both regular and irregular plural morphologies were included in the research design. The subjects received linguistic input in a laboratory so that their exposure and proficiency could be monitored. As frequency was a variable being measured, the subjects received half of the plural forms five times more frequently than the other half. Their data were consistent with the predictions using a connectionist model: Learning is more likely to take place when the frequency is higher. Pinker (1991), however, suggested that we need a rule-based system to acquire regular plural morphology and an associative system to learn irregular morphology. Ellis and Schmidt (1997) concluded that the connectionist mechanism can explain the acquisition of plural morphology, irrespective of whether they are regular or irregular.

虽然较少二语习得的研究是以连结主义为基础，近来一些学者仍企图将连结主义应用在他们的研究中(Sokolik, 1990; Soklik and Smith, 1992; Ellis & Schmidt, 1998; Kempe & Mac Whinney, 1998; MacWhinney, 1999, 2001; Ellis, 2003)。 Ellis & Schmidt (1997)通过一个人工语言，研究在连结主义模型下成人如何习得复数的形态结构。研究设计包含了规则与不规则的复数形态结构。被试在一个实验室里接收语言输入，因此他们接触语言的机会以及语言能力的发展都在严密的监控之下。由于频率是测量的变量之一，所以在测试中有一半的复数形式比另一半的出现频率高出五倍。实验数据和连结主义模型预测的一致。当频率较高的时候，学习较有可能发生。然而，Pinker (1991)提议，我们使用一套以规则为导向的系统来习得规则复数形态结构，以及一套连结系统去学习不规则的形态结构。Ellis & Schmidt (1997)总结指出，连结主义机制可用来解释复数形态结构的习得，无论是规则或是不规则的形态。

3.3 TAP Theory 适当迁移加工理论

As cognitive psychology has become more influential, researchers have started to examine the relationship between cognitive psychology and SLA. TAP theory suggests that learning to use languages in a communicative context is helpful for retrieving it in a similar context (Segalowitz & Lightbown, 1999). In other words, a good learning environment connects the classroom and the real world, enabling learners to rapidly and accurately retrieve what has been learned when they encounter similar contexts.

随着认知心理学影响力的提升，学者开始检视认知心理学和第二语言教学的关联性。适当迁移加工理论(Transfer appropriate processing; TAP)强调，在交际语境中学习使用语言有助于在相似的语境中提取知识(Segalowitz & Lightbown, 1999)。换言之，一个好的学习环境可以把教室和外面世界做连结，让学习者在遇到相似语境时能快速而准确地提取他们所学的知识。

However, not every language feature can be naturally acquired in communicative contexts (Lightbown, 2008). Some low-frequency and low-salience language features are rarely used in natural speech. Also, some features, which are misleadingly similar to learners' L1, compete for attention in instruction and communication (Doughty & Williams, 1998). To deal with these issues, TAP researchers suggest using special instructional tasks to strengthen form-meaning connections.

并非所有的语言特征均可在交际语境中自然地习得(Lightbown, 2008)。某些低频率和不明显的语言特征,在自然的口语中很少出现。此外,有些特征与学习者的母语相近,因此会误导学习者,或在教学与交际时和目标语结构竞争学习者的注意力(Doughty & Williams, 1998)。为了解决这个问题,适当迁移加工理论学者建议,通过使用特殊的教学任务来强化形式与意义的联系。

Gatbonton and Segalowitz (1998; 2003) proposed opportunities for form-meaning mapping practice, in which learners repeatedly use certain expressions or sentence patterns to accomplish classroom tasks. Then, the learners engage in a consolidation activity, in which they focus explicitly on the forms and meaning of each form. Finally, students participate in more open-ended communicative tasks, in which the practiced patterns are very likely to be used. This instructional model promotes automatization by repetition and practice.

Gatbonton and Segalowitz (1998; 2003)提议,通过强化形式与结构联系的练习活动,学生必须重复使用某些词组或句型以完成课堂任务。之后藉由一个巩固活动让学生把重心放在语言的形式结构以及和每个形式结构相对应的意思上。最后,在开放式的交际任务中,学生可能必须使用先前练习的句型完成任务。这个教学模型通过重复练习促进了自动化的实现。

3.3.1. Processing and Learning in an L2 Classroom
　　适当迁移加工与二语课堂教学

Bjork (1994) emphasized on the close relationships between processing approaches and L2 classroom learning. He argued that learning becomes more effective if classroom activities are desirably difficult. When learners work on a more challenging task, they need to work harder during learning. As a result, the learning effect can be retained longer. Based on Bjork (1994)'s proposal, five TAP desirable difficulties for creating a more challenging communicative environment in a L2 classroom have been suggested.

　　Bjork(1994)强调加工理论与二语课堂教学的密切关系,主张如果课堂活动的难度十分理想,学习会更有成效。当学习者投入一个较具挑战性的任务,他们必须付出更高的努力才能达到目的。因此,学习的效果也较持久。根据Bjork(1994)的提议,在二语课堂中打造一个较具挑战性的交际环境有五个TAP理想的难度:

First, TAP theorists suggest varying the conditions of practice, because the more situations in which the language features are encountered, the greater is the likelihood that they will become adequate triggers for retrieval in different situations (Lightbown, 2008). Second, it is suggested to provide contextual interference during learning. In a grammar translation or audiolingual classroom, learners acquire language features in a disconnected order, such as AAABBBCCC (Lightbown, 2008). In contrast to traditional drills in language instruction, contextual interference allows learners to review what they have learned in the communicative contexts created in the classroom. Therefore, the pattern of instruction is ABCABC. With contextual inference, we can intentionally include low-frequency or low-salience features in language instruction (Lightbown & Spada, 2006).

　　首先,适当迁移加工论者主张变化练习的条件与情境,因为当学习者接触越多情境中的语言特征,这些特征就越有可能成为将来在不同情境中提取记忆的触发器(Lightbown, 2008)。

　　其次,适当迁移加工论者也提议在学习中提供语境的推论与线索。在以语法翻译法或是听说法为主的课堂,学习者通过一个如AAABBBCCC般不连续的次序习得语言的特征(Lightbown, 2008)。不同于语言教学中传统的反复操练,情境推论让学习者能在课堂打造的交际语境中复习他们习得的知识。因此,教学的模式为ABCABC。在情境推论的辅助下,我们可以特意地将低频率或是不突出的特征融入语言教学中(Lightbown & Spada, 2006)。

Third, instead of studying intensively in a single learning session, materials are better remembered if learned in multiple brief study sessions (Seabrook et al., 2005). Distributing the focus of learning over time allows learners to review, restructure, and internalize previously learned material. Fourth, to enhance learners' sense of self-monitoring, Lightbown (2008) suggested that teachers need to reduce their feedback and encourage learners to take greater responsibility for their output. Lastly, tests can be used as a tool for retrieving previously learned materials. The retrieval can create a learning event and allow learners to obtain diagnostic information about their progress.

第三,相较于在单一期间内密集学习,若能将同样的材料分散在多个短期区段内反复练习,学习者的记忆成效较佳(Seabrook et al., 2005)。将学习的重心分散在不同的时间可以让学习者拥有复习、重整以及内化先前所学材料的机会。

第四,为了提高学习者自我监控的意识,Lightbown (2008)建议教师减少反馈,并鼓励学习者对他们自己的口语表现多担负一些责任。最后,考试可被用来当做提取过去所学材料的工具。提取的过程也可视为一种学习,并能让学习者了解他们学习的进展与其中的问题。

3.4 Chaos/Complexity Theory 混沌/复杂理论

With the development of SLA field, researchers have proposed different views about language acquisition and the pertinent focus of SLA research. There is an increasing debate between cognitive-based approach and socio-based approach in language acquisition. Over the past decade, Diane Larsen-Freeman proposed the chaos/complexity theory (C/CT) to accommodate diverse perspectives of SLA

(Larsen-Freeman, 1997, 2002, 2008).

随着二语习得研究的发展,研究者通过不同的方法提出各种与语言习得有关的观点以及二语习得研究的重点。因此,这也引起了以认知为基础的学派以及以社会为根本的学派针对语言习得的争论。在过去十年,Diane Larsen-Freeman 提出了"混沌/复杂理论"(chaos/complexity theory, C/CT) 来容纳不同二语习得学派的观点 (Larsen-Freeman, 1997, 2002; Larsen-Freeman & Cameron, 2008)。

Borrowed from a Greek myth, chaos refers to the initial state, nothingness, and total emptiness from which the universe emerged. After chaos, the universe evolved unpredictably, interacting with a variety of factors. As described by Waldrop (1993), the world is not like a clock governed by simple rules. Instead, it is similar to a kaleidoscope; changing patterns make the world new and different. C/CT has influenced many research fields, including applied linguistics. Language should be seen as a nonlinear dynamic system made up of interrelated cognitive and sociocultural elements that allow us to think and act in the society.

借自希腊神话,混沌代表最初的状态,也就是"无"或是来自宇宙的完全虚空。混沌之后,在与许多因素的相互作用下,宇宙的进化是无法预测的。如 Waldrop (1993) 所描述,世界并非像一个时钟里的分针秒针,按着简单的规则运转。相反,世界像个万花筒,在花样图案的不停变化中,世界总是以新的样貌呈现在我们的眼前。混沌/复杂理论影响了许多研究领域,包括应用语言学在内。语言应被视为一个由相互关联的认知与社会文化要素组成的非线性动态系统,这些要素影响了我们在社会中的思考与行动。

As shown in Figure 3.8, SLA involves a complicated process that develops through dynamic and constant interaction among the subsystems as well as alternating moments of stability and turbulence. Any change in a subsystem can affect the other elements in the network. As complex systems are in constant movement, learning occurs when a new order arises as an evolving process after chaos (Larsen-Freeman & Cameron, 2008).

如图3.8所示,二语习得是一个复杂的过程,其中涉及不同子系统之间动态的交互作用,稳定以及混乱的状态交替出现。任何子系统中的变动都会影响网络中的其他要素。由于复合系统处于持续不断的变动中,学习发生于混乱之后新的秩序产生之际(Larsen-Freeman & Cameron, 2008)。

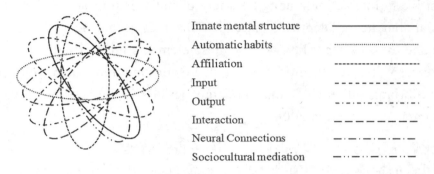

Figure3.8　Second Language Acquisition is a complex system

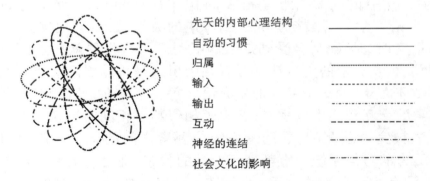

图3.8　二语习得是一个复杂的系统

As we are different individuals, our SLA processes, which are mediated by innate mental structures, contexts, and cultural artifacts, are different. However, we still can find similar patterns from different individuals' SLA processes. Out of chaos emerges a new language, which is a product of a variety of elements involved in the process. In the SLA process, L1 can be seen as the initial condition. The L1 and L2 work as attractors, which refer to regions or poles of a system (Larsen-Freeman & Cameron, 2008). A language learner is initially attracted to

his/her L1 and then to L2 when he/she attempts to acquire a new language. Language development swings between these two poles, in which a learner is attracted or repelled by one of these competing forces. Out of this cycle of attraction and repulsion emerges learners' interlanguage. Each interlanguage phase is highly sensitive to interaction among a variety of individual or social factors and yields similar, but never identical, patterns. This means that acquisition is not predictable and evolves according to how these elements interact with each other in the system. A live acquisition system is in constant movement and never reaches equilibrium, although it may undergo periods of higher/lower stability (Larsen-Freeman & Cameron, 2008).

由于我们是不同的个体,我们的二语习得过程受到内在心理结构、情境与文化因素的影响下也会有所不同。然而,我们仍可在不同个体的二语习得过程中发现相似的模式。在混沌之后衍生的新语言是许多要素相互作用下的产物。在二语习得的过程中,母语可被视为最初的状态。母语和二语作为系统中的两极,拥有磁吸的作用(Larsen-Freeman & Cameron, 2008)。一个语言学习者最初会先受到母语的吸引,之后当他/她企图习得一个新的语言时,他/她又会受到外语的吸引。语言发展就在这两极之间摇摆,这两股相互竞争的力量让学习者在吸引或是排斥之间摇摆。在吸引与排斥的循环之外,就是学习者的中介语。每一个中介语阶段对各种个人或社会因素的交互作用十分敏感,产生了相似却不相同的模式。这意味着习得是无法被完全预测的,它随着系统内要素之间的交互作用而演变发展。充满活力的习得系统一直都处于变动的状态,即使它的稳定度或低或高,它永远没有达到平衡的一天(Larsen-Freeman & Cameron, 2008)。

3.4.1. Complexity Theory in an L2 classroom
复杂理论在二语教学中的应用

From a complexity theorist's perspective, language classroom actions are dynamic and unpredictable because any action in language teaching and learning is connected and co-adaptive. According to Larsen-Freeman and Cameron (2008), there are four components in the process of language teaching and learning.

从复杂理论的角度,语言课堂活动是动态而不可预测的,因为任何语言教学与学习的活动都是相互连结以及相互适应的。Larsen-Freeman and Cameron (2008)指出,在语言教学和学习的过程中有四个要素:

First, complexity theorists emphasize that learning is a continuous process that involves the individual brain and body, a speech community, and the sociopolitical context of language learning. Actions in language learning and teaching are connected. A language class can be seen as a complex system, in which agents and elements, such as learners, teachers, textbooks, the language items being learned, and the physical environment are closely related and adapted to each other.

第一,复杂理论强调学习是一个持续的过程,当中涉及个人的心理生理、语言社群以及语言学习的社会政治条件。语言学习和教学中的行为都是相连的。一个语言课堂可以被视为一个复合系统,当中包含了各种中介以及要素,像是学习者、教师、教材、学习的语言点以及实际环境。这些中介与要素相互连结彼此调适。

Second, according to complexity theory, language is dynamic. Even when presented in a frozen or stabilized formin a syllabus, grammar book, or exam paper, once it is released into the classroom or into the minds of learners, language becomes dynamic (Larsen-Freeman & Cameron, 2008:199). In a classroom, the use of language between a teacher and students and in student group discussions leads to the emergence of language resources and classroom dialects. It creates opportunities for language growth in each individual.

其次,在复杂理论者眼里,语言是动态的。即使像在课程大纲、语法书或是考试卷中,语言呈现的状态是凝结不动或是固定的,一旦语言成了课堂的活动,或是进入学习者的心里,语言就变成动态的了(Larsen-Freeman & Cameron, 2008:199)。在课堂中,教师和学生之间或学生之间语言的使用构成了语言资源以及课堂专属的"方言"。这也创造了个人语言成长的机会。

Co-adaptation refers to change in the connected systems, where change in one system creates change in the other. In the dynamic systems of the language classroom, co-adaptation occurs all the time between a teacher and students, among the students, and between a teacher or students and the learning contexts. As language action emerges from co-adaptation, which is inevitable, neutral, and undirected, it is important to note that co-adaptation is not always positive. Also, teaching is not simply transferring knowledge from the teacher to the students.

相互调适是指相连的系统中的任何改变,都会对另一个系统造成影响。在语言课堂的动态系统中,相互调适的现象在教师和学生之间、学生彼此之间以及学习环境与教师或学生之间不断地发生。由于相互调适的现象是无法避免的、中性的以及无法规范的,语言行为又是在相互调适之中形成的,我们必须明白语言调适并非都是正向的。此外,教学也并非简单地由教师将知识转移给学生。

As learning does not have a predictable linear growth, learners make their own language acquisition paths. Teachers cannot precisely control or monitor their students' progress. A teacher can only manage the dynamics of learning and exploit the complex adaptive nature of language action, while also ensuring that co-adaptation works for the benefit of learning (Larsen-Freeman & Cameron, 2008).

因为学习并非是一个可预测的线性成长曲线,学习者打造各自的语言习得轨迹。教师无法准确地控制学生的语言进展。教师能做的就是管理学习的动态,发掘语言行为中复杂的调适本质,以及确保相互调适的现象能有益于学习 (Larsen-Freeman & Cameron, 2008)。

3.5 Learner Variables 学习者因素

Some individuals are better in learning L2 than others. A number of learner variables, including aptitude, motivation, age, personality and learning style, affective factors, and social distance, may be responsible for these differences. In this section, we focus on aptitude and self-efficacy, which are mostly cognitive. In Chapter 4, we will concentrate on factors such as motivation and identity, describing the relationships between identity, motivation, and language acquisition. These above-mentioned factors are essential for the development of Iowa's instruction model which is extensively discussed in Chapter One. We also provide two instructional examples for reference in Chapter Ten.

在学习第二个语言时,有些人的学习效果明显优于其他人。许多学习者因素,包括天资、动机、年龄、性格与学习风格、情感因素以及社交距离,均可能影响学习的成效。在这几小节中,我们将把重心放在与认知较为相关的天资以及自我效能上。在第四章,我们将探讨动机和身份认同等意念因素,研究语言习得与动机和身份认同的关系。上述因素对于爱荷华大学中文部汉语口语教学模式的形成与发展十分重要,我们已在第一章深入介绍爱大汉语口语教学模式,并在第十章提供两个具体的教学方案实例以供参考。

3.5.1. L2 Aptitude
二语潜质

Aptitude refers to the potential for acquiring new knowledge or skills (Gass & Selinker, 2008). When it is applied to SLA, it appears that some people acquire a new language easily, while others seem to struggle. According to the Modern Language Aptitude Test (MLAT) developed by the Harvard psychologist, John Carroll, in 1953, three cognitive abilities are essential indicators of L2 aptitude: grammatical sensitivity, phonetic coding ability, and memory capacity (Modern Language Aptitude Test, 2000—2001 (Modern Language Aptitude Test); Carroll, 1981; Ortega, 2009). Grammatical sensitivity refers to the ability to recognize the functions of linguistic parts in linguistic wholes. Phonetic coding ability refers to a special capability to identify different sounds and make sound-meaning connections. Memory capacity denotes the ability for rote and decontextualized learning of sound-meaning associations.

潜质(天资)指一个人习得新知识或者新技巧的潜力 (Gass & Selinker, 2008)。当潜质这个概念应用在二语习得上,代表某些人习得一个新的语言比其他人容易。根据哈佛心理学家 John Carroll 在 1953 年发表的当代语言潜质测验(Modern Language Aptitude Test，MLAT)，有三种认知能力可以当做二语潜质的重点指标：语法敏锐度、语音编码能力以及记忆容量(Modern Language Aptitude Test, 2000—2001; Carroll, 1981; Ortega, 2009)。语法敏锐度代表识别语言成分在整体中的功能的能力。语音编码能力代表辨认不同声音以及形成语音和意义连结的特殊能力。记忆容量意指反复背诵和在没有语境的辅助下学习音义连结的能力。

3.5.1.1. L2 Aptitude: Memory Capacity
二语潜质：记忆容量

Memory capacity is seen as a privileged component of L2 aptitude. As memory is involved in information processing, people with greater working memory capacities are expected to learn a new language more efficiently. Therefore, working memory capacity has become an indicator of learning rate and ultimate attainment in foreign language acquisition (Ortega, 2009). Elisabet Service and her colleagues. (1992, 1995) found that Finnish elementary students, who were good at repeating random non-word lists, were also better in learning English vocabulary. Their results are consistent with the findings that adults with low short-term memory capacities have difficulty in remembering new words (Chun & Payne, 2004). Harrington and Sawyer (1992) investigated the correlation between memory span and L2 performance. They found that individuals with greater memory spans achieved higher scores on the grammar and reading sections of the TOEFL.

  记忆容量被视为二语潜质中很特别的一部分。因为记忆与信息处理有关，拥有较大工作记忆容量的人被期待能更有效率地习得一个新的语言。因此，工作记忆容量成为外语习得速率以及最终成就的一个指标(Ortega, 2009)。Elisabet Service 和她的同事(1992, 1995)发现，在芬兰的小学生中，善于复述随机的非文字字表的人学习英语词汇的成效也较好。他们的研究发现和另一个与成人被试有关的研究一致。另一个研究发现短程记忆容量较低的成人在记忆新的生词时困难重重(Chun & Payne, 2004)。 Michael Harrington & Mark Sawyer (1992)探讨记忆广度与二语表现的相关性。他们发现记忆广度较大的人在托福考试的语法和阅读部分的分数也较高。

However, increasing number of researchers are questioning the validity of memory tasks and proficiency measures, because differential learning rates and L2 ultimate attainments are more complex. Masoura and Gathercole (2005) found that vocabulary learning is boosted after the accumulation of a threshold size of vocabulary knowledge. This means that memory alone cannot explain L2 learners' vocabulary development.

不过,越来越多的研究质疑记忆测试和能力量表的信度,因为不同的学习速率和二语最终成就远比我们想象的复杂。Masoura & Gathercole (2005)发现,在积累了一定的词汇知识之后,词汇学习就会快速提升。这意味着记忆不仅仅能解释二语学习者的词汇发展。

O'Brien et al. (2006) found that good memory facilitates different aspects of language learning at different stages. They observed the L2 changes among 43 learners of Spanish over one semester and found that good memory helps vocabulary learning at the beginning stages. Later, good memory is beneficial for acquiring grammar rules.

O'Brien 和他的同事(2006)发现,较佳的记忆能力能够在不同阶段促进语言学习的不同方面。他们观察了43个西班牙语学生在一个学期内的二语变化,发现较佳的记忆能力能在刚开始的阶段帮助词汇的学习。之后,较佳的记忆能力有助于语法规则的习得。

3.5.1.2. Instruction and L2 Aptitude
二语潜质与教学应用

According to Skehan (2002) and Robinson (2002), instruction can facilitate L2 learning for students with different L2 aptitude profiles. In an aptitude-treatment interactions research study conducted by Wesche (1981), a group of Canadian public servants were placed in different types of French courses on the basis of their MLAT scores. Those who had a high score on phonetic coding test were assigned to a class taught with audiolingual and audiovisual methods, in which aural and visual input and repetitive drills were extensively used. Those who had a better score on grammatical sensitivity test were directed to take a traditional grammar explanation course. Three months later, these students who were assigned to these courses based on their test scores greatly outperformed their peers who were randomly assigned to these two courses. L2 aptitude seems to be an effective indicator of learner's strength and an efficient way to match a student to an appropriate instructional approach.

根据 Skehan (2002) 和 Robinson (2002) 的研究，对于二语潜质不同的学生，教学可以促进他们的二语学习。在 Wesche (1981) 所进行的一个潜质实验互动研究中，有一组的加拿大公务员因职业需要必须学法语。他们根据各自的当代语言潜质测验 (MLAT) 成绩被分到采用不同教学法的法语班。语音编码分数较高的被分到以听说法或视听法教学为主的班级，在课堂中接受大量听觉、视觉的输入以及反复的操练是常态。在语法敏锐度部分表现较佳的人则被分到采取传统语法解释的法语班。三个月后，这些依照他们测验成绩分班的学员表现远远超过那些被随机分到这两种法语班的学员。二语潜质似乎成为一个探查学习者潜能的有力指标以及一个将学生与适合的教学法配对的方法。

However, as pointed out by Ortega (2009), the aptitude-instruction matching is more complicated. In Robinson's (2002) and Skehan's (2002) models, an L2 learner may have a higher performance in some aptitude categories and lower in others (HL), or high in all categories (HH) or low in all categories (LL). These two models allow us to better understand how instructional approaches can be designed to promote effective L2 learning to satisfy different learners' needs.

不过，Ortega (2009) 指出，潜质与教学配对比我们想象的复杂。在 Robinson's (2002) 和 Skehan's (2002) 提出的模型中，一个二语学习者可能在某些潜质类别表现较佳，而在另一些类别表现较差 (HL)，或是在所有的类别都有很高的潜质 (HH)，或在所有的类别都没有突出的表现 (LL)。这两个模型让我们更了解应该如何设计教学法以满足不同学习者的需求以及提高二语学习的成效。

3.5.2. Self-efficacy
自我效能

3.5.2.1. Self-efficacy and Learning
自我效能与学习

Every individual can identify goals that he/she wants to accomplish and things that he/she wants to change or achieve. However, most people shy away from goal setting when they realize that putting these plans into action is not easy. Bandura (1986) claimed that an individual's self-efficacy plays an essential role in accomplishing goals and overcoming challenges, and this applies to L2 learning.

　　每个人都能指出他想要完成的目标以及他想要达到或改变的事。但是，在理解到实现这些计划并不容易之后，大多数的人会回避设定的目标。Bandura (1986)主张，一个人的自我效能与他是否能完成目标以及克服挑战有关，而这个概念也可适用于学习第二外语。

As a theory of motivational psychology, self-efficacy refers to belief about the ability to produce a desired outcome. The theory originated from observations that people who strongly believe in their capabilities tend to perform better than those who doubt themselves. The sense of self-efficacy is developed from mastery experience, observing other people and feedback from others (Bandura, 1986).

　　源自动机心理学理论，自我效能代表一种信念，相信自己有能力取得理想的成果。这个理论源于那些对自己能力较为自信的人比那些总是怀疑自己能力的人有更突出的表现。自我效能的意识通过个人成功的经验、观察他人以及他人反馈而形成(Bandura, 1986)。

As shown in Figure 3.9, people with a strong sense of self-efficacy identify their aims and know how to use different kinds of resources and efforts to achieve their goals. They are confident of their own ability and potential. According to Bandura (1994), people with high self-efficacy view challenging problems as tasks to be mastered. They develop a strong commitment to the activities in which they are interested. They usually recover quickly from setbacks and disappointments. On the contrary, people with low self-efficacy avoid challenges and think difficult tasks are beyond their ability. They easily become frustrated and need longer to recover from failures because they put too much emphasis on negative outcomes (Bandura, 1994).

如图3.9所示,拥有较强自我效能意识的人辨识他们的目标、知道如何利用不同的资源以及努力去达到目的。他们对自己的能力与潜力十分自信。Bandura(1994)指出,自我效能高的人将挑战与问题视为要去征服的任务。对于有兴趣的活动,他们有强固的承诺去完成。他们不轻易被挫折或失意打倒,总能很快地恢复精神,整装再战。相反的,自我效能低落的人回避挑战,并认为困难的任务是他们能力之外的挑战。他们很容易感到挫败,因为他们太过看重负面的结果,所以需要很长的时间才能从失败中恢复(Bandura, 1994)。

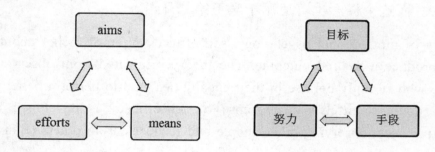

Figure3.9　Self-efficacy Triangle.　　　图3.9　自我效能三角

According to Bandura (1994), self-efficacy is a living developmental process, which continues to evolve over time as people acquire new skills and have new experiences. Generally, there are four primary sources of self-efficacy. First, as described by Bandura, the most effective way to develop self-efficacy is through mastery. Successful experience makes us more confident in our ability. Second, witnessing the successes of others allows us to believe that similar tasks are within our ability (Bandura, 1994). Third, people can be persuaded that they have the potential to carry out tasks. Being encouraged by friends, supervisors, or family members motivates us to achieve a goal and protect us against self-doubt. Finally, moods, emotional states, physical reactions, and stress levels directly influence feelings about personal capabilities; learning to minimize stress and elevate moods when encountering challenges can improve our sense of self-efficacy.

　　Bandura (1994)指出，自我效能是一个动态发展的过程，随着人们习得新技能以及拥有新的经验而不断地演变。大体上，自我效能的形成有四个主要的来源。第一，如 Bandura 所述，形成自我效能最有效的方法就是通过精通或娴熟某个技能的成功经验。成功的经验让我们对自己的能力更有自信。其次，亲眼目睹别人成功的经验也会让我们相信自己也能完成类似的任务(Bandura, 1994)。第三，人们可以被说服自己有潜力去完成任务。朋友、领导或是家人的鼓励帮助我们努力达到目标以及摆脱自我怀疑。最后，心情、情绪状态、生理反应以及压力程度都直接影响人们对自己能力的感觉；学习在面临挑战时纾解压力以及振作心情能增进我们的自我效能。

3.5.2.2. Academic Self-efficacy and Instruction
学术自我效能与教学应用

When the concept of self-efficacy is applied to learning and academic performance, the term "academic self-efficacy" is used. Academic self-efficacy refers to a student's belief that he/she can successfully accomplish course-specific tasks, demonstrate the competency skills required for the course, satisfactorily complete assignments, pass the exams, and meet the requirements to continue his/her major. The higher the academic self-efficacy is, the greater is the goal aspirations and the firmer is the commitment to achieving goals. In this situation, a learning activity should foster self-efficacy by creating a learning environment in which peer competition is de-emphasized. Instead, self-comparison is stressed for developing a sense of self-efficacy and promoting academic achievement (Peer & McClendon, 2002).

　　当自我效能的概念应用在学习或是学业表现上时，我们使用"学术自我效能"这个术语。学术自我效能指一个学生相信自己能够成功地完成课程相关的任务、完美地展现课程所需的技能、满意地做完作业、通过考试以

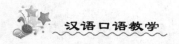

及达到所选专业的要求。学术自我效能越高,达到目标的渴望也就越强,而完成任务的承诺也就越坚定。在这个情况下,学习活动必须能助长自我效能。我们可以打造一个减低同侪竞争的学习环境,强调自我比较以发展自我效能的意识,从而促进学术上的自我实现(Peer & McClendon, 2002)。

Pedagogically, methods of stimulating self-efficacy and presenting Chinese language as learnable are very important. First, an instructor should encourage learners by telling them that they are capable of performing designated tasks in class and using Chinese to express themselves in the real world. Second, it is necessary to provide environmental conditions, such as instructional strategies and appropriate technology tools, to promote a learner's self-efficacy. Third, an instructor should create opportunities for learners to experience successful learning. As we know, character recognition is the most challenging task for beginner-level Chinese speakers. If an instructor uses various kinds of scaffolding tools, such as introducing Chinese radicals, then learners can build their sense of self-efficacy through successful recognition of characters. Subsequently, this will motivate them to increase their efforts to achieve their learning goals.

　　教学上,运用激发自我效能的方法以及让学生理解汉语的"可学性"十分重要。首先,教师必须说服学生,让他们相信自己有能力完成课上交付的任务以及在现实世界中用汉语表达自己的想法。其次,必须提供充分的环境条件,例如教学策略、恰当的技术手段来促进学生的自我效能。第三,教师必须为学生创造机会,让他们拥有成功学习的经验。我们知道,识读汉字对汉语二语初学者来说是个艰巨的挑战。倘若能运用包括部首在内的各种辅助方法,学习者就可通过成功识读汉字的经验建立起他们的自我效能。这会激励学习者更加努力完成他们的学习任务。

Chapter Four 第四章
Language Socialization Theory and Research
语言社会化理论与研究

4.1 The Social Turn in the Language Learning Field
语言学习领域的社会化趋势

In this chapter, we focus on the increasing social turn in the language learning field, in which language learning is understood essentially as a social activity. Among the language theories and empirical research that are related to this perspective, we look at sociocultural theory, which is closely associated with the Russian psychologist, Lev S. Vygotsky. Following the direction of mainstream language teaching and learning, we then address the theoretical basis and research principles of language socialization in second language acquisition (SLA). With the social turn in language acquisition research, language students are no longer treated as reactive learners who receive and process input, but rather as proactive language users whose personal characteristics, such as their language background, identity, and motivations, will have an impact on language learning outcomes. Following this social perspective, we briefly review the rise of identity as well as the motivational factors in the language learning process. With these discussions on the social perspectives of language learning, we introduce an interface between these sociocultural perspectives and the second language (L2) teaching field—task-based language instruction (TBLI), which as one important approach to communicative language teaching has been implemented in the curriculum in the Chinese Program at the University of Iowa.

在这一章，我们将关注语言学习领域的社会化趋势，语言学习被视为一个社会活动。在与这一语言视角相关的语言学理论和实证研究中，我们将先介绍由俄国心理学家列夫·维果茨基Vygotsky提出的社会文化理论。秉承当前语言教学的主流发展方向,我们接下来将讨论二语习得中语言社会化理论的理论基础和研究准则。随着语言习得研究越来越关注社会因素,语言学习者不再被视为被动吸收、加工知识的学习者,而是作为一个主动活跃的语言使用者积极地参与学习的整个过程。在这一动态过程中,他们的个人因素,像语言背景、身份认同和学习动机都直接影响他们的学习效果。在这种社会性视角的引导下,我们将简短回顾身份认同和学习动机对语言学习的影响。综合这些关于语言学习领域的社会性的讨论,我们将在本章最后介绍语言社会化理论和语言教学交互作用下的"任务型教学法"(以下简称TBLI)。作为交际型语言教学的一个主要模式,任务型教学法被引入到爱荷华汉语口语教学模式中,成为该中文项目汉语口语教学及评估的重要组成部分。

4.1.1. Sociocultural Perspectives on Language Learning and Research
语言学习和研究的社会文化层面

Based on the work of Vygotsky (1978, 1987), the field of SLA has witnessed a significant increase in researchers who use a sociocultural theoretical framework (SCT) to guide their work (Block, 2003; Lantolf, 2000; Lantolf & Thorne, 2006; Swain, 2000, among the others). In contrast to cognitive models of SLA, researchers using SCT theoretical perspective attempt to account for the social and cultural aspects in acquiring L2 and to explain how those variables affect language learning as it happens in a particular context.

以列夫·维果茨基的相关理论为基准 (Vygotsky, 1978, 1987),第二语言习得领域出现了一批以社会文化理论为理论指导的新兴研究者(Block, 2003; Lantolf, 2000; Lantolf & Thorne, 2006; Swain, 2000, etc.)。不同于二语习得中的认知模式,这批以社会文化理论为出发点的研究者的关注重点在于理解习得一门语言过程中的社会与文化方面的因素,并同时解释这些变量如何在特定的语境中影响语言的学习。

James Lantolf, a leading scholar in SCT, began applying Vygotskian insights to SLA since the early1990s. Through his work, SCT and its associated theoretical approaches have become well known to SLA audiences (Lantolf & Appel, 1995; Lantolf, 2000; Lantolf & Thorne, 2006). According to Lantolf (2006), language learning is a process mediated partially through learner's developing use and control of mental tools, namely, language. Language serves as a tool that mediates between social individuals and their environment. Through the scaffolded interaction between a novice and an expert (e.g., learner and teacher), a notion that was later expanded by SLA researchers to include pair and group work among peers (Donato, 1994; Swain & Lapkin, 1998; Swain, 2000), learners achieve desired learning outcomes within the zone of proximal development (ZPD). The ZPD is conceived as a metaphorical space between what the learner is able to achieve independently and what he/she would be able to achieve with help. It is within this ZPD that language learners develop sensitivity to their current abilities and their potential development. The notion of the ZPD also emphasizes on context from linguistic, situational, interactional, and cultural perspectives, which is shaped by people in communication with a variety of roles and statuses (Kramsch, 1993). From this perspective, the process of interaction itself constitutes learning. Researchers who work within this sociocultural framework (Donato, 1994; Brooks & Donato, 1994; Swain & Lapkin, 1998, 2003) more often look broadly at what is happening in the social setting that both surrounds and is embedded in the language learning context, particularly in the language classroom. This line of research examines language acquisition as a collaborative construction of opportunities (Swain & Lapkin, 1998), which Swain and Lapkin (1998) directly regarded as occasions for learning.

　　James Lantolf 作为社会文化理论的领军人物,早在90年代初就开始把列夫·维果茨基的理论应用到二语习得的领域。通过他的研究成果,越来越多的二语习得者了解到社会文化理论及其相关的理论架构(Lantolf & Appel, 1995; Lantolf, 2000; Lantolf & Thorne, 2006)。Lantolf (2006) 指出,语言学习是一个过程,受到学习者对语言这个工具的使用和掌控的影响。语言同时肩负连接个体和个体所处社会环境的媒介角色。通过一个新手与专家(比如:学生和教师)之间的互动交流,学习者在最近发展区内取得理想的学习效果。这一理念随后由二语习得的研究者扩展到同学间的两人成对或小组的交流。"最近发展区域",顾名思义,是一个差距空间的隐喻,描述"学习者能够独立完成"和"须通过外界帮助方能成就"的差距。这一概念从语言学、社会性、交际性和文化性方面强调了语言学习的环境。这个环境随着交际者所处社会角色和地位的不同而变化(Kramsch, 1993)。根据这个观点,学习在交际中开展。相关的许多研究(Donato, 1994; Brooks & Donato, 1994; Swain & Lapkin, 1998, 2003)大多关注语言学习的语境,例如语言课堂以及其所处的社会大环境。

Unlike the claim that comprehensible input leads to learning, we wish to suggest that what occurs in collaborative dialogues is learning. That is, learning does not happen outside performance; it occurs in performance. Furthermore, learning is cumulative, emergent, and ongoing... (Swain & Lapkin, 1998, p. 321)

这些研究将语言习得视为一个协力创造机会的过程(Swain & Lapkin, 1998),Swain & Lapkin (1998)更直接认为:"不同于那些认为可理解输入会产生学习的观点,我们认为合作性对话的过程即为学习。换言之,学习并非发生在表现之外,而是在表现当中呈现的。更进一步来说,学习本身是累积的,自发的,不断进行的……"(Swain & Lapkin, 1998, p.321)

After initially proposing the output hypothesis (1985), Swain later modified it, because she shifted from regarding output as a language product to understanding it as a cognitive tool, a part of the learning process (Swain, 2000, 2005). Learners, therefore, take a proactive role in their language development.

从Swain1985年提出她的输出假说以来,她一直致力于修正、完善她的假说,最初她把语言输出视为一种语言产出,但后来语言输出被当做一种认知工具,甚至是语言学习过程的一部分(Swain, 2000, 2005)。因此,学习者在语言发展过程中扮演积极主动的角色。

The sociocultural approach, which challenges the compartmentalization of the social and psycholinguistic aspects of language learning, has gained a wide acceptance in SLA. Although sociocultural theory offers a rich theoretical and conceptual framework for reconceptualizing relationships between learners, language, and their sociocultural context, its comparatively recent introduction to the field of SLA indicates that many of its methodological implications are yet to be adequately debated and explored. Thus, we turn to our next topic, language socialization, which is one of the sociocultural approaches in SLA research.

不同于语言学习中将社会与心理语言学因素完全区分的概念，社会文化框架在二语习得领域得到了广泛的关注和认同。尽管社会文化理论从理论和概念层面提出了一个重新认识学习者、语言以及他们所处的社会文化环境的框架，但作为一个二语习得领域的新兴理论框架，它在研究方法方面仍有待进一步的探讨和研究。以此为出发点，我们将在下一小节介绍二语习得社会文化理论中的一个分支——"语言社会化"。

4.1.2. Language Socialization in SLA
二语习得中的语言社会化

As discussed earlier, the field of SLA has seen increasing debate over questions that relate to the nature of language and language learning. For many years, the dominant voice in SLA research, including research related to language classroom learning, has understood interaction as a cognitive process (Gass, 1997, 2006; Long, 1996; Long & Doughty, 2003, among the others). This cognitively oriented view of SLA has been challenged in recent years (Block, 2003; Firth & Wagner, 1997; Lantolf, 2000; Lantolf & Thorne, 2006). An early centerpiece of the debate was a special issue of the *Modern Language Journal* (1997), in which the lead article by Firth and Wagner was followed by a series of responses from a variety of perspectives. Ten years later, when the *Modern Language Journal* reviewed the topic in a focus issue (2007), it was clear that the professional consensus has shifted significantly away from a cognitive and mentalist orientation and moved towards a sociocultural perspective.

正如前段所述，二语习得领域就语言和语言学习的本质的争论日趋激烈。在很长一段时间内，包括语言课堂相关研究在内的二语习得领域的主流论点，都主张把互动交际视为一种认知加工的过程(Gass, 1997, 2006; Long, 1996; Long & Doughty, 2003, etc.)。然而，这一从认知角度出发的二语习得观点受到越来越多的质疑与挑战 (Block, 2003; Firth & Wagner,

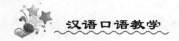

1997; Lantolf, 2000; Lantolf & Thorne, 2006)。早期的一个焦点辩论始于 *Modern Language Journal* (1997)发行的一期特刊,由 Firth & Fagner 发表的文章和二语习得界其他研究者从各个视角的回应文章组成。十年后,*Modern Language Journal* 发行了一期回顾这一历史性辩论的特刊(2007),这两场关于二语习得本质、跨度十年的辩论,清楚地呈现出二语习得领域从以认知和个体发展为中心向社会文化视角转换的趋势。

Currently, SLA researchers increasingly recognize the relevance and importance of sociocultural factors in the language learning process (Atkinson, 2002; Block, 2003; Kramsch & Whiteside, 2007; Lafford, 2007; Lantoff, 2000; Lantolf & Johnson, 2007; Lantolf & Thorne, 2006; Larsen-Freeman, 2007; Walsh, 2006; Young & Miller, 2004; Young, 2009). However, not everyone agree on precisely how to bring these sociocultural factors into play in a theoretically coherent way in research or teaching. Language socialization, one of the main theoretical strands in the field of sociolinguistics, provides an integrative perspective to understand the cognitive, social, cultural, and political complexity of language learning. Researchers following the language socialization tradition regard language and culture as an inseparable unit. By considering a language socialization perspective, many SLA researchers use ethnographic and longitudinal methods to examine language learning and pertinent learning outcomes (Duff, 2002, 2009; Schmidt, 1990; Siegal, 1995; Watson-Gegeo, 1992, 2004).

到目前为止,二语习得研究者已经逐渐认识到语言学习过程中社会文化因素的相关性和重要性(Atkinson, 2002; Block, 2003; Kramsch & Whiteside, 2007; Lafford, 2007; Lantolf, 2000; Lantolf & Johnson, 2007; Lantolf & Thorne, 2006; Larsen-Freeman, 2007; Walsh, 2006; Young & Miller, 2004; Young, 2009)。然而,众人对于如何将这些社会文化因素系统地体现在研究和教学中仍未达成共识。语言社会化作为社会语言学领域的一个主要理论分支,为语言学习的认知性、社会性、文化性以及政治复杂性提供了更全面的视角。从社会文化性传统出发的研究者认为,语言和文化是一个不可分割的整体。以这一立场为基础,很多二语习得研究者采用了人种志和纵向研究方法来重新认识语言学习和其相关的学习效果 (Duff, 2002,

2009; Schmidt, 1990; Siegal, 1995; Watson-Gegeo, 1992, 2004)。

Siegal (1995) discussed the cases of two white western upper middle-class women, Arina and Mary, living and studying in Japan. She described the difference in their sociolinguistic competence. Both had the desire to speak politely and they knew that to speak competently in Japanese, honorifics were necessary. In addition, both were somewhat ambivalent about using honorific language. Siegal argued that to understand individual differences in sociolinguistic competence in L2 community, it is necessary to consider the conscious and unconscious desires of the learner to maintain his/her image and the resulting language use, which might deviate from native speaker norms. This study provides a good paradigm of language socialization research, in which the role of language subjectivity in the acquisition of sociolinguistic competence in L2 is well articulated in its social, cultural, and cognitive framework.

　　Siegal (1995) 在研究中讨论两位西方上层的中产阶级白人女性 Arina 和 Mary 在日本生活学习的事例。她着重描述两人在社会语言能力上的差异。两人都希望能得体地用日文表达，她们也深知要想说好日文，敬语的使用是非常必要的。但是，两人对敬语使用又都有所保留。Siegal 指出，要了解在二语语境中社会语言能力的个体差异，就必须要考虑学习者潜意识或有意识地保持其从母语衍生的自我形象以及与此相关的语言使用。Siegal 的研究为语言社会化研究提供了一个很好的范例。这类的研究强调在二语习得的过程中，语言主观性对社会语言能力的掌握格外重要。研究本身也充分展现了其社会、文化和认知方面的兼容并包性。

Following her longitudinal previous linguistic system (L1) socialization study in nine families (1992), in which multi-year ethnographic and discourse analytic studies were conducted in nine families' home and community contexts in Solomon Islands, Watson-Gegeo (2004) claimed that language socialization paradigm serves as a theoretical and methodological basis for socially situated SLA research. She listed five key premises of the language socialization paradigm for SLA: a) Linguistic and cultural knowledge are constructed through each other and that language-acquiring children and adults are active and selective agents in both the processes; b) There is no context-free language learning, and all communicative contexts involve social, cultural, and political dimensions that affect the linguistic forms that are available or taught and how they are represented; c) Language socialization theory has to deal with the complexities of context essential to analysis; d) Children and adults learn culture largely through participating in linguistically marked events, whose structure, integrity, and characteristics are primarily understood through verbal cues to such meanings; and e) Cognition is built from experience and is situated in sociohistorical and sociopolitical contexts.

在先前一个母语社会化纵向研究的基础上，Watson-Gegeo 2004 年发表了一个后续研究。在 1992 年的研究中，Watson-Gegeo 对九个家庭以及它们位于索罗门群岛的社会环境进行了人种志和语篇分析的研究调查。Watson-Gegeo (2004) 主张，语言社会化可为以社会视角为基础的二语习得研究提供理论和方法的研究范例。她同时列举出五个二语习得语言社会化范例的前提：1) 语言和文化知识是共同建构的。在语言习得过程中的孩童与成人在共建过程中皆扮演积极主动的决策者的角色；2) 无语境的语言学习根本不存在。所有交际环境都涉及社会、文化和政治等诸多方面，这些方面同时对体现其特点的语言形式产生直接的影响；3) 语言社会化理论主要着眼于分析复杂语境；4) 孩童和成人大多通过参与有语言形式特点的活动来学习文化，通过在这些活动中的言语信息对活动的结构、综合性和特点有所了解。5) 认知是通过经验以及置身于社会历史和社会政治的复杂语境中建立的。

As summarized by Ortega (2009), "second language socialization studies help reconceptualize as social not only the process of language learning but also its outcomes" (p. 239). This integrative perspective would transform SLA research, making it more relevant to language learners' experience. In addition, it has transformed the way in which we design materials and how we teach languages in classrooms. These broader societal approaches in research and theory allow exploration of issues, such as how identity, motivation, social status, and values influence L2 learning outcomes.

Ortega (2009)指出,"二语社会化研究帮助我们重新认识社会性不仅是语言学习的过程,也是其结果。"(p. 239)这种一体化的观点将从根本上改变二语习得研究,使其与语言学习者的学习经历有了更加紧密的联系。除此以外,它也影响了我们教学材料的设计以及课堂上语言教学的方式。从理论上和研究上都更趋宏观的社会化模式使我们有机会进一步探讨关于语言学习者的身份认同、学习动机、社会地位以及价值观念对二语学习效果的影响。在下一小节,我们将讨论二语习得中的身份认同问题。

4.1.3. The Rise of Identity in SLA
二语习得领域中的身份认同的崛起

A recent area of research related to the issue of language socialization deals with how one's identity is positioned and constructed by the self or others during discursive interactions of various kinds. L2 learning also involves the construction of an L2 identity. The study of identity has become an increasingly vibrant research area in SLA research. Bonny Norton formulated the most influential model of L2 identity theory (Norton Peirce, 1995; Norton, 2000). Norton Peirce (1995) made a first call for a comprehensive theory of social identity that integrates the language learner and the language learning context. Since then, considerable work has been published featuring identity as a key construct in L2 learning (Block, 2003, 2007; Kinginger, 2004; Lantolf & Genung, 2003; Norton, 2000; Pavlenko & Blackledge, 2004; Siegal, 1995).

目前语言社会化研究的一个重要议题在于关注一个人在交流互动中形成身份认同的过程。很多时候,二语的学习同时也意味着第二个身份的建构。相关的研究在二语习得研究中日趋活跃。其中,Bonny Norton 提出了最具影响力的二语身份理论(Norton, 1995; Norton, 2000)。在 Norton Pierce (1995)提出结合语言学习者和语言学习环境的综合性的社会身份理论之后,二语习得领域出现了大量分析二语学习中语言身份因素的相关研究。(Block, 2003, 2007; Kinginger, 2004; Lantolf & Genung, 2003; Norton, 2000; Pavlenko & Blackledge, 2004; Siegal, 1995)

One of the most frequently quoted studies on identity in the foreign language

instructional context is Lantolf and Genung (2003). They reported on the experience of one of the authors, Genung, in learning Mandarin Chinese at an American university. Genung was presented as an experienced and successful language learner, who had studied up to varying degrees of proficiency in several languages. At the time of the study, she was a colonel in the U.S. Army. In the course of her Chinese study in a classroom that she characterized as being filled with hostility, Genung's social learning motives (the desire to communicate with others and self-related motives, including a drive towards self-fulfillment) shifted to cognitive motives, including the learning of facts and achieving a high grade.

  Lantolf & Genung 在 2003 年发表一个关于身份认同的研究，这个研究在外语教学领域被广泛引用。他们在研究中重现了同为研究者之一的 Genung 在一所美国大学学习汉语的经历。在研究中，Genung 的形象是一个学过好几门语言的成功的语言学习者。除此之外，她还是一名美国陆军上校。在她描述为火药味十足的汉语课堂学习过程中，她的社会学习动机（与人交流的愿望，自身的学习动力，包括一种达到自我实现的动力）逐渐转换为掌握具体的语言点并取得优异成绩的认知动机。

Kinginger (2004) investigated the trials and tribulations of Alice, a highly motivated learner who had to overcome significant personal, social, and material obstacles to her learning of French in the study-abroad context. Unlike some of the other participants in her program, Alice did not end her stay in France with a realization that she could never be taken seriously as an L2 speaker; instead, she changed from a parochial American to an intellectually more sophisticated French-speaking person, knowledgeable of and interested in world affairs. Over time, she was able to gain membership in different communities of practice with French students, a process that opened up the prospect of new subject positions for her.

  在海外留学的情境下，Kinginger (2004) 观察了 Alice 在海外学习法语的甘苦。Alice 是一个有着高度学习积极性的语言学习者。不同于其他参与留学项目中的学习者，Alice 克服了重重困难，无论是个人的、社会的还是物质上的。她在法国的学习旅程并未因为无法融入当地生活以及得到当地人的认同而画上休止符。Alice 在留学过程中逐步从一个狭隘的美国人的小我走出来，逐渐成长成为一个有着广阔视野，老练的法语使用者。同时她也和法国学生一起融入当地各种团体活动，为她之后的发展开辟了新的可能性。

The above-mentioned studies support Firth and Wagner's (1997, 2007) call for more research on the social identities that L2 learners may adopt in their L2 learning experience. Following the social nature of human beings, language learners' identities are not something fixed, but rather are fragmented and contested in nature (Norton Peirce, 1995), because it is socially constructed and situated. In the following section, we present a discussion on motivation, another socially situated phenomenon, as noted by Dörnyei (2001).

　　上述的研究充分响应Firth & Wagner (1997, 2007)的呼吁，强调应该有更多二语学习者在学习过程中逐步形成第二种身份认同的相关研究出现。人类本身即是社会性的动物，在此前提下，语言学习者的身份认同绝对不是一成不变的，由于身份认同的社会性本质，身份认同是片段且充满矛盾与冲突的(Norton, 1995)。在下一个小节，我们将进一步讨论学习者的学习动机问题。正如Dörnyei (2001) 所言，学习动机也是一个社会性的现象。

4.1.4. Motivational Factors in Language Learning Tasks
　　语言学习中的动机因素

One of the individual differences frequently used to explain why some L2 learners are more successful than others is motivation. The concept of motivation is diversely defined. Generally, there are two widely recognized types of motivation: integrative and instrumental. Integrativeness is defined as "a genuine interest in learning the second language in order to come closer to the other language community" (Gardner, 2001: 5, as cited by Ortega, 2009: 170). Integrative motivation, therefore, is based on interest in learning the L2, with the intention to participate in or integrate oneself into the L2 using speech community. On the other hand, instrumental motivation involves perception of purely practical value in learning an L2, such as increasing job and business opportunities, accessing information, or just passing a course in school. Among many forms of motivation,

Gardner (2001) believed that integrative motivation is optimal and most facilitative.

在讨论为什么某些二语学习者比其他同学学得好的时候,我们常常提到的一个个体差异因素就是学习动机。然而,学习动机的概念却有各种不同的定义。一般来说,有两种广为人知的动机:综合动机和策略动机。综合动机即指为了接近另一种语言的文化环境而真心诚意地学习第二语言的主观能动性 (Gardner, 2001:5, as cited by Ortega, 2009:170)。因此,综合动机的目的在于学好二语以便能够参与和融入二语的语言使用环境。策略动机则与学习二语的实用价值有关,包括工作上的晋升和生意机会,得到某个信息,甚至于满足某个课程学分要求。在各种形式的学习动机中,Gardner (2001) 相信综合动机最优化、也最具有促进作用。

Most of the research on motivation have been conducted using data collected with questionnaires that ask participants to report on their reasons for language learning (Gardner & Lambert, 1972; Gardner, 1985, 2001). Among them, the Attitude/Motivation Test Battery (AMTB) developed by Gardner and Lambert has become the dominant instrument in L2 learning motivation.

大部分关于学习动机的研究都主要采用让参与者回答关于他们语言学习初衷的相关问卷调查 (Gardner & Lambert, 1972; Gardner, 1985, 2001)。在这些问卷调查中,以 Gardner & Lambert 研发的学习态度和动机标准化测试工具 (AMTB) 最为有名,已成为二语学习动机研究中最主要的测试工具。

Dörnyei and Ottó (1998) proposed a three-phase model of motivation: the pre-actional stage, actional stage, and post-actional stage. This model is intended to show that different motives may be involved in different time periods and that they may change over time. More recently, Dörnyei et al. (2006) proposed the construct of the L2 Motivational Self System, which is made up of the following three main components:

Dörnyei & Ottó (1998)提出一个三阶段学习动机模型:动机前期、活动期、动机后期。这个模型显示,学习动机会随着时间的推移而改变。最近几年，Dörnyei (2006) 提出"二语自我动机体系"。这个体系主要由三个方面组成：

1. "Ideal L2 Self", referring to the L2-specific facet of one's "ideal self"—if the person we would like to become speaks an L2, the ideal L2 self is a powerful motivator to learn the particular language because we would like to reduce the discrepancy between our actual and ideal selves.

第一，"理想化二语自我"，即二语层面的理想自我。如果我们想变成一个会说某个语言的人，那么理想化二语自我就是学习这门二语的有力动机，因为人们总是希望缩减现实自我与理想自我之间的差距；

2. "Ought-to L2 Self", referring to the attributes that we believe we ought to possess to avoid possible negative outcomes—this motivational dimension may therefore bear little resemblance to our own desires or wishes.

第二，"期待的二语自我"：为了避免负面结果的产生，人们相信自己应该具有某种特征。这个动机方向并不等同于我们的愿望和期待；

3. "L2 Learning Experience", which concerns executive motives related to the immediate learning environment and experience. (Dörnyei et al., 2006：145)

第三，"二语学习经历"：这个动机层面主要与语言学习环境和经历的决策型动机有关。(Dörnyei et al., 2006：145)

Based on the results of a large-scale motivation survey involving over 13,000 teenage language learners in Hungary on three successive time periods (in 1993, 1999, 2004), the current construct has wider implications on the dynamics of motivational factors and language globalization over the examined 12-year period.

以此模式为基础，一项在匈牙利的研究通过大规模问卷在三个不同时间段(1993年、1999年和2004年)调查语言学习的动机。大约13000名青少年语言学习者参与了这项问卷调查。在研究进行的12年间，这个动机模式就学习动机的动态和语言的全球化做出了更佳的诠释。

As discussed earlier, even though the motivational factors differ from person to person, motivation, as a situated phenomenon, is also frequently influenced by external social factors. The discussion on identity, motivation, and attitude doesnot occur in vacuum or isolation. These are dynamic constructs changing with the immediate learning environments, more macro-level contexts such as social, political and historical factors, and different phases of learning period.

  虽然每个人的学习动机各不相同,但是学习动机作为一种社会现象,常常受到外在社会因素的影响。如同我们先前关于学习身份认同和学习态度的讨论,学习动机并非完全孤立的现象。这些动态结构随着周遭的学习环境的改变而改变,同时也受到大环境诸如社会、政治、历史和不同学习阶段等因素的影响。

When it comes to speaking instruction, the dynamics of motivational factors has provided both language learners and language educators some important insights. From the learners' perspectives, instructional practices should give them a sense of ownership of their learning, which includes, but not limited to, the personal relevance of the learning content, their involvement in the learning process, etc. With regard to the language teachers and curriculum designers, several aspects need to be considered when learners' motivational factors are a part of the concerns. First, teaching objectives should be incorporated with learners' needs and interests through mutual planning. Consequently, pertinent teaching and learning activities need to be designed cooperatively and interactively to achieve these objectives. Second, pertinent methods, materials, and assessment criteria and process should also represent the voice of the learners.

  这些关于学习动机的讨论为语言学习者和语言教育者在口语教学方面提供了很多启示。从语言学习者的角度,他们在教学演练中应该拥有学习的所有权,这个权利包括了相关学习内容与其自身经历的相关性,以及学习者在学习过程中的全程参与性。从语言教师和课程设计者的角度来看,需要强调以下几点。首先,教学目标应该结合学习者的兴趣需要,并通过师生双方共同的规划来完成;而教学需与学习活动相互结合,以达成学习的目标。其次,教学方法、教学材料以及教学的评估过程和标准皆应该体现学习者的主导作用。

4.2 Interface of Theory and Practice on L2 Instruction: TBLI
二语教学理论与实践的交集:任务型语言教学模式 (TBLI)

The sociocultural constructs to address L2 learning greatly enrich our insights into classroom learning environment, in which the nature of language, language learners, and language learning processes are important. Considerable empirical effort has thus been invested to describe these aspects in practice. In the last few decades, L2 instruction has become more communicative, with more emphasis placed on students' ability to use the L2 in real-life situations, namely, their communicative competence (Hymes, 1972; Canale & Swain, 1980). TBLI is one of the increasingly popular approaches to Communicative Language Teaching (CLT) (Bygate, Skehan, & Swain, 2001; Nunan, 2004; Skehan, 1998). Thus, the language pedagogy moved from the traditional focus on form to an approach that promotes, besides grammatical skills, the ability to interact to achieve communicative goals in the real world. As pointed out by Richards and Rodgers, "Task-Based Teaching can be regarded as a recent version of a communicative methodology and seeks to reconcile methodology with current theories of second language acquisition" (2001: 151). By implementing TBLI in our instructional model of spoken language development, the Chinese program has provided meaningful interactive practice to engage students in communication while allowing them to develop their communicative competence.

在我们重新审视二语学习的社会文化性的同时,我们对于课堂学习环境有了更多元的认识。这个新的视角涵盖语言本身、语言学习者以及语言的学习过程。这些理念也一一在实践中体现。在过去的几十年里,二语教学越来越强调交际的重要性和学生在真实语境中使用语言的能力,也就是学生的语言交际能力(Hymes, 1972; Canale & Swain, 1980)。其中,被视为交际型语言教学的一个主要模式——任务型语言教学模式(简称为 TBLI)逐渐受到广泛关注。由此可以看出,语言教学的重心由传统的语法形式教学,逐渐转换为促进学习者综合语言能力的发展。这种转换强调发展语法在内的综合语言能力,进而达到在真实语境中交流的目的。Richards & Rodgers 回顾语言教学方法的发展,指出:"作为一个新形式的交际型教学模式,任务型教学完美地调和了二语习得理论和方法论之间的差距。"(2001:151) 爱荷华的口语教学模式正是采用了任务型教学法为学生提供有意义的口语交际训练,使他们在交流互动的同时发展和提升他们的交际能力。

To understand TBLI, we need to first define what a task is. In the context of language instruction, Bygate, Skehan, and Swain (2001) defined tasks as "an activity which requires learners to use language, with emphasis on meaning, to attain an objective" (p. 11). Brown (2007) provided a very similar, yet, according to him, a better-understood definition of tasks by quoting one of Skehan's earlier description: "a task is an activity in which meaning is primary, there is a problem to solve and relationship to real-world activities, with an objective that can be assessed in terms of an outcome" (p. 242). Skehan, based on a review of task-based literature, presented several main features of a task in instruction:

要了解任务型语言教学模式,我们首先必须了解什么是任务。在语言教学界,根据 Bygate, Skehan and Swain 2001 年发表的研究,任务被定义为一种要求学习者通过语言的使用达到某种目标的有意义的活动(p. 11)。以上述定义为基础,Brown (2007)提出了一个非常相似,但在他看来更为恰当的定义。他引用 Skehan 早期关于任务的描述:"任务是一种以意义为核心的活动。这一活动的目的在于解决一个与现实生活相关的问题。同时,活动结果可以用来评估检验活动目标的完成度。"(p. 242) 在综合与任务相关的文献后,Skehan (1997:95)提出任务在语言教学中最显著的几个特点:

- Meaning is primary
- Learners are not given other people's meanings to regurgitate
- There is some sort of relationship to comparable real-world activities
- Task completion has some priority
- The assessment of the task is in terms of outcome. (Skehan, 1998, p. 95)

- 意义是关键
- 学习者不是简单复述其他人所表达的意义
- 任务与现实生活中的活动相关

- 任务完成具有某种程度的优先性
- 任务的评估取决于任务的结果

Nunan (2004) went further to distinguish target tasks (uses of language in the world beyond the classroom) and pedagogical tasks (those designed to be used in the classroom). From these descriptions on tasks, we can observe its multiple perspectives in language pedagogy: teachers and teaching, learners and learning, and assessment. TBLI, therefore, is a language teaching approach that emphasizes on communicative interaction, learner-centered teaching, simulating the situations in real life, assessment involved in language development, and enhancing students' problem-solving abilities and interlanguage development.

Nunan (2004)进一步地区分了目标型任务(即在教室以外的环境中应用语言的任务)和教学型任务(即那些专为课堂设计的任务)。通过上述与任务定义相关的讨论,我们可以更了解任务在语言教学中的多面性。综上所述,任务型语言教学模式是一种语言教学的方法,它强调交际性的互动和以学习者为中心的教学。在真实世界的启发下,任务型教学的评估方式包括语言的发展、学生解决实际问题的能力和中介语的发展。

As one of the approaches to CLT, TBLI has been influenced by a wide range of intertwined theoretical dimensions, which cover psychological, cognitive, sociocultural, and linguistic perspectives (Ke, 2006). This integrative teaching approach seems to provide language teachers, researchers, as well as curriculum developers a very promising direction towards language teaching and learning. Following the communicative learning direction, building of tasks within the language classroom, such as syllabus design and classroom teaching procedures, has much potential with careful and detailed planning. All the tasks need to fit well-defined goals and learning objectives, the tasks should be interrelated to one another, and the assessment criteria regarding the tasks should be valid. Only in this way will the language instruction become one meaningful activity after another and the language learning process move steadily from less to more student output. For a detailed introduction of TBLI as a pedagogical approach, please refer to Chapter 6 on pedagogical theories and research. Nevertheless, TBLI should work eclectically with other instructional approaches to best promote learners' language development in the language classroom and beyond.

　　作为交际语言教学法的一个分支,任务型语言教学模式受到多个互为关联的理论影响,这些理论涵盖了心理学、认知学、社会文化学和语言本体论等相关理论(Ke, 2006)。这个兼容并包的教学模式为语言教师、研究者以及课程规划者提供了一个非常可行的语言教学方向。在交际学习原则的指导下,语言课堂内的任务建构,像课程大纲的设计与课堂教学过程都需要仔细审慎的计划。当然,所有的任务都应该与相关的教学目标相契合。任务之间应该是互相关联的。同时与任务相关的评估标准也必须是可行而有效的。这样课堂教学才可以说是一连串有意义的活动的整合,而语言学习过程才能激发越来越多的语言输出。本书的第六章将对任务型教学提出更全面的阐述。本书强调任务型教学应该与其他的教学方法有机地结合,以求帮助语言学习者在语言课堂和课堂外的真实环境中有效地提高语言能力。

Based on our discussion regarding the increasing social turn of the field of SLA, many implications in language instruction and curriculum design could be noted. First, the complex social nature of language itself and language learning as well as teaching process seems to provide more questions than answers when it comes to concrete curriculum design. However, a better understanding of how the systems operate is essential for us to transform our curriculum and pertinent teaching practices. With regard to speaking instruction in language education, language learners should no longer be taken as passive recipients, but rather as language users who play an active role in their own language development. Therefore, the language structures and other linguistic knowledge introduced in the class should include these L2 users' own efforts throughout the process. In other words, it can be stated that the traditional lecture-style language teaching and learning process no longer fits the changing picture of language acquisition and instruction, in which the language learners as well as language teachers work closely to co-construct knowledge in the classroom, and the language learners are proactive negotiators for meaningful communication both inside and outside the classroom.

二语习得领域社会化趋势的讨论对语言教学和课程设置启示良多。总体来看,语言及语言教学过程社会方面的特质似乎在课程设置方面提出了更多问题和挑战,而不是提供解答。但是我们也认识到,唯有更清楚地了解整个语言系统的运作,我们才可以进一步探讨如何在课程和教学实践上进行变革。在口语教学中,语言学习者不再是一个被动的知识接收者,而是能够影响、掌控自身语言能力发展的语言使用者。因此,在课堂上介绍语言结构和相关的语言知识时,我们应该让这些语言使用者充分参与这个过程。换言之,随着我们对语言学习社会化的进一步认识,传统的课堂授课方式应该做出相应的调整。在新兴的语言课堂上,语言教师和学习者通力合作,共建新知。无论在课堂内外,语言学习者都以积极协商者的身份使用语言进行有意义的交流。

Chapter Five　第五章
SLA Theory and Research
第二语言习得理论与研究

In this chapter, we introduce the theoretical approaches of second language acquisition (SLA) that we believe are well established and the most significant to second language (L2) speaking acquisition and instruction, followed by the discussion on how these theoretical approaches of SLA have impacted L2 Chinese speaking teaching and learning. Reflecting the variety and multiple disciplinary perspectives of the field of SLA, we first provide a brief overview to the field. Our overview of the theoretical traditions is far from exhaustive, because we have been selective in reviewing these SLA theories as well as pertinent empirical studies. Overall, our goal is to provide an overview of key concepts and empirical research that recur throughout the book in our discussions of various approaches to L2 speaking teaching and learning.

我们将在本章重点介绍与二语口语习得和教学有直接联系的第二语言习得理论，并就其对汉语口语教学的具体影响进行讨论。鉴于二语习得领域的多元化与多样性，我们将先对其进行简单的综述。需要指出的是，我们对二语习得领域的理论介绍是非常有选择性的。本章的总体目标在于阐述全书在二语口语教学中依循的主要概念以及介绍相关的实证研究。

5.1 SLA Theory: An Overview　二语习得理论：概论

SLA is a complex field. It discusses a variety of topics, which include, but are not limited to, the nature of language, language learning process, cross-linguistic influences, the relationship between L2 learning and L2 use, views of language learners, and the social and cultural contexts of language learning. These topics cover a wide range of disciplines, such as linguistics, psychology, language education, communication, and sociolinguistics (Doughty & Long, 2003; Gass & Selinker, 2008; Ortega, 2009).

二语习得是一个错综复杂的领域。这一领域涵盖许多话题,例如:语言的本质、语言学习过程、语际影响、二语学习和二语应用之间的辩证关系、语言学习者以及语言学习所处的社会和文化环境等等。而这些话题涵盖了很多不同领域,诸如语言学、心理学、语言教育学、交际学与社会语言学等等 (Doughty & Long, 2003; Gass & Selinker, 2008; Ortega, 2009)。

Looking through the disciplinary perspectives of SLA, it is safe to state that the dominant theoretical traditions have been cognitive and psycholinguistic. Within this tradition, language learning is mainly about information processing following certain internal developmental mechanisms. From this perspective, language learners have been viewed as individuals with relatively fixed characteristics, from their identity to their language learning motivation, which play certain roles in their ultimate language learning outcomes. The first approach following this tradition is VanPatten's (1996, 2004) input processing, which deals with the comprehension of utterances and form-meaning relationships.

纵观二语习得界的理论构架,其理论主体和传统更偏重认知学和心理语言学。在这种理论体系的引导下,语言学习通常被视为在特定内在发展机制中进行的信息处理和转换。因此,无论是他们个人的身份认同还是他们的语言学习动机,语言学习者被视为拥有相对固定特征的一群个体,而这些特征在某个程度上影响他们最终的语言学习效果。本章介绍的第一个理论是 VanPatten (1996, 2004) 提出的输入加工理论。这个理论旨在理解话语本身以及形式与意义之间的关系。

5.1.1. Input Processing Model
输入加工模式

According to VanPatten (2004), input processing "as the starting point for acquisition" (p. 25) mainly concerns "the initial process by which learners connect grammatical forms with their meanings" (p.5). Following its main meaning priority principle, this model argues that L2 learners first focus on meaning when attending to language input, and hence, they can acquire forms only when processing for meaning has become automatic. VanPatten presented the following model of processes involved in acquisition: (VanPatten, 2004, p. 26)

  VanPatten (2004) 提出，输入加工是习得的始发点。这个理论主要关注学习者将语法形式与其意义相联系的初步加工处理。在意义先行的理论基础引导下，这个理论模式认为，二语学习者在处理语言输入时会先注意语言的意义，因而他们只有在意义加工已经自动化的前提下才有可能习得有关的形式。VanPatten (2004, p. 26)提出的习得加工模式如下：

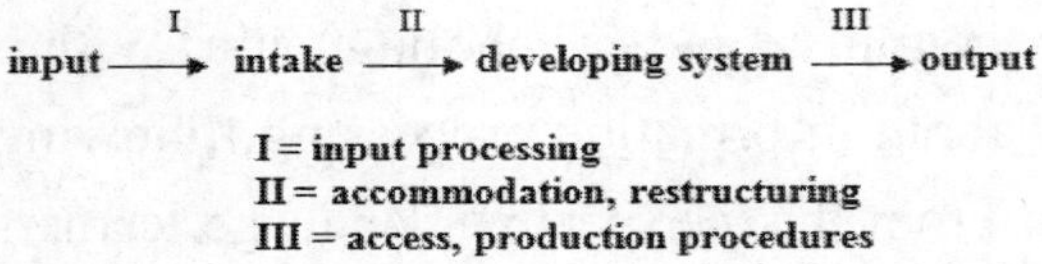

```
        I              II                III
input ──→ intake ──→ developing system ──→ output
         I = input processing
         II = accommodation, restructuring
         III = access, production procedures
```

```
         I          II           III
输入 ──→ 摄入 ──→ 发展系 ──→ 输出
                    统
         I = 输入加工阶段
         II = 适应重组阶段
         III = 存取生成阶段
```

Figure 5.1 A Sketch of Basic Processes in Acquisition (VanPatten, 2004, p. 26)

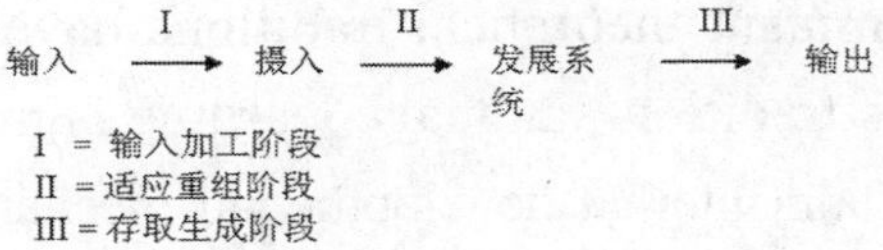

图 5.1 习得加工模式 (VanPatten, 2004, P. 26)

Based on this model, processing instruction (PI), a pedagogical tool, is designed to manipulate the developmental process of the input processing mechanisms. Following this approach, other theoretical approaches and hypotheses related to, but distinct from, input processing in SLA have been introduced and discussed.

  根据这个模式，加工教学 (PI)被当做一项教学工具，用于操控输入加工机制的发展过程。同时，延续这个理论基础，又有别于输入加工理论的其他二语习得理论与假说也逐渐出现。

5.1.2. Noticing
  注意假说

One of the most influential scholars in the field of SLA, Schmidt (1990), argued from a psycholinguistic perspective that subliminal L2 learning is impossible and learners need to engage in conscious noticing for learning to occur. Intake, therefore, is what learners consciously notice. However, what learners notice is constrained by a number of factors, such as instruction, frequency, perceptual salience, skill level, and task demands. Schmidt (1990) also claimed that his noticing theory can be incorporated into many different SLA theories. For example, in the theories of parameter settings in L2 acquisition (as in Universal Grammar introduced by Chomsky, 1965), whenever triggers are required to set parameters, they must be consciously noticed.

在二语习得界深具影响力的学者Schmidt(1990)基于心理语言学的观点，否定潜意识的二语学习的可能性。Schmidt主张，为了启发学习，学习者必须投入有意识的注意活动中。因此，摄入(intake)可以理解为学习者有意识地注意到的东西。然而，学习者可以注意到的东西受到多方因素的制约，比如教学、语言的频度、感知的凸显性、技能水平以及任务要求。Schmidt(1990)也提出，他的注意假说可以和其他诸多二语习得理论结合。例如，二语习得中的参数设定理论（以乔姆斯基的普遍语法为代表，1965），在任何需要设定参数的过程中都应该涉及有意识的注意。

5.1.3. The Output Hypothesis
输出假说

Traditionally, output was seen not as a way of creating knowledge, but as a way of practicing it, or it was simply understood as the learning outcome, the product. In the context of L2 learning, Swain (1995, 1998, 2005) defined three functions of output:

传统上，输出被视为一种学习结果、产品或者一种语言实践，而不是生成知识的方式。在二语学习环境中，Swain(1995, 1998, 2005)提出输出所具有的三项主要功能：

1) **Noticing (triggering function):** The activity of producing the target language may prompt L2 learners to consciously recognize some of their linguistic problems, and this awareness triggers cognitive processes that might generate linguistic knowledge that is new for the learner or consolidate the learner's existing knowledge.
2) **Hypothesis testing:** Learners may use their output as a way of trying out new language forms and structures as they stretch their interlanguage to

meet the communicative needs in their target language.

3) **Metalinguistic (reflective function):** Learners use language to reflect on language produced by others or by themselves.

1）注意（触发功能）：目的语的输出活动可能触发学习者认识到自身存在的语言问题；这种有意识的关注引发促使学习者在整合现有语言知识的基础上创造新的语言知识的认知加工过程。
2）假说测试：当学习者通过中介语的发展以达到用目的语完成交流目的时，他们将输出作为一种检验新的语言形式和结构的方式。
3）元语言（反思功能）：学习者用语言反思他们自身或别人所输出的语言。

These three functions of output are expected to raise L2 learners' awareness of both their interlanguage and target language, which mediates L2 learning. The output hypothesis has shown a major shift from regarding output as a language product to output as a cognitive tool, as a part of the learning process.

这三项关于输出的功能旨在提高二语学习者对自身中介语和目的语的关注。根据输出假说，语言输出最初被视为一个语言成品，但之后则被看做学习过程中的一种认知工具。

5.1.4. Interaction Hypothesis
互动假说

Many SLA theories so far have suggested that learners need to interact with the target language to acquire it (Larsen-Freeman & Long, 1991; Mackey, 1999; Pica, 1994). The modifications and collaborative efforts that take place in social interactions facilitate SLA, as Long (1996) claimed in his interaction hypothesis: negotiation for meaning, and especially negotiation work that triggers interactional adjustments by the NS or more competent interlocutor, facilitates acquisition because it connects input, internal learner capacities, particularly selective attention, and output in productive ways. (Long, 1996, pp. 151-152)

截止目前为止，许多二语习得理论都提出：学习者唯有在目的语的交际互动中才能习得该语言(Larsen-Freeman & Long, 1991; Mackey, 1999; Pica, 1994)。学习者在互动过程中的协作与调整促进了二语的习得。Long (1996, pp.151—152)在其提出的互动假说中指出：语义协商,特别是在与母语者或语言能力更强的学习者互动下所引起的调整,可有效促进二语的习得。因为这个过程有机地结合语言输入、学习者内在能力(特别是选择性注意力)以及语言的输出。

According to the interaction hypothesis, learning may take place during the interaction, or negotiation may be an initial step in learning, which may serve as a priming device representing the setting of the stage for learning. Many studies support this hypothesis. Pica et al. (1987) reported that in an experiment on picture completion instructions, the group that was allowed to interact outperformed the modified input group. Mackey (1999) noted a positive relationship between interaction and development, in that learners who were involved in structure-focused interaction moved along a developmental path more rapidly than those who were not. Tarone and Liu (1995) found that interaction can change the route of development depending on the context.

　　根据互动假说,学习可能在互动中发生,或者说协商即是学习的第一步。协商可以作为学习的启动装置,呈现学习时的情境设置。许多研究发现支持这个假说的论点。根据Pica等人1987年发表的研究,在一项学习者配对合作找出图片缺失信息的教学实验中发现,在图片表述的过程中,允许互动合作的实验组的总体表现优于修正输入实验组。Mackey (1999)也注意到互动与语言发展之间的正面相关性,积极参与互动的学习者比没有参与互动的学习者更快地掌握语言结构。Tarone & Liu (1995)发现,根据语言环境的不同,互动会改变语言的发展路径。

5.1.5. Input-Interaction-Output Model
　　　输入—互动—输出模式

Gass, one of the leading scholars in cognitive-based theory in SLA, persisted in advancing her model: Input-Interaction-Output (IIO) (as cited in Block, 2003：26). In her response to Firth and Wagner (1997), Gass (1998) stated that her "emphasis on input and interaction studies is on the language used and not on the act of communication" (p. 84, emphasis in the original) and that her main work is "to understand what types of interaction might bring about what types of changes in linguistic knowledge" (p. 84). According to Gass (1997), L2 learning starts from certain input in the learning environment. This prerequisite of language learning has to be apperceived at certain point through features, such as frequency, affect (e.g., motivation, attitude), attention, and learners' prior knowledge, which is a prior stage to noticing. The comprehended input resulting from apperception represents the beginning of analysis from two distinct levels: a superficial level that involves comprehension of meaning for immediate communication purposes and a deeper level that involves the comprehension of syntax for long-term learning. This is followed by intake, which is "the processing of assimilating linguistic material" (Gass, 1997, p. 5). In this stage learners process their prior linguistic structures and procedural memory as well as learnability. As a result of accommodation or restructuring, the development and storage of changes occur in the learners' grammar. This process occurs in three possible ways: (a) When hypothesis confirmation or rejection occurs; (b) By strengthening a rule that the learner already knows; or (c) After intake, language may be stored for later use, but not actually integrated into the present system. Output, serving as a part of a feedback loop to the intake stage, forces syntactic, rather than semantic, analysis. It is not the endpoint, but is rather a potential catalyst for starting up the entire process again (see summary by Block, 2003, pp. 26-30). Gass's IIO model is regarded as one of the most comprehensive models explaining the language acquisition process of L2 learners.

　　Gass 作为二语习得领域中强调认知理论的领军人物之一,不断地发展和完善她称之为输入—互动—输出的语言加工模式(以下简称为IIO) (as cited in Block, 2003:26)。Gass (1998:84) 在回应 Firth & Wagner (1997)所发表的文章里指出,她之所以强调输入和互动方面的研究是因为她关注这个过程中所使用的语言,而非交际的过程;她主要的重心集中在了解互动类型与引发语言知识变化的关联性。Gass (1997) 提出,二语学习始于语言学习环境中的输入。作为语言学习的前提,语言输入必须通过某些特点呈现。这些特点包括交感(比如动机、学习态度)、注意力、学习者的既有知识体系等先于注意阶段的特点。

可理解输入通过两个不同的层面呈现出分析的起点：以直接交流为目的、对语言意义的粗浅理解，以及涉及句法理解的长期学习。在这个阶段中，学习者对他们先前已有的语言结构，过渡记忆以及可学性进行加工重整。在经历适应与重组的阶段后，语言的发展与变化的储存体现在学习者的语法中。这个过程有三种可能性：1)对假说的确认和否定出现时；2)强化学习者已知的一个语法规则；3)在摄入输入以后，语言可能处于储存阶段以供以后使用，但尚未融入当前的语言系统。输出作为在摄入阶段反馈圈的一部分，促成了对相对应的句法而非语义方面的分析。由此理解，输出并不是学习的终端而是开启一个全新加工过程的潜在催化剂(See summary by Block, 2003, pp. 26—30)。Gass 的 IIO 模式被公认为是用以解释二语学习者语言习得过程的最全面的一个认知模式之一。

5.2 Communicative Competence 交际能力

By directly investigating the use of language in social contexts, sociolinguist, Hymes (1972, 1974), proposed the term ethnography of communication, which focuses on the communicative and contextual factors in language use. Communicative competence (CC) became the fundamental concept in sociolinguistics, and has been widely adopted in the field of SLA. Saville-Troike (2003) defined it as what a speaker needs to know to communicate appropriately within a particular language community (p. 18). Canale and Swain (1980) extended the earlier work on CC and presented their seminal work which has a great impact on L2 teaching and testing. In their construct of CC, which was initially proposed in 1980, but was expanded 3 years later, there are four components: (Canale, 1983, pp. 2-27)

社会语言学家 Hymes (1972, 1974)通过探究语言在社会环境中的使用，提出"交际人种学"的概念。这个概念强调在语言使用过程中交际和语境方面的因素。交际能力因而逐步成为社会语言学领域的一个基本概念，在二语习得领域被广泛接受。根据 Saville-Troike (2003:18)的定义，交际能力为任何一个说话者在其所处的特定语言环境中，为了有效而适宜地实现交

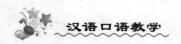

际目的而需要了解的知识和技巧。Canale & Swain (1980)在总结先前交际能力相关研究后,发表之后对二语教学和测试产生深远影响的"交际能力的理论框架"。这个框架(1983,pp. 2—27)主要包括四个要素:

1) **Grammatical competence:** the aspect of CC that include "knowledge of lexical items and rules of morphology, syntax, sentence-grammar semantics, and phonology".
2) **Discourse competence:** the competence to connect discrete sentences to whole discourse, including both spoken conversation and written texts.
3) **Sociolinguistic competence:** the component of the knowledge of "sociocultural rules of use and rules of discourse".
4) **Strategic competence:** the component "made up of verbal and nonverbal communication strategies that may be called into action to compensate for breakdowns in communication due to performance variables or to insufficient competence".

1) 语法能力:包括词汇的知识和与词汇有关的形态学、句法学、句法语义学以及语音学方面的知识;
2) 语篇能力:结合分散语句与篇章的能力,可在口语交流以及书面表达中体现;
3) 社会语言能力:社会文化方面的语用规则和组织语篇的细则;
4) 策略能力:由言语和非言语交际策略构成,用以弥补交流中因表现变量或是语言能力不足所造成的交际中断。

This influential framework has had great implications in L2 learning. Since the 1980s, CLT has become the main direction of language teaching. Regarding language as communication (Hymes, 1972, 1974), CLT has adopted an approach to language teaching, which emphasizes on the functional and communicative use of language (Richards & Rodgers, 2001). Chapter 6 provides a more comprehensive introduction of CLT as a language teaching method.

  这个理论框架对二语教学影响深远。从八十年代起,交际语教学模式(以下简称CLT)已逐步成为语言教学的主流。在"语言即交际"的思潮影响下(Hymes, 1972, 1974)，CLT 强调语言的交际性和功能性。本书第六章将特别阐述 CLT 作为一种教学模式在二语教学界的发展和特点。

5.3 Classroom-Based Research on L2 Speaking 二语口语的有关课堂研究

The field of L2 teaching has witnessed a major change in recent years with respect to the methodologies of language teaching and their underlying theoretical frameworks, with a dominant emphasis on communicative competence. The great impact of communicative competence on the language teaching field has resulted in more discourse analysis studies examining how the interactions and discourse in L2 contexts facilitate or provide opportunities for language learning and development.

　　近年来，二语教学界历经了一场教学方法及其理论指导基础的根本性变革，其中以对交际能力的强调最为突出。这场变革引出语言教学界更多关于话语分析的研究。这些研究探讨二语环境中的互动和话语如何促进第二语言的学习和发展。

5.3.1. The Discourse Analysis Approach
　　　　话语分析方法

5.3.1.1. What is Discourse Analysis?
　　　　　什么是话语分析？

Originating from different disciplines, discourse and discourse analysis have been diversely defined in the literature. For language educators and researchers in SLA, discourse analysis is an approach to analyze language development in real interactions, which moves beyond its purely structural functions (Hatch, 1978; Hatch & Long, 1980). One of the definitions that reflect the majority of language teachers' perspectives on discourse analysis was proposed by McCarthy (1991): "Discourse analysis is concerned with the study of the relationship between language and the contexts in which it is used" (p. 5).

　　源于不同的领域，话语和话语分析在文献中的定义各不相同。对语言教育者和二语习得研究者来说，话语分析的重心并非在语言的结构性功能，而是侧重真实交流中的语言发展(Hatch, 1978; Hatch & Long, 1980)。McCarthy (1991:5) 对话语分析的定义受到大多数语言教师的认同。他认为话语分析主要就是"研究语言和其所处的环境之间的关系"。

5.3.1.2. Classroom Discourse Analysis
课堂话语分析

Classroom discourse analysis mainly examines language use in classroom interactions. It may be regarded as a type of naturally occurring talk in the space of the classroom, where teachers and learners jointly construct learning opportunities. By exploring language use and its context in classroom-based interaction, classroom discourse analysis studies focus on the ongoing spoken interaction in the language classroom, how speakers talk, and what they do through talk.

课堂话语分析着眼于课堂互动中的语言使用。从这个角度，课堂话语分析可以被视为一种在语言课堂中由教师和学生共同建构的交流方式。着眼于在课堂互动中的语用和对应的语境，课堂话语分析主要研究语言课堂里进行的口语互动，以及说话者表达的方式和对话的目的。

To produce a descriptive system by examining the linguistic aspects of classroom interactions, Sinclair and Coulthard (1975) conducted a research project on classroom discourse regarding the English used by teachers and students. They found that the typical structure of classroom discourse followed a sequence of well-ordered moves: I (teacher initiation)→ R (student response)→E/F (evaluation or feedback by teacher). Walsh (2006) presented a new framework for analyzing classroom discourse: Self-Evaluation of Teacher Talk (SETT). SETT is used to describe the classroom interaction context through the identification of "locally negotiated microcontexts" (modes) (p. 61). It revealed the dynamic and complex nature of L2 classroom context and interactions. Recently, Young (2009) extended the scope of classroom discourse analysis by proposing the discursive practice approach in L2 context. With regard to discourse as a social action that is context grounded and always emergent and situated, Young's discursive practice approach provides a more current framework to understand verbal, nonverbal, and interactional activities that L2 users employ in their language learning and usage contexts.

  Sinclair & Coulthard (1975)从课堂互动的语言层面研究师生间的语言使用。他们发现,典型的课堂语言大都遵循着一定的步骤:教师提问→学生回答→教师评价/反馈。以此为基础,Walsh (2006)提出一个分析课堂语言的新框架:教师言语的自我评估(以下简称SETT)。SETT先辨识出课堂中"协商的微观环境",再描述课堂互动中的语言环境。这个新的框架体现了二语课堂环境和互动的多元性与复杂性。Young (2009)扩展课堂话语分析的观点,提出二语环境中话语实践的新模式。Young 认为,言语是一种社会行为,必须在语境中呈现,同时不断地进行变化。他的话语实践模式呈现的理论框架让我们能更全面了解二语使用者在语言学习和语境中的语言、非语言(non-verbal)以及互动的活动。

Till date, many language educators and researchers have carried out studies that have closely examined classroom discourse and interactions (Bateman, 2002, 2004; Donato, 2004; Duff, 2002; He, 2000; Kearney, 2009; Swain & Lapkin, 1998; Wang, 2007, among others). Bateman (2004), extending his previous study on using ethnographic interviewing techniques in a foreign language classroom (2002), conducted a qualitative case study among first-year Spanish students, in which he asked the students to work in pairs to conduct a series of three ethnographic interviews with a native speaker of Spanish. The results indicated students' enhanced awareness, attitudes, and communicative competence towards Spanish speakers. Duff (2002) employed ethnography of communication framework to observe "how students' identities and interpersonal differences are created and manifested through interaction patterns during classroom discussions" (Duff, 2002:315). He (2000) examined the ways in which language teachers in Chinese Heritage Language Schools in the U.S.A.convey Chinese cultural values through teachers' directives in classroom discourse. Locating the teachers' directives in the regular language classroom as a speech event, identified as instructional/initiatingdirectives and disciplinary/responsivedirectives, His study indicated that the grammatical and interactional organization of these classroom

directives provide teachers the discourse tool to engage these young Chinese heritage language learners to co-construct the cultural knowledge, even sometimes with students' subversive responses. More recently, Kearney (2009) analyzed the classroom discourse and interaction surrounding the use of images in an intermediate French course, with a specific focus on the ways that facilitate culture learning. Swain and Lapkin (1995, 1998) coined the term language related episodes (LRE), which identifies "any part of a dialogue in which language students talk about the language they are producing, question their language use, or correct themselves or others" (Swain & Lapkin, 1995), arguing the effectiveness of classroom scaffolding between the instructor and the students as well as peer collaboration. Wang (2007), by discussing the different types of group work tasks used in communication-based language classrooms as well as their designing guidelines and considerations, provided some suggestions regarding how various group work tasks can be applied in teaching Chinese in an L2 context.

截至目前,语言教学者和研究人员从多方面进行了与课堂语言和互动相关的研究(Bateman, 2002, 2004; Donato, 2004; Duff, 2002; He, 2000; Kearney, 2009; Swain & Lapkin, 1998; Wang, 2007, among others)。在人种志采访的研究基础上,Bateman (2004)发表了一个在一年级西班牙语课堂中进行的质化个案研究。在这个研究中,学生两人一组与一个西班牙语母语者进行一系列为数三次的人种志采访。结果显示,学生在与西班牙语母语者进行交流时的交际能力、态度以及觉察力都有显著的提高。Duff (2002)采用了交际人种学的框架,通过课堂讨论过程中的互动模式观察学生的身份认同和人际差异的生成与呈现。何纬芸研究美国华裔中文学校里的教师如何通过课堂中的语言传播中华文化的价值(He, 2000)。何纬云选取教师在课堂中教学与提问的指令,以及维持纪律与回应性的指令作为研究的重点。她发现,这些课堂指令可以被当做一个语言工具,让教师与华裔学习者可以共同建构文化知识。Kearney (2009) 在最近的一个研究中分析某个法语中级班的课堂互动,在研究中,Kearney 特别强调促进文化学习的交流方式。 Swain & Lapkin (1995, 1998) 提出"语言相关片段"的概念,用以表示学习者就自己陈述的语言进行讨论,对自己的语言使用发出质疑、或纠正自己或他人在对话中的错误。同时,Swain & Lapkin 也强调课堂教学中教师和学生间互助的有效性和学生间协作的重要性。王瑞峰在2007年发表的研究中讨论交际课堂中小组活动的任务设计方式与原则,并对对外汉语教学中的小组活动任务的设计提出许多有建设性的建议。

Many of the above-mentioned research studies have taken a sociocultural perspective by viewing classrooms as social contexts where the language learners, as well as the language instructor, are actively involved in the dynamics of classroom interaction. As we have seen in this chapter, theoretical approaches to L2 speaking have evolved over time. SLA studies in cognition, psychology, and sociology have influenced the development of L2 speaking acquisition theories and have consequentially modified L2 language teachers' pedagogical approaches of teaching L2 speaking. The predominantly cognitive theoretical tradition of SLA research has seen a notable expansion in recent years, from an increasing focus on the sociocultural perspectives of language learning and language use, to further study of topics such as language learners' identities and motivational factors as well as the dynamics of language learning contexts and language socialization. This new trend of combining the social and cognitive perspectives in L2 learning and usage has led to a new direction of understanding L2 speaking acquisition and instruction, which will continue to guide us in the subsequent theoretical development and empirical study design in L2 speaking, with a new sociocognitive construct that incorporates the cognitive and social elements of L2.

  上述研究大多采用社会文化的角度,视课堂为一个社会的环境,在这个环境中语言学习者和教师积极地投入课堂的互动。正如我们在本章开始时提到的,二语口语的相关理论与框架不断地演变。认知学、心理学、社会学等方面的研究都对二语口语习得理论和相关教学实践产生了冲击。以认知理论为主导的传统二语习得研究在近年来逐步向语言的社会文化方向扩展。语言学习者的身份认同、学习动机、语言学习环境的动态性以及语言的社会化等相关课题在二语习得研究中一一出现。这个新趋势也提供我们一个了解二语口语习得和教学的新方向,即是在整合二语的认知性和社会性的基础上,采用全新的社会认知结构进行二语口语的教学与研究。

Chapter Six 第六章
Pedagogical Theories and Research
教学法理论与研究

Language instruction has caught more attention in second language acquisition (SLA) research since the twentieth century. Changes in language teaching have reflected changes in theories of the nature of language and language learning, as well as the changing perceptions of the kind of proficiency that learners need to achieve, as indicated by, for example, the shift in focus from reading comprehension to oral proficiency. In this chapter, we briefly discuss the major trends as well as pertinent approaches and methods in language teaching. Through this chapter, readers will not only get an extensive understanding of the development of pedagogical theories, but also better understand the pedagogical theoretical basis of Iowa's instructional model.

自20世纪起，语言教学在二语习得的研究上受到更多的关注。语言教学的转变也反映出这个领域其他方面的改变，包括语言本质和语言学习相关理论的转变，以及我们对于学习者语言能力的要求的不同，例如，语言学习的重心从阅读理解转为口语表达能力。本章我们将简单介绍语言教学的主要潮流与非主流方法以及20世纪以来的语言教学法。通过本章的介绍，读者不仅将对语言教学法的发展脉络有更广泛的了解，更对爱荷华大学中文部的口语教学模式的教学法理论基础有了更深入的认识。

6.1 Grammar-Translation Method 语法翻译教学法

Similar to English, Latin was the dominant language for education, commerce, religion, and government in the Western world 500 years ago. However, when French, Italian, and English gained attention as a result of political changes in Europe, English gradually became the dominant language used in international communication. In the seventeenth and eighteenth centuries, Latin diminished from a living language to a subject in language curriculum. Nevertheless, as Latin was still regarded as the classical and the most ideal form of language at that time, it affected the approaches to language study and curriculum design. The analysis of classical Latin grammar and rhetoric became the primary model for foreign language study between the seventeenth and nineteenth century. Students were taught through rote learning of grammar rules and by practicing translation of passages and writing sample sentences. With the introduction of "modern languages" in the curriculum of European schools in the eighteenth century, they were taught with the same approach as that used for teaching Latin. Speaking and communication were never considered goals for foreign language study. The Grammar-Translation Method dominated Europe and the whole foreign language teaching field from the 1840s to the 1940s.

如同今日的英语,拉丁文在五百年前的西方世界是教育、商业、宗教以及政治上的主要语言。然而,随着欧洲政治情势的改变,法语、意大利语以及英语的重要性大为提高,拉丁文逐渐成为一个在国际交流场合使用的语言。在十七八世纪,拉丁文更从一个使用中的语言衰退为一个语言课程的科目。但由于拉丁文被视为一个代表古典以及理想语言的形式,它仍对语言学习的方法以及语言课程的设置有极大的影响。古典拉丁文语法和修辞分析在17世纪到19世纪期间成为外语研究的主要模式。学生通过反复背诵的方式学习语法规则、练习翻译段落与书写例句。当"现代语言"在18世纪开始被引进欧洲学校的课程时,教师教授这些语言的方式和拉丁文并无不同。在当时,口语以及交际沟通并非语言学习的目标。从1840年到1940年,语法翻译法在这百年间一直是欧洲外语教学的主流。

6.1.1. Grammar-Translation Method: Classroom Practice
语法翻译法:课堂实践

According to the Grammar-Translation Method, the goal of foreign language learning is to read the literature or benefit from the intellectual developments of another culture. Therefore, reading comprehension and understanding grammar rules of the language are the focus of this method. In other words, the ability to communicate orally with speakers of the target language is not considered as one of the learning goals.

根据语法翻译法,学习外语的目的在于阅读文学作品,或受到另外一个文化的启发,在理解思维上有所成长。因此,阅读理解以及熟悉语法规则是语法翻译教学法的核心。换言之,学习者是否有能力与目的语的使用者沟通并非教学的目标。

Grammar-Translation is a way of studying a language initially through detailed analysis of its grammar rules, and then by applying this knowledge to the task of translating sentences and texts in and out of the target language. Hence, it views language learning simply as memorizing rules and facts to understand and manipulate the morphology and syntax of the foreign language. Here, teachers are the center of the foreign language classroom, delivering linguistic knowledge to students, while students are passive, serving as recipients of knowledge.

语法翻译法学习语言的方式是先通过详细分析语法规则,再将规则应用在翻译句子与篇章的任务上。因此,语言学习对语法翻译法而言,仅仅是记诵规则以求理解掌握外语的结构形态与句法。教师是外语课堂的中心,传授语言知识给学生。学生则是被动的知识接收者。

Grammar is taught deductively in a Grammar-Translation classroom. Instructors first present and explain the rules and ask students to undergo intensive translation practices. The student's native language is the primary language of instruction because it is used to explain new rules and make comparisons between the target language and the students' native language. There is little active use of the target language in a Grammar-Translation classroom. Accuracy is strongly emphasized and every error is corrected. Under the Grammar-Translation instruction in the late eighteenth and early nineteenth centuries, students were expected to learn to do very accurate translations of the target language in their process of preparing for formal written examinations.

在语法翻译的课堂上,语法规则通过演绎法来讲授。教师首先介绍以及解释语法规则,并要求学生做密集的翻译练习。在以语法翻译为主的课堂中,学生很少有主动使用目的语的机会。学生的母语是课堂中主要的媒介,用来解释新的语法规则以及比较目的语和母语的异同。在课堂上教师十分强调准确度,纠正学生的每一个错误。在18世纪末以及19世纪初,语法翻译教学下的学生为了准备之后的正式笔试,在课上必须以目的语精确地完成翻译练习。

In a typical language textbook designed for the Grammar-Translation classroom, chapters or lessons are organized around grammar points. Each chapter consists of a vocabulary list and several grammar points. Vocabulary is taught in the form of isolated word lists, with explanations in learners' native language. Grammar rules are illustrated with usage explanations and sample sentences. All the sentences and dialogs are prepared for the purpose of explaining grammar rules and practicing Grammar-Translation exercises. Little attention is paid to the content of the texts, which are treated as exercises in grammatical analysis.

在语法翻译教学法所使用的课本中,每一章或每一课都以语法点为中心来编排。每一章都包含了一个词汇表以及数个语法点。词汇是用学生的母语按表上的顺序个别介绍。语法规则则通过用法说明以及例句来阐述。所有的句子与对话都是为了解释语法规则以及语法翻译练习做准备。课堂上很少留意课文的内容,课文仅当做语法分析练习的材料。

The Grammar-Translation Method has been criticized for treating languages as a collection of isolated and fragmented words. It has also been blamed for dampening learners' motivation due to its monotonous and tedious instruction style and boring translation exercises. The type of error correction can even be harmful to students' learning process, attitudes, and self-confidence. As most class time is used for grammar instruction and translation exercises, there are few opportunities for students to frame their own sentences in the target language.

语法翻译法常被批评将语言视为单字的集合,而非一个整体。语法翻译法单调乏味的授课方式以及无趣的翻译练习也被认为会大大降低学习者的动机。而纠错的方式更不利于学生的学习过程、动机以及自信心。由于多数的课堂时间被用来介绍语法以及做翻译练习,学生很少有机会能够发展他们的口语能力。

6.2 Direct Method　直接教学法

In the mid and late nineteenth century, oppositions to Grammar-Translation Method gradually developed in several European countries. Researchers and educators started to see the importance of oral proficiency in foreign languages and started to seek an alternative. Frenchman F. Gouin (1831—1896), L. Sauveur (1826—1907), and other specialists observed how children learn their first language, and were inspired by the Natural Method. These followers of Natural Method started to develop a language teaching approach, which came to be known as the Direct Method.

在19世纪中后期，许多欧洲国家里出现了反对语法翻译教学法的声潮。学者和教育工作者开始正视外语中口语能力的重要性，并开始寻求替代语法翻译法的教学方式。Frenchman F. Gouin (1831—1896)、L. Sauveur (1826—1907) 以及一些其他的专家观察孩童学习母语的过程并深受自然教育法的启发。这些自然教育法的追随者开始研发一个新的语言教学法，也就是后人所称的直接教学法。

6.2.1. Direct Method: Classroom Practice
　　　直接法：课堂实践

Direct Method proponents believe that foreign language acquisition is similar to first language acquisition. Therefore, achieving native-like pronunciation and oral communication skills are the primary goals.

直接教学法的支持者相信外语习得的过程和母语习得并无不同。因此，达到如母语者一样的发音以及口语交际技巧是直接教学法的主要目标。

In a Direct Method classroom, lessons begin with conversational-style dialogs in the target language. Only the vocabulary and sentences used in daily life are selected for instruction. Concrete vocabulary is taught through pictures, visual objects, and teachers' gestures, while abstract vocabulary is introduced through stories or association of ideas. Known words are used to introduce new vocabulary. In a small intensive class, students' oral communication skills are developed through a carefully graded progression of lessons organized around question-and-answer exchanges between teachers and students (Richards & Rodgers, 2001).

  在一个实践直接教学法的课堂，课程始于一个用目的语所进行的当代口语形式的会话。只有日常生活会用到的词汇以及句子才会在课程中出现。学生通过图片、实物以及教师的肢体动作学习具体的词汇，而抽象的词汇则是借由故事或相关的概念来习得。已知的字被用来介绍新的词汇。在一个小型的密集课堂中，教师与学生之间围绕课程主题进行层层递进的问答，学生得以逐渐提高他们的口语交际技巧(Richards & Rodgers, 2001)。

The students' first language is never used during instruction. Teachers use the target language to introduce new teaching points orally. Unlike the Grammar-Translation Method, grammar is taught inductively. Learners are guided to discover the rules through the teacher's use of adequate linguistic forms in the target language. There is no translation in class and the preferred type of exercise is a series of questions in the target language based on dialogs or anecdotal narratives. Pronunciation errors are corrected to achieve native-like pronunciation.

  教学中禁止学生使用母语。教师使用目的语口头介绍新的课程要点。不同于语法翻译法，在直接教学法中，语法教学是以诱导、归纳的方式进行的。教师以目的语带出语言结构的使用，引导学习者发掘规则的存在。课中没有翻译的活动，最常出现的练习形式是根据对话或趣闻故事以目的语所进行的问答。为了让学习者拥有母语般的发音，教师主动纠正学生发音的错误。

In a Direct Method classroom, the textbook is replaced by the teacher's demonstration and actions. Teachers take the center stage in the classroom, providing students with sufficient target language exposure by speaking only the target language. Learners are recipients of the oral input, who also participate in the conversations and dialogs.

在直接教学法的课堂里，课本被教师的演示以及动作所取代。教师是教学的中心，通过不带口音的发音，提供学生充分接触目的语的机会。学习者是口语输入的接收者，他们也是对话以及会话的参与者。

The Direct Method has been criticized for overemphasizing the similarities between natural acquisition of a first language and learning a foreign language. It has also been blamed for failing to consider the practical realities of the classroom and lacking a rigorous foundation in applied linguistic theories.

直接教学法常被批评过于重视甚至曲解了母语和外语在自然习得上的相似性。直接教学法也被攻击未能考虑课堂的实际情况以及缺乏应用语言学的基础。

6.3 Audiolingual Method 听说教学法

Audiolingual Method is a foreign language teaching method in the 1950s. After the World War II, the U.S.A. sent a large number of servicemen all over the world. It was therefore necessary to provide these soldiers who were sent abroad with at least basic verbal communication skills. Not surprisingly, in response to the U.S. government's urgent demands of personnel with foreign language skills, many universities in the U.S.A. established foreign language programs to provide foreign language training for military personnel. To enhance learners' oral skills in a short period of time, the new method relied heavily on the prevailing scientific methods of time, observation, and repetition. Because of the military influences, early versions of the Audiolingual Method were also called the "Army Method".

听说教学法是1950年代外语教学方法的主流。在二次世界大战后，美国派遣大量的军人到世界各地。因此，让这些派驻在外的军人拥有基础的外语沟通技巧是必要的。当然，为了回应美国政府亟需大量外语技术人才的需求，许多美国大学成立了外语项目以提供军事人员外语训练。为了在短期内提高学习者的口语技能，这个新的教学法依赖盛行的科学方法，强调掌控时间、观察以及重复练习。由于听说教学法的起源受到军方的影响，先前也称做"军队教学法"。

Derived from structural linguistics, languages is viewed as a system of structurally related elements for meaning encoding, the elements being phonemes, morphemes, words, structures, and sentence types (Richards & Rodgers, 2001). Structural linguists claim that the primary medium of languages is speaking, because many languages do not even have a written form. Human beings learn to speak before acquiring literacy skills. As a result, it is assumed that speaking should be a priority in language instruction. As American linguist, William Moulton, proposed in a report prepared for the 9th International Congress of Linguists in 1961, "Language is speech, not writing. A language is what its native speakers say, not what someone thinks they ought to say" (Richards & Rodgers, 2001).

　　源自结构语言学,语言被视为一个含有各种语义编码要素的系统,这些要素包括是音素、词素、字、结构以及句型(Richards & Rodgers,2001)。结构语言学家主张,因为许多语言没有文字的形式,语言的主要媒介就是口语,而且我们在习得读写之前,已经先学会说话。因此,听说法的支持者认为口语在语言教学中比其他技能更重要。根据美国语言学家William Moulton在1961年第九届国际语言学大会上提出的报告,"语言就是口语,并非写作。语言就是母语者说的话,而不是某个人认为他应该说的话"。(Richards & Rodgers,2001)

According to behaviorists, an individual acquires new skills through a process of habitual formation. Based on behaviorist theories, proponents of the Audiolingual Method believe that foreign language skills can be learned through a system of reinforcement. Reinforcement is essential in the learning process, because it serves to mark whether a response is considered appropriate or inappropriate by either encouraging repetition or suppressingincorrect responses. A correct response receives positive feedback, while incorrect response receives negative feedback.

　　行为学家表示,一个人习得一项新的技能是一个习惯养成的过程。根据行为学派理论,听说教学法的支持者相信外语技巧的习得可以通过系统的强化。强化对于学习的过程十分重要,因为强化可用来标注某个行为适当与否,以及之后用来鼓励学习者重复正确的行为以及抑制不正确的表现。正确的表现将得到正面的反馈，而错误的表现将得到负面的反馈。

Influenced by Behaviorism, followers of the Audiolingual Method apply the

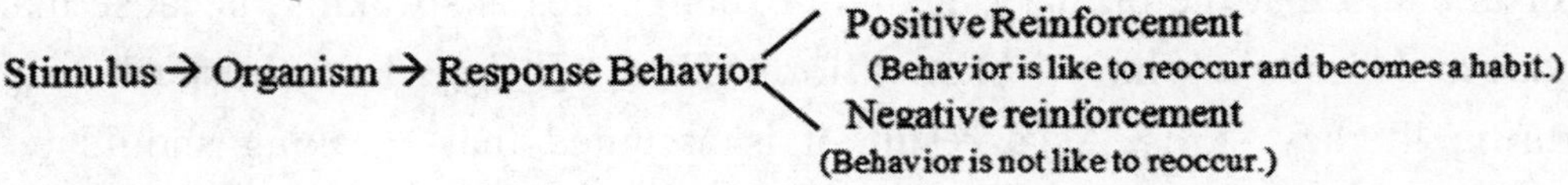

Stimulus → Organism → Response Behavior 〈 Positive Reinforcement (Behavior is like to reoccur and becomes a habit.) / Negative reinforcement (Behavior is not like to reoccur.)

Figure 6.1　Audiolingual method: Stimulus, response and reinforcement

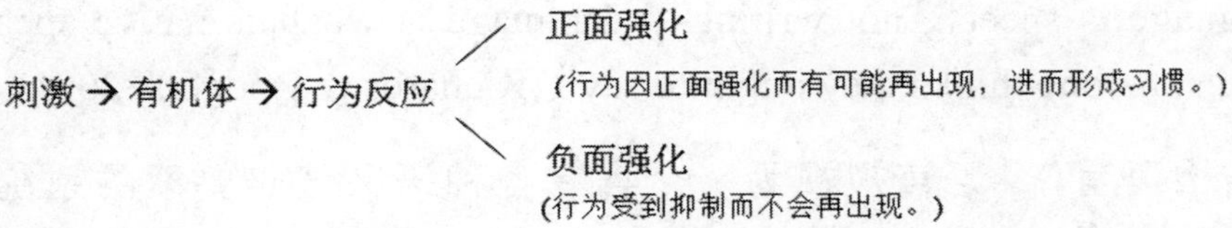

刺激 → 有机体 → 行为反应 〈 正面强化 （行为因正面强化而有可能再出现，进而形成习惯。） / 负面强化 （行为受到抑制而不会再出现。）

图6.1　听说法：刺激、反应和强化

following learning principles to foreign language instruction:

受到行为学派的影响，听说法的追随者将下面的学习原则应用在外语教学上：

1. Foreign language learning is a process of mechanical habit formation. Good habits are formed after receiving positive reinforcement of correct responses. To maximize the possibility of getting positive reinforcement, memorization of dialogs and performance of pattern drills are required. Mimicry, memorization of set phrases, and over-learning are essential in this method.
2. Language skills are learned more effectively if the items to be learned are presented in the spoken form of the target language.
3. Analogy is better than analysis in providing a foundation for language learning, because analogy involves a process of generalization and discrimination. In the Audiolingual Method, grammar is taught inductively, and not deductively. Hence, drills are very helpful for habit formation and correct analogy formation.

1. 学习外语是一个机械性的习惯养成过程。好习惯的养成是通过正面反馈的强化。为了能最大限度地得到正面的强化作用,背诵对话以及反复操练句型是必要的。模仿、记诵词组以及过度学习都是听说教学法的重点。
2. 若学习的语言点是以目的语的口语形式呈现,语言技巧的习得将会更有成效。
3. 类比比分析更能提供语言学习的基础,因为类比牵涉一个归纳以及辨别的过程。在听说教学法中,语法是透过诱导、归纳的方式习得的,而非演绎法。因此,操练有助于习惯的养成以及正确类比的塑造。

6.3.1. Audiolingual Method: Classroom Practice
听说法:课堂实践

According to Brooks (1964), an audiolingual language curriculum has both short-term and long-range objectives. Short-term objectives include having control of sound, form, and order in the new language, and being familiar with content-related vocabulary items and knowing how to apply these into sentence structures. With regard to the long-range objectives, learners are expected to reach native-like proficiency level.

Brooks (1964)指出,听说法的语言课程设置有短期和长期的目标。短期目标包括掌握一个新语言的发音、语法形式以及语序,熟悉与内容相关的词汇以及了解如何将这些应用在句子结构中。至于长期目标,期望学习者能达到母语般的能力水平。

At the early stages, the focus of language learning is on oral skills. Accuracy in pronunciation, fluency, and the use of grammar in spoken communication are emphasized. The target language is taught in a specific order: first listening, then speaking, reading, and writing. Listening comprehension is used to develop learners' aural discrimination of basic sound patterns. The target language is entirely presented orally at first, followed by more complex reading and writing tasks at more advanced levels.

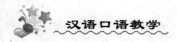

在早期阶段,语言学习的重心在口语技巧。发音与语法使用的准确性以及口语交际的流利度都受到高度的重视。目的语的教学依据特定的顺序,首先通过听力,之后才是口语、阅读以及写作。听力理解用来培养学习者对基本声音模式的识别力。语言先通过口语的形式进行教学,之后在高级班才带入较复杂的阅读以及写作任务。

Similar to the Direct Method, the Audiolingual Method suggests that students be taught in the target language directly, without using the students' native language. However, unlike the Direct Method, the Audiolingual Method does not focus on teaching vocabulary. Rather, dialogs and drills are used for repetition and memorization. As little or no grammar explanations are provided in an audiolingual class, grammar is taught inductively. Structures are sequenced and taught one at a time. Structural patterns are taught using repetitive drills. After students memorize the text of a dialog, the teacher selects specific grammatical patterns from the dialog and uses repetitive drill exercises.

如同直接教学法,听说教学法建议直接以目的语进行教学。而不需要使用学生的母语解释新词或语法。然而,不同于直接教学法,听说法并不侧重词汇的教学。对话与口语操练用于反复练习以及记诵。由于听说法课堂中语法解释的比例很小,甚至几乎没有,语法教学是以归纳、诱导的方式进行。课堂上将语法结构排序,依序介绍,句型结构通过反复操练的方式习得。在学生记诵对话内容之后,教师从对话中选择特定的语法句型,通过反复的口语操练提高学生对这个句型的熟练度。

Use of drills and pattern practice is a distinctive feature of the Audiolingual Method. According to Brook (1964), different types of drills are used in an audiolingual language class. Those audiolingual practices include repetition, inflection, replacement, restatement, completion, expansion, transformation, and integration.

运用口语操练以及句型练习是听说教学法的主要特色。Brook (1964)指出,听说法的课堂中运用的口语操练有许多不同的形式。这些听说练习包括了重复练习、词性变化、替换练习、重述练习、完成句子、句子伸展、改写句子以及合并练习。

- Repetition: Students are asked to follow and repeat an utterance spoken by the teacher.

  Example: I want to eat an apple — I want to eat an apple.

- Inflection: When repeating an utterance, students are asked to change the form of the teacher's original utterance.

  Example: I want to eat an apple — I want to eat apples.

- Replacement: When repeating an utterance, students are asked to replace one word in the utterance with another word.

  Example: I want to eat *this apple* — I want to eat it.

- 重复：要求学生跟着老师，重复说出老师说的话语。

  例子：师：我要吃一个苹果。生：我要吃一个苹果。

- 词性变化：当重复老师的话语时，学生必须改变老师原话的形式。

  例子：师：我要吃一个苹果。生：我要吃苹果（复数）。

- 替换练习：当重复老师的话语时，学生必须将老师原话中的某个字替换成另一个字。

  例子：师：我要吃这个苹果。生：我要吃那个。

As the Audiolingual Method is a teacher-dominated teaching approach, instructional materials are only used to assist the teacher during instruction. At the early stages of learning, students focus on listening, repeating, and responding to the teacher's utterances. Textbooks and printed materials only provide texts of dialogs and cues to the needs for drills and exercises. Tape recorders, audiovisual equipment, and language laboratories are important for an audiolingual class, because they facilitate drill work and provide an alternative to classroom practice.

  由于听说法是一个以教师为中心的教学法，教学材料仅用于辅助教师的教学。在学习的初期，学生把注意力集中在听力、重复以及回应老师的话语。课本以及其他印制的材料仅用于提供会话的原文以及口语操练所需的提示。录音机、视听设备以及语言实验室对以听说法为主的课堂十分重要，因为这些器材能够辅助口语的操练以及提供课堂练习其他替代的选择。

In the Audiolingual Method, learners are treated as amenable to conditioning, able to produce correct responses with intensive training and reinforcement. They have little control over the content, pace, or style of learning. Learners are discouraged from initiating interactions because this may lead to errors (Richards & Rodgers, 2001).

　　在听说法中,学习者被视为能服从于条件反射作用,在密集的训练以及强化作用之下可以做出正确的反应。他们几乎没有办法掌控任何与学习有关的内容、节奏以及形式。学习者被劝阻尝试任何同学间的互动,因为互动可能导致错误的产生(Richards & Rodgers, 2001)。

In contrast, teachers' role is active and central in the Audiolingual Method. The teacher provides modeling for students, controls the pace and direction of learning, and monitors students' progress and corrects students' errors. Intensive drills and active verbal interactions between teachers and students are believed to result in effective language learning.

　　相反的,在听说教学法中教师扮演主动且核心的角色。教师提供学生一个榜样,掌控学习的步调以及方向,监控学生的进展以及纠正学生的错误。密集的口语操练以及积极的师生口语互动被认为可以提高语言学习的效果。

Audiolingual Method has been criticized for failing to make a connection between classroom instruction and real-life communication. Students also complain that sitting in an audiolingual lab and repetitive drills is boring.

　　听说法因未能将课堂教学与现实生活联系起来而饱受批评。学生也抱怨坐在以听说为主的语言实验室里,不停地重复口语操练十分无趣。

6.4 Total Physical Response　全身反应法(TPR)

Total Physical Response (TPR) is a language teaching method developed by James Asher, a psychology professor at San Jose State University. It focuses on the coordination of speech and action, and attempts to teach a language through physical activities. After observing the process of children's native language acquisition, Asher found that children respond to oral commands physically before they are able to respond verbally. Therefore, he claimed that adults should follow the same process. According to Asher (1977), the grammatical structure of the target language and vocabulary items can be learned from instructor's skillful use of commands. Verbs are the most important element of commands. TPR can also be linked to the theoretical trace of memory in psychology, which argues that the more intensively a concept is reinforced by physical movements or association with other things, the stronger will be the memory and the greater will be the possibility for it to be retained. Associating verbal utterances with motor actions strengthens memory retention and increases the possibility of successful recall.

全身反应法(TPR)是圣何塞州立大学心理学教授James Asher所提出的一种语言教学方式。这个教学法注重口语和肢体的协调,并企图通过肢体活动来教授语言。在观察孩童的母语习得的过程之后,Asher发现孩童在接收到口头命令时,身体会比言语先做出反应。因此,他主张成人应该也依循同样的过程。

Asher(1977)指出,通过教师熟练地使用口头指令,可让学生学习目的语的语法结构及词汇。动词是命令中最关键的要素。

全身反应法(TPR)也与心理学中的记忆痕迹理论有关联。记忆痕迹理论主张,当某个概念通过肢体动作或其他事件进行强化时,对此概念的记忆就越深刻,也更可能被保留。把语言和动作联系起来,让记忆得以继续保留,也增加了成功提取记忆的可能性。

As a natural method, Asher's TPR emphasizes on the similarities between first language acquisition and foreign language learning, and is connected with brain lateralization learning theory. Similar to first language learners, foreign language learners should acquire a language through physical movement at first, which involves right-hemisphere activity. After creating a cognitive map of the target language by listening to the instructor's oral utterances, learners' left hemisphere will be triggered to produce language and to initiate more abstract language processes. Unlike other language learning approaches, which focus on abstract forms and rules of the target language, TPR aims to use physical movements to liberate learners from stressful learning situations.

如同自然法,Asher 的全身反应法强调母语和外语习得之间的相似性,更认为和大脑左右半球侧化理论有关联。和母语学习者一样,外语学习者先通过肢体动作习得语言,而这与右脑半球的活动有关。通过聆听教师的口语表达,学习者建立一个目的语的认知地图,这时他们的左脑半球将会受刺激而输出语言,并启动更抽象的语言加工。

不同于其他注重目的语抽象形式以及规则的语言学习方法,全身反应法强调使用肢体动作来把学习者从紧张的学习情境中释放出来。

6.4.1. TPR: Classroom Practice
全身反应法:课堂实践

TPR aims to teach beginning-level speaking skills. As pointed out by Richards & Rodgers (2001), TPR does not have a specifically elaborated instructional objective because it always takes learners' particular needs into consideration. However, all the objectives must be attainable through the use of action-based drills in the imperative form.

全身反应法的目的在于教授初级的口语技巧。Richards & Rodgers (2001)指出,TPR 并没有一个特别具体的教学目标,因为它总是将学习者的特别需要纳入考虑。然而,通过口语命令形式、以动作为基础的操练,所有的学习目标都必须是可达成的。

Unlike grammar or structural based approaches, at the early stages of learning a language, TPR focuses on meaning and introduces grammar inductively. In a TPR language classroom, to ensure that learners understand differentiation and assimilation, a fixed number of items are introduced. Imperative drills, which are used to coordinate speaking and actions, are the primary in-class activity. In addition to drills, role playing in scenarios that imitate daily life are frequently used in a TPR class.

不同于以语法或是以结构为基础的方法，TPR 的重心放在语义，以诱导、归纳的方式教授语法。在一个 TPR 课堂，为了确保学习者理解观念的异同，只教授固定数量的语言点，协调口语和动作的命令式操练是主要的课堂活动。除了口语操练之外，在设定的情境中模拟日常生活的角色扮演也是 TPR 课堂的常用活动。

According to Asher (1977), a typical TPR class begins with a fast-moving warm-up review. After the review, new commands are introduced and practiced with physical actions. As the students get familiar with the new commands, the teacher allows the student to give the commands to each other. Finally, the teacher summarizes new vocabulary items and sentences and the students write or perform what he/she reads.

Asher (1977)表示，一个典型的 TPR 课堂会以一个节奏很快的热身复习拉开序幕。在复习之后，教师会介绍新的口令并通过肢体活动来练习这些新口令。随着学生越来越熟悉这些新指令，教师会让学生对班上其他同学发号施令。最后，教师总结新的词汇以及句子，而学生写下或是表演老师说的指令。

In a TPR class, the use of instructional materials depends on learners' proficiency levels. For beginners, the teacher's oral commands, actions, and gestures are the primary instructional tools. As learners' language proficiency advances, the teacher may include visual aids or supplementary materials to support in-class activities. Special instructional tools related to specific scenarios, such as the home, grocery store, restaurant, and beach, are often created by TPR teachers to facilitate students' learning.

在一个 TPR 课堂里，教材的使用取决于学习者的语言程度。对初级者来说，教师的口头指令、动作以及手势都是主要的教学工具。随着学习者语言程度的提高，教师可能加入一些辅助课堂活动的视觉教具或补充材料。TPR 教师也常制作一些与家庭、杂货店、参观、海滩等特定情境有关的特殊教具来帮助学生的学习。

Learners are primarily listeners and performers in a TPR class. They listen to the teachers' oral commands and respond physically. They are encouraged to use previously introduced words or patterns to create their own sentences. Based on their physical performances, learners also monitor and evaluate their own progress.

学习者在TPR课堂里主要扮演聆听者和表演者的角色。他们聆听教师的口令并以肢体动作回应口令。教师鼓励学生使用之前学过的词汇或句型造他们自己的句子。根据他们的肢体表现,学习者也能监控评估他们的进展。

As the person who decides the teaching content, selects supplementary materials, and does the modeling in class, the TPR teacher plays an active and direct role in instruction. Similar to the role that parents play in children's acquisition of a first language, the TPR teacher gives feedback to the students. At the early stages, the teacher exhibits greater tolerance of errors to avoid frustrating students. However, as the students' proficiency levels go up, teachers' intervention and corrections increases.

身为决定教学内容、筛选补充材料以及亲身示范者,TPR教师在教学上扮演直接主动的角色。如同父母亲在孩童习得母语时扮演的角色,TPR教师给予学生反馈。在初期,为了避免让学生轻易受挫,教师对错误的容忍度较大。但是,随着学生语言程度的提高,教师的介入以及纠错也增加了。

TPR was popular in the 1970s and 1980s due to its emphasis on the significance of comprehension in SLA. Krashen (1981) claimed that performing physical actions in the target language is a way of learning and reduces stress. However, TPR has been criticized as only suitable for beginners. TPR is more effective in teaching concrete vocabulary items, but fails to teach abstract concepts that are acquired at advanced levels of language learning. Second, grammatical features and vocabulary items are selected not according to their frequency of use in the target language, but according to the situations in which they can be used during instruction. Also, when compared with other language teaching method, TPR is very time-consuming. Some students, especially older learners, who are not used to using their bodies to learn a language, may find TPR activities embarrassing.

TPR 在70年代和80年代因其重视二语习得中理解的重要性而广受欢迎。Krashen (1981)主张，目的语种肢体动作的表演是一种学习和降低压力的方法。不过，有人认为TPR教学法只适合初学者。TPR对教授具体词汇较为有效，但未必能用来讲解各阶级语言学习时常遇到的抽象概念。此外，语法特征以及词汇的选择并非依据它们在目的语里使用的频率，而是依据教学中它们适用的情境。还有，相较于其他语言教学法，TPR相当费时。有些学生，特别是年纪较大的学习者并不习惯使用肢体来学习语言，有可能觉得TPR活动让他们感到十分尴尬。

6.5 Communicative Language Teaching　交际语言教学法

Communicative Language Teaching (CLT) is a foreign language teaching method, which emphasizes on interaction as both the means and the ultimate goal. It was developed in response to growing dissatisfaction with Grammar-Translation Method and Audiolingual Method in foreign language instruction. Critics felt that students, who were taught using these methods, lacked the ability to communicate appropriately and deal with real-life situations in the target language. For this reason, in the 1970s, researchers and language instructors became interested in developing communicative teaching methods to bridge the gap between classroom instruction and real-life communication(Savignon, 2005).

交际语言教学法(CLT)是一个以人际互动为工具和终极目标的语言教学法。为了回应对语法翻译教学法和听说教学法在外语教学上日渐高涨的不满，交际语言教学法开始萌芽。批评者认为，在这两个教学法指导下的学生缺乏适当的交际能力，也没办法用目的语应付现实生活中会遇到的情况。因此，在1970年代，学者以及语言教师开始对交际语言教学法的发展感兴趣，并期望能藉此弥合课堂教学与现实生活交际之间的差距(Savignon, 2005)。

Generally, CLT has a rich theoretical foundation in language theories. It views languages as a system for expression of meanings and sees the primary function of languages as facilitating interaction and communication.

一般而言,交际语言教学法有坚实的语言理论基础。它视语言为一个表达意义的系统,并认为语言的主要功用在于促进互动以及沟通。

In contrast to Chomsky's (1965) theory of linguistics, which characterizes the ability to produce grammatically correct sentences in a language as abstract and universal, Hymes (1972b) insisted that linguistic theories need to incorporate a more comprehensive account of communication and culture. From Hymes' perspective, learners acquire communicative competence to appropriately participate in a speech community.

不同于Chomsky (1965)强调普遍语法的语言学理论,Hymes (1972b)坚持语言学理论必须结合交际以及文化。根据Hymes的观点,学习者习得交际的能力是为了能够适宜地参与一个语言社区。

Halliday (1970) also emphasized on the functional goals of language learning. Children learn language primarily as a means to an end; to get things, to control the behavior of others, to interact with others, to express feelings, to learn new knowledge, and to create work of imagination. CLT draws from these theories by emphasizing the function of language (Halliday, 1975). In the Communicative Approach, the goal of language instruction is to develop communicative competence (Hymes, 1972b).

Halliday (1970)也强调语言学习的功能性目标。孩童学习语言主要是把语言当做一个工具;可以用来取得物件、控制他人行为、与他人互动、表达感觉、学习新知以及打造想象空间。交际语言教学法源于这些强调语言目的性的理论(Halliday, 1975)。在交际教学法中,语言教学的目标在于培养学生的交际能力(Hymes, 1972b)。

Although there are a few discussions on the relationship between CLT and learning theories, there are several learning principles of CLT. The first is that real communication promotes learning. The second is the task principle stating that meaningful tasks promote learning. The third is the meaningfulness principle: Meaningful and authentic learning activities, which are designed or selected to enhance learners' engagement, facilitate language learning.

Canale & Swain (1980)指出了交际能力的四个面向。这四个面向包括了语法能力、社会语言能力、篇章言谈能力以及策略能力。语法能力表示知道如何使用一个语言的语法、句法以及词汇；社会语言能力指在既定的环境、话题以及交谈人关系下知道如何使用及适当地回应语言。篇章言谈能力是指能准确完整诠释信息以及发掘信息和整段话语的关系的能力。策略能力指的是能够察觉与修补交际中断，以及知道如何利用有限的语言能力完成交际任务。

虽然关于 CLT 和学习理论关系的讨论并不多，仍有一些 CLT 的学习原则。第一个原则是实际的交际有助于学习。第二个是任务原则：有意义的任务有助于学习。第三个原则是有意义原则：选择或设计有意义且真实的学习活动，能够提高学习者积极性且促进语言学习。

6.5.1. CLT: Classroom Practice
交际语言教学法：课堂实践

The primary objective of CLT is to enhance students' communicative competence. Students learn to use language as a means of expression, making judgments, and meeting communication needs.

交际语言教学法的主要目的在于提升学生的交际能力。学生学习将语言作为一种表达思想、做判断以及满足交际需求的工具。

CLT makes use of real-life situations that necessitate communication. The teacher sets up a situation that students are likely to encounter in real life. Unlike the Audiolingual Method, which relies on repetition and drills, the communicative approach can leave students in suspense with respect to the outcome of a classroom exercise, which varies according to their reactions and responses. The real-life simulations change from day to day. Students' learning motivation comes from their desire to communicate in meaningful ways about meaningful topics.

交际语言教学法利用现实生活的情境来使交际成为必要。教师在课上设置一个学生在现实生活中可能遇到的情境。不同于依赖重复口语操练的听说教学法，CLT教学法可以让学生自行决定课堂任务的结局，也就是依照他们反应来完成任务，因此，一个任务可能有许许多多的结局。模拟现实生活的任务每天都在转变。学生学习的动机来自他们想要进行有意义的交际任务的渴望。

Classroom activities or tasks are often designed to promote interaction through a process of negotiating meaning or information sharing. According to Littlewood (1981), two types of activities are commonly used in a communicative class. One is "functional communication activities", which include comparing pictures and identifying similarities and differences, sequencing an event from a set of pictures, discovering a missing feature from a map or picture, working in pairs to complete a jigsaw task, and solving programs from shared clues. The other type of activities is "social interaction activities", such as conversations and discussion on a specific topic, dialogs, and role plays, simulations, skits, improvisations and debates (Richards & Rodgers, 2001).

课堂活动或任务一般通过意义协商或是分享信息的过程来促进互动。Littlewood (1981)提出两种交际语言教学法常用的活动。其中一个是"功能性交际活动"，包括比较图片辨识异同、将图片按照时间顺序排序、找出地图或图片上缺少的部分、两人一组完成一个拼图任务，以及从共享的信息中解决问题。另一种活动是"社交互动活动"，包括讨论一个特定的议题、两人对话和角色扮演、虚拟实境、喜剧小品、即兴演说以及辩论(Richards & Rodgers, 2001)。

Various types of materials are used in CLT. According to Richards and Rodgers (2001), there are three main types:

交际语言教学法使用多种不同的课程材料。Richards & Rodgers (2001)归纳出三种主要的类型：

1. Text-Based materials: A large number of textbooks are designed for CLT. According to their tables of contents, there are specific grading criteria and

a sequence of language exercises, which use a communicative approach.
2. Task-Based materials: A variety of games, simulations, role plays, and task-based activities are used in CLT classes. To prepare those activities, materials such as exercise books, cards, and activity sheets can be created.
3. Realia: Authentic materials, such as magazines, advertisements, newspapers, or other media resources, are also adapted and used in CLT classes.

1. 课文为主的材料：大量的课本是为了交际语言教学课堂而设计的。根据这些课本的目录，我们可以发现有一个根据交际语言教学法而设定的特定评分标准以及语言练习的先后次序。
2. 任务为主的材料：交际语言教学课堂中应用各式各样的游戏、模拟、角色扮演以及任务型活动。为了准备这些活动，教师可以制作一些像是练习册、卡片、活动单的材料。
3. 真实语料：包括杂志、广告、报纸或是其他媒体资源在内的真实语料也常常在交际语言教学的活动中出现。

There are some advantages of using the CLT approach. First, it allows learners to use the target language in meaningful contexts and brings the real world into the classroom. CLT learners are active participants and negotiators in the classroom. They are encouraged to speak their mind and use their knowledge to create conversations. As learners collaborate in various types of group work, they take joint responsibility for the effectiveness of the communication.

使用交际语言教学法有一些优点。第一，交际语言教学法让学习者能在有意义的语境中使用目的语，并把现实世界带入教室。交际语言教学法的学习者是课堂中主动的参与者与协商者。他们被鼓励表达自我以及利用所知的语言知识自己创造对话。由于学习者在各种不同的小组活动中相互合作，他们一起担负交际成效的责任。

In addition, this approach can be adopted at different levels of language classes. It is also suitable for classes comprising students with different linguistic backgrounds and various levels of communicative competence. With specific task design, in which learners play different roles in group work and contribute to the collaborative task, learners are able to interact with each other according to their levels of proficiency. In a CLT classroom, teachers are able to step back and take a role of facilitator. Through a variety of tasks, the teacher can monitor students' learning progress and make necessary adjustment.

  此外,CLT 教学法适用于不同程度的语言课程,也能适用于班级学生语言背景和交际能力参差不齐的情况。

  在特别的活动设计下,学习者可以在小组活动中扮演不同的角色,并在协作任务中贡献一己之力,学习者根据自己的语言水平和同学进行互动。在一个以 CLT 为主的课堂,教师可以退居为一个辅助者。通过各式各样的任务,教师可以监控学生的学习进展以及做必要的调整。

As a teaching method focusing on oral fluency, CLT is blamed for putting too much emphasis on the use of language in everyday situations and ignoring the significance of linguistic accuracy. Also, CLT approach gives the learning priority to functional aspects of the language and language use. Furthermore, the various categories of language functions are overlapping and are not graded systematically (Al-Humaidi, 2007). For this reason, CLT instruction is criticized for neglecting the importance of language structures and rules. Moreover, a major premise underlying this approach is the importance of individual learners' needs and interests. However, in real-life situations, it is very difficult to take every learner's needs into consideration. To create a learner-centered environment, CLT teacher should not be the center of classroom activities. Nevertheless, CLT teachers need to be highly competent and imaginative to design various types of classroom tasks. Inexperienced teachers may influence the effectiveness of CLT instruction.

  作为一个强调口语流利度的教学法,CLT 被批评过于重视日常生活中语言的使用,而忽略了语言准确度的重要性。此外,语言交际教学法把语言的功能面向以及语言使用视为应优先考虑的事。然而,不同类别的语言功能相互重复,也没有像语言结构一样系统化地分级(Al-Humaidi, 2007)。为此,CLT 教学因忽略语言结构与规则的重要性而饱受批评。

再者，这个教学法的一个主要前提在于关切个别学习者需求和兴趣的重要性。然而，实际上很难将每一个学习者的需求都纳入考虑。为了打造一个以学习者为中心的环境，CLT 教师不是课堂活动的重心。不过，CLT 教师需要非常有能力，更要在设计课堂活动上充满创意。缺乏经验的教师可能影响交际语言教学的成效。

6.6 Content-Based Instruction　内容教学法

Content-Based Instruction (CBI) refers to an approach designed to teach a language by content. CBI proponents believe that a learner is successful when the focus is on content rather than on mastery of the language. The word content is interpreted as the use of subject matter as a vehicle for L2 or foreign language teaching. CBI is an innovation in teaching a language. In its best form, language lessons are blended with stimulating content. Engaging with the content of the subject matter is prioritized in the learning process. Language-related skills are acquired automatically in the process of learning content. CBI is built on the principles of CLT. Classrooms need to be filled with real and meaningful communication when information is exchanged or shared.

内容教学法(CBI)是一个利用内容来教授语言的教学法。内容教学法的支持者相信，当教学的重心在内容而非语言时，学习者的学习效果最好。内容一词就是指二语教学中相关的学习主题。内容教学法(CBI)在语言教学上是一个创新。在最理想的情境，语言的课程与刺激有趣的内容结合。在学习的过程中学生优先从事与学科有关的内容，在学习内容的过程中学生会自动习得与语言有关的技能。CBI 的出现是根据交际语言教学法的原则。在信息交换或共享的时候，课堂中必须充斥真实、有意义的交际沟通。

According to Richards and Rodgers (2001), a number of assumptions about the nature of language underline CBI. First, CBI sees language as a tool for learning content. This means that the purpose of language teaching is to help learners to comprehend how meaning and information are communicated and constructed through texts and discourse. Second, CBI views language as a process involving several linguistic skills simultaneously. In a CBI course, materials are presented in topics or themes, which provide a good basis for connecting knowledge, language, and skills, as well as promoting coherence and continuity across skill areas. In addition, CBI approach uses language for specific purposes, which can be academic, vocational, social, or recreational. The purpose of language use gives direction and meaning to discourse and texts. Learners start at sentences and move through clauses, phrases, and speech events, and construct a text at the final stage. For example, by discussing "environmental issues in China", students not only can better understand the current environmental situations in China, but can also acquire vocabulary knowledge related to various kinds of pollution and environmental protection policies in Chinese. During class discussion, students have an opportunity to enhance their reading, speaking, listening, and writing skills.

  Richards & Rodgers (2001)指出，根据内容教学法，有一些关于语言本质的假设。首先，CBI认为语言是学习内容的一个工具。这意味语言教学的目的在于帮助学习者去理解如何通过文字和谈话建构语义和交换信息。第二，CBI视语言为一个同时牵涉数个语言技能的进程。在一个CBI的课堂中，上课材料以话题或是主题的方式呈现，为知识、语言和技能的连结提供一个良好的基础，也促进了不同技能间的连续性与持续性。此外，CBI教学法为了特定的目的运用语言，这个目的可以是学术、职业、社交或娱乐。语言运用的目的呈现了谈话和文字的意义。学习者始于句子，接着通过分句、短句、言语活动以及在最后一个阶段建构篇章。例如，借由讨论"中国的环境问题"，学生不只可以了解目前中国的环境情况，更可以学到与污染以及环保政策有关的汉语词汇知识。在课堂讨论中，学生有机会提高他们在阅读、口语、听力以及写作方面的技巧。

Brinton et al. claimed that successful language learning occurs when students are presented with meaningful and contextualized materials in the target language (Brinton, Snow, & Wesche, 1989). Language learning is more motivating when the materials are perceived as interesting, useful, and close to learners' learning goals. When students are interested in and motivated by the materials that they are learning, it is easier for them to make connections to their personal lives.

Brinton 和他的同事主张,当学生接收以目的语传达的有意义且情境化的材料时,语言学习就会有成效(Brinton, Snow, & Wesche, 1989)。当学生感到材料有趣、有用,更能帮助他们达到理想目标时,他们的学习动机就会更高。而在他们对学习材料感到兴趣高昂时,他们就会在学习和个人生活之间创造更多、更紧密的联系。

由于 CBI 教学法因适应学生的兴趣以及需求选择内容,学生的学习动机较高,进步也较大。此外,CBI 的材料是根据学生的知识以及之前的经验所制作。能为课堂贡献已知,学生的学习动机也变得更强。

6.6.1. CBI: Classroom Practices
内容教学法:课堂实践

In a CBI class, content learning and language acquisition occur simultaneously. As learners are expected to acquire language knowledge through content learning, a CBI curriculum should have clear objectives.

在 CBI 课堂中,内容学习和语言习得是同时发生的。由于学生应该通过学习内容而习得语言知识,内容教学法的课程设置必须有清楚的教学目标。

To enhance language proficiency, a variety of learning and teaching activities are used in CBI classrooms. These activities are categorized according to their instructional focus, such as language skills improvement, vocabulary building, discourse organization, communicative interaction, study skills, and synthesis of content materials and grammar (Stroller, 1997).

为了有效提高学生的语言能力,CBI 课堂中使用了许多教学活动。这些活动根据教学的重心分成不同的类别,像增进语言技巧、词汇学习、组织会话、交际互动、学习技巧以及整合材料的内容和语法(Stroller, 1997)。

In CBI, a wide range of authentic materials are used to facilitate language learning. These materials are directly related to the subject matter, including, but not limited to, TV broadcasts, newspaper advertisements, railway timetables, magazine articles, and tourist guidebooks.

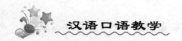

  CBI教学法使用了大量的真实语料来辅助语言学习。这些材料与学科内容直接相关,包括电视节目、报纸广告、铁路时刻表、杂志文章以及旅客导览手册等。

However, with complicated sentence structures, rarely used vocabulary, and lengthy passages, many authentic materials are not suitable for beginning and intermediate learners. CBI researchers and language instructors emphasize that some materials need modification to achieve maximum comprehensibility.

  然而,复杂的句型结构、不常用的词汇以及过长的段落,使得许多真实语料不是那么适合初级或是中级的学习者。内容教学法研究者以及教师强调,为了确保学生能够理解内容,某些真实语料需要进一步的修改。

CBI learners are active participants in the process of learning, who collaborate actively in team work. As CBI courses incorporate learners' interests and needs into the curriculum, learners are well-informed and know what they want to learn.

  CBI教学法下的学生在学习的过程中是积极的参与者。他们在团队任务中相互合作,与教师一同选择主题以及设计活动。由于CBI教学将学习者的兴趣以及需要融入课程规划,学习者必须见多识广且明确知道自己想要学什么。

Unlike traditional language instructors, CBI teachers have to be good analysts of students' learning needs. They have to consider their students' prior knowledge and special needs in the curriculum design while trying to balance between authenticity and comprehensibility when they select materials for the class.

  不同于传统的语言教师,CBI教师必须善于分析学生的学习需求。他们得将学生既有的知识以及特定的需求纳入课程规划中,并在选择上课材料时在真实度以及理解度之间保持平衡。

CBI has been criticized for setting an extremely high standard for instructors. As most of the language teachers have been trained to teach language skills rather than a specific subject of content, they may lack sufficient content knowledge or skills when it comes to a particular subject matter.

CBI 因对教师设定过高的标准而受到批评。由于大多语言教师之前所受的培训是教授语言技能而非教授某个学科的内容,他们可能对特定学科的内容缺乏了解。

6.7 Task-Based Instruction　任务教学法

According to Kris Van den Branden (2006), a task is an activity in which a person engages to attain an objective, which necessitates the use of language. Task-Based Instruction (TBI), which is emerging as a major focal point of language teaching practice worldwide, focuses on meaningful communication in class.

　　Kris Van den Branden (2006)指出,任务即一个有目的性的活动,在这个活动中语言的使用是必要的。任务型教学(TBI),在世界各地已经成为了语言教学领域的主要焦点,重视在课堂上使用有意义的任务以及真实语料。

In-class tasks, which simulate real-world situations, such as visiting the doctor, bargaining during shopping, and conducting an interview, are all used to develop students' target-language fluency, enhance their problem-solving ability, and help them successfully use the target language to communicate in the real world. Assessment is primarily based on the completion of tasks, and not on the accuracy of language forms. Hence, it effectively boosts students' motivation and confidence.

　　课堂上的任务通过模拟真实生活中看病、讨价还价以及进行访问等情境,用来提高学生目的语的流利度和使用目的语解决问题的能力,帮助学生在真实世界中成功使用目的语进行交际。课堂评估主要是根据任务的完成度,而非语言形式的准确度。因此,任务教学法有效地提升了学生的学习动机和自信。

6.7.1. TBI: Classroom Practices
　　任务教学法:课堂实践

Unlike traditional approaches and the communicative approach, TBI approach seeks a balance between form and meaning. To effectively enhance students' language accuracy, complexity, and fluency, TBI not only emphasizes on providing students enough exercises to ensure accuracy in language forms, but also stresses on language functions and connections to the real world.

不同于传统的教学法以及交际语言教学法,任务教学法试图在形式和意义之间取得平衡。为了有效提高学生语言的准确度、复杂度以及流利度,任务型教学不仅强调提供学生充分的练习机会以确保他们在语言结构与形式使用上的准确度,更重视语言的功用以及课堂活动与现实世界的联系。

According to Wills (1996), the components of a TBI framework can be categorized into three phases: a pre-task phase, task cycle, and language focus phase.

Wills (1996)指出,任务型教学框架代表任务型教学模式的实施过程,其中有三个阶段:任务前置阶段、任务环以及语言焦点。

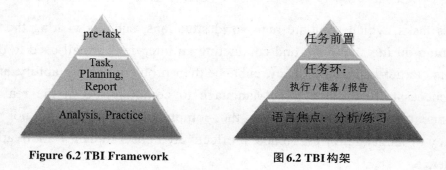

Figure 6.2 TBI Framework　　　图6.2 TBI构架

1) Pre-task phase: Introduction to Topic and Task

The teacher introduces the topic and explains what the students need to accomplish in the class. Useful words, phrases, and sentence patterns are highlighted. The teacher also helps the students to understand the instructions and makes sure that the goals are clear. The teacher has to ensure that students have enough time to prepare.

1) 任务前置阶段(Pre-task):介绍任务与主题

教师先介绍主题,解释学生需要完成的任务,同时强调进行任务时会用到的单词、短语以及句型。教师帮助学生理解任务内容,确保任务目标的明确性。教师也必须保证学生有足够的时间准备任务。

2) Task cycle: Task, Planning, and Report

There are three components of the task cycle, namely, task performance, report planning, and report presentation.

Task: Students are asked to perform a task, typically in pairs or small groups. The teacher circulates, provides necessary assistance, and encourages all attempts at communication. In this phase, the teacher only serves as an observer or a counselor.

Report Planning: Students prepare to report their progress and their findings to the whole class. The instructor simply monitors the students and provides necessary help.

Report Presentation: Students present their reports to the rest of the class. The teacher acts as a chairperson, provides immediate feedback, and sums up at the end of discussion.

2) 任务环(Task cycle):任务、准备、报告

  任务环阶段有三个部分:执行任务、准备报告以及总结报告。

  执行任务:学生必须两人一组或是以小组的形式完成一个任务。教师在课堂里巡视,提供学生必要的帮助,并鼓励学生使用目的语交际沟通。在这个阶段,教师仅扮演观察者或是顾问的角色。

  报告准备:学生准备向全班汇报任务执行的过程、发现及任务的结果。教师监控学生的语言表达,并同时提供必要的帮助。

  报告总结:学生向全班报告他们的任务执行过程、结果与发现。教师担任主席的角色,提供学生即时反馈以及在讨论的最后进行总结。

3) Language Focus: Analysis and Practice

Analysis: Students examine the reports and exchange opinions. In this phase, the teacher helps the students to review what happened during the task, especially problems that the students may have encountered.

Practice: The teacher conducts practice activities to review words and patterns occurring in the analysis phase.

3) 语言焦点:分析与练习

分析:学生检视报告的内容,彼此交换意见。在这个阶段,教师协助学生复习任务中出现的语言点,特别是学生遇到的问题。

练习:教师进行练习活动,通过这些活动复习分析阶段出现的单词以及句型。

The teacher serves as a selector, planner, and facilitator in TBI. As many tasks are done in pairs or small groups, students are also monitors because they need to "attend" to and analyze what they did during the task. In addition, learners are risk-takers and innovators because many tasks require learners to interpret and create new messages in the target language.

在任务式教学中,教师是选择者、筹划者以及辅助者。由于TBI里的许多任务是通过配对或是小组的形式进行的,学习者也是任务进行的监控者,因为他们必须关注、分析自己以及同伴在任务中的表现。此外,学习者也是冒险者以及创新者,因为许多任务需要学习者用目的语制造或是诠释信息。

As a student-centered method, TBI provides learners more freedom to choose what they want to say and encourages them to use all the vocabulary that they know, rather than to repeat drills. As tasks are closely related to students' personal needs and real-life situations, the students are more likely to participate actively in the task work. Tasks provide students the opportunities for revision and repetition, and give teachers the options to assess learners' progress. Tasks also provide clear objectives in terms of what participants should be able to do by the end of the lesson. Also, as cooperative efforts area part of TBI, it creates a supportive, non-threatening environment for participants to work together.

作为一个以学生为中心的教学法,TBI提供学习者更多的自由去选择他们想要表达的话,以及鼓励学习者使用已知或是正在学习的词汇,而不是一味地进行重复式的口语操练。

由于任务与学生的需求息息相关,也和现实世界的情境紧密连结,学生更可能积极地全身心投入。任务提供学生一个修正以及知识反刍的机会,也让教师有评估学生进展的机会。任务的明确目标也让我们得知学习者在任务最后应该达到的能力。此外,团队合作是任务型教学的一部分。它为学习者创造了一个支持的、不具威胁的环境,可以身处其中与同学协力合作。

However, TBI is not flawless. It has been criticized by many SLA researchers and instructors. First, task-based language instruction demands more classroom management skills and time than traditional approaches. The teacher's experience and time limits may affect the effectiveness of TBI. Under the time pressure, there is a risk that learners will achieve fluency at the expense of accuracy. Second, TBI requires a high level of creativity and initiatives on the part of the teacher. If teachers are accustomed to more traditional methods or do not have time to design and plan tasks, this type of teaching may be impossible.

With the development of educational technology, computer-assisted language learning (CALL) has become an essential element of language instruction. In the next chapter, we discuss the connection between technology and language teaching and how technology has been applied in speaking acquisition and instructional practices.

然而,任务型教学并非完美,它受到不少二语习得学者与教师的批评。首先,相较于传统的教学法,任务型教学对课堂管理技巧以及时间的掌握要求较高。缺乏经验的教师以及时间的不足都可能影响任务型教学的成效。在时间压力下,学习者有可能牺牲准确度来换取较高的口语流利度。其次,任务型教学需要教师高度的创造力以及主动性。倘若教师习惯于传统的教学法或没有时间设计规划任务,任务教学法就不太可能实现。

随着教育科技的发展,电脑辅助语言学习已经成为语言教学的重要一环。在下一章,我们将探讨科技与语言教学的关系以及科技如何被应用在口语的习得。

Chapter Seven 第七章
CALL Theory and Research
电脑辅助语言教学理论与研究

In the previous decades, educational technology was treated as one of the many possible tools in language instruction and had not entered the mainstream of foreign language instruction (Grabe, 2004). However, with the development of more sophisticated programs, the relationship between computer-assisted language learning (CALL) and second language acquisition (SLA) has changed. As emphasized by Chapelle (2004), everyday language use is closely related to technology in the twenty-first century, and hence, learning a language through technology has become a part of life. In the following sections, we first discuss the relationship between educational technology and SLA. Then, we investigate how educational technology has been applied in language instruction and how it can be used to effectively enhance learners' oral proficiency. Through this chapter, readers are expected to better understand how educational technology is closely connected with classroom language teaching practice in the Iowa Speaking Instruction Model.

在过去十年，教育技术在语言教学上一直被视为可以用来辅助教学的工具之一，并未成为外语教学领域的主流(Grabe, 2004)。然而，随着越来越多复杂程序的研发，电脑辅助教学(CALL)与二语习得的关系也有了改变。Chapelle (2004)强调，在21世纪，人们日常的语言使用与科技息息相关，因此通过科技来学习语言已经成为许多人生活的一部分。在下面的章节里，我们将先讨论教育技术与二语习得的关系。之后我们会探究如何将教育技术运用在语言教学，以及用教育技术有效提高学习者的口语能力。通过本章的介绍，读者将更深入了解紧密结合教育科技与课堂教学的爱荷华口语教学模式。

7.1 The Connections between CALL and SLA
电脑辅助语言教学与第二语言习得的相关性

With the increasing application of technology tools in language instruction, researchers have sought to demonstrate the connection between SLA and CALL. According to Chapelle (2009), theoretical approaches in SLA can be used to develop and evaluate CALL materials and tasks. In addition, expanding use of technology has also impacted the development of SLA theory and pertinent research.

　　随着越来越多科技工具被应用在语言教学上，学者开始探究电脑辅助语言教学(CALL)与二语习得的关系。Chapelle (2009)表示，二语习得的理论可以用来研发与评估电脑辅助教学的材料与活动。此外，科技的广泛使用也影响了二语习得理论的发展，更让投入二语习得研究的学者越来越多。

As pointed out by Doughty (1987), CALL can be used in assessing the effects of instructional conditions and gathering evidence of learners' knowledge strategies. However, she also stressed that the design of CALL needs to have a strong theoretical foundation to ensure that the tasks provided are meaningful. Over the past two decades, a variety of SLA approaches have been developed, all of which have more or less provided implications for CALL design. According to Chapelle (2009), there are four primary camps in SLA theory, which are useful for CALL design.

　　Doughty (1987)指出，CALL可以应用在评估教学效果以及收集学习者知识策略的证明。然而，为了确保设计的任务是有意义的且能精确地用来收集数据，她也坚持CALL的设计必须有坚实的理论基础。
　　在过去20年间，学者提出了许多二语习得的理论，而这些理论的主张也落实在电脑辅助语言教学的设计上。

7.1.1. Cognitive Linguistic Approaches
　　　　认知语言学理论

Cognitive linguistic approaches, such as Universal Grammar and Caroll's (2007)

Autonomous Induction Theory, focus on the internal mechanisms responsible for linguistic development and seek to discover the order of language acquisition. Proponents of cognitive linguistic approaches believe that appropriately sequenced instruction might accelerate the process of language acquisition. From this perspective, CALL activities should be organized in a way that are consistent with the orders of grammar acquisition (Chapelle, 2009). In cognitive linguistic approaches, oral production is not specifically addressed because it is regarded as a part of the linguistic progress.

包括普遍语法以及Carroll (2007)提出的自主诱导论在内的认知语言学理论强调与语言发展有关的内在机制，并寻求发现语言习得的顺序与轨迹。认知语言学理论的支持者相信循序渐进的教学可能加快语言习得的过程。认知语言学派认为，电脑辅助学习的活动应该符合语法习得的次序 (Chapelle, 2009)。口语输出并非认知语言学者关注的重点，因为他们认为口语输出是为语言发展的一部分。

7.1.2. Psycholinguistic Approaches
心理语言学理论

According to Chapelle (2009), three theories are classified as psycholinguistic approaches, including Pienemann's (2007) processability theory, VanPatten's (2007) input processing theory, and cognitive interactionist theories established by Gass (1997), Long (1996), and Pica (1994).

Chapelle (2009)指出，有三个理论被归类为心理语言学理论，其中包括Pienemann (2007)的可加工式理论、VanPatten's (2007)的输入加工理论以及Gass (1997)、Long (1996)与Pica (1994)等人提出的认知互动理论。

Processability theory explains how second language (L2) learners process linguistic information, and learn the language over time. Similar to cognitive linguistic approaches, supporters of processability theory emphasize the need for sequencing CALL activities in accordance with the order in which grammatical structures are learned (Chapelle, 2009).

可加工式理论解释二语学习者加工处理语言信息以及学习第二语言的过程。类似认知语言学派，可加工式理论的支持者强调，CALL 活动次序的编排必须符合语法结构习得的顺序(Chapelle，2009)。

VanPatten's input processing theory emphasizes on the importance of input materials and activities that are likely to trigger form-meaning mapping. Generally, learners are more likely to attend to the meaning of the input that they receive. Therefore, in designing CALL tasks, it is important to provide input that draws learners' attention to the target form-meaning mappings (Chapelle, 2009).

VanPatten 的输入加工理论强调语言输入及可能引出形义连结的活动的重要性。根据这个理论，学习者较容易把注意力集中在语言输入的意义上。因此，在设计 CALL 的任务时，提供能让学习者把注意力放在特定形义连结关系的语言输入十分重要(Chapelle，2009)。

According to interactionist theory, language learning is triggered through communicative pressures. In addition to obtaining comprehensible input, learners are pushed during interactions to modify their utterances to avoid communication breakdowns. The process of meaning negotiation allows learners to notice gaps and discover the difference between their observed input and their deviated utterances. In this situation, learners' attention is directed to the linguistic elements and the connections between form and meaning. Therefore, to facilitate language acquisition, it is necessary to provide learners sufficient opportunities for meaning negotiation. The arguments of interactionist theory have provided a theoretical base for CALL design, which aims to create meaning-oriented activities and offer sufficient learner-computer interactions or learners' paired communications. A variety of computer-mediated communication (CMC) studies have drawn on interactionist theories to conceptualize meaning negotiation during interactions. In the last section of this chapter, how different types of CMC are applied in language learning and instruction would be discussed.

根据互动理论，交际的压力带动了语言学习。除了获得可理解的语言输入，学习者在交际中会被迫调整他们的口语表达以解决交际中断的问题。语义协商的过程让学习者可以注意到自己的口语表达和所观察到的语言输入的差异。在这个情况下，学习者的注意力会被导向语言要素以及形式和意义的连结。因此，为了促进语言的习得，提供学习者充分的机会进行语义协商是很重要的。互动理论的这个主张为CALL设计提供了理论基础，进而打造以语义为本的活动，提供学习者与电脑或学习者彼此之间充分的交际活动。许多网络互动交际研究(CMC)利用互动理论将互动中的语义协商概念化。在本章的最后一节，我们将讨论不同形式的网络互动交际在语言学习以及教学上的应用。

7.1.3. General Human Learning Approaches
普遍人类学习理论

Theories, such as DeKeyser's (2007b) skill acquisition theory, claim that the process of language acquisition is similar to those that govern other human learning. Associative-cognitive CREED theory suggests that learning is through repetition, which is consistent with a behaviorist perspective. Skill acquisition theory emphasizes on the importance of practice, which enables the advance of declarative knowledge to procedural knowledge as language use becomes more automatic and habitual (Chapelle, 2009). These approaches suggest that it is necessary to provide opportunities for repetition and practice in CALL tasks. These arguments have presented the design of intensive and repetitive multimedia materials, such as those focusing on the practice of pronunciation and grammar.

　　包括DeKeyser (2007b)所提出的技能习得理论在内的这一个学派主张，语言习得的过程与其他技能的习得并无不同。连结认知理论(Associative-cognitive CREED theory)与行为学派的观点一致，认为学习是通过反复的练习获得的。技能习得理论强调练习的重要性，练习能让陈述性知识转化成程序性知识，语言使用则越来越趋向自动化，进而成为一个习惯(Chapelle, 2009)。这个学派认为，在CALL的任务中提供反复练习的机会是必要的。上述的主张对设计以发音与语法为主、强调密集反复练习的多媒体材料形成一定的影响。

7.1.4. Language Learning Approaches in Social Context
   社会环境下的语言学习理论

As mentioned in Chapter 4, increasing number of SLA researchers have recognized the importance of sociocultural factors in the process of language acquisition. In contrast to cognitive perspectives, these SLA researchers focus on how language is acquired in its social contexts. The proponents of social approaches are interested in understanding how learners construct knowledge through collaborative work, how their identities change during group participation, and how they accomplish social action through conversation. With the development of Internet technology, the scope of social approaches and their empirical applications have expanded.

  在第四章中曾提及,越来越多的二语习得研究者开始意识到语言习得过程中社会文化因素的重要性。不同于认知学派的观点,这些研究者关注语言在社会环境下被习得的过程。社会学派的支持者希望能更深入了解学习者如何通过协力合作建构知识、学习者的个人认同在参与团队活动时的变化,以及他们在交谈中如何完成社交行为。社会理论的范畴及其在实证上的应用也随着网络科技的发展而有了进一步的扩展。

Sociocultural theory has provided a theoretical foundation for tele-collaboration tasks, in which learners work together in the target language. According to sociocultural theory, communication, in which language learners engage with peers and others using the target language, is critical to the development of language and intercultural competence. As it requires multiple contextual factors to provide an ideal circumstance for effective communication, the goal of instructional design should be to maintain the flow of communication to increase opportunities for group collaboration and knowledge co-construction.

  社会文化理论为学习者使用目的语进行合作的网络协作任务提供了理论基础。社会文化理论认为,学习者与同学或别人用目的语进行交际对于语言的发展以及跨文化沟通能力的养成十分重要。由于提供一个有效交际的理想环境需要许多环境因素,根据社会文化理论,为了增加团队协作与合作建构知识的机会,教学设计的目标在于让交际得以延续。

7.1.5. How CALL Development has Changed SLA Research
CALL 的发展对二语习得研究的影响

In the past two decades, the focus of CALL research has changed (Chapelle, 2009). In the past, the teachers had the power to decide whether technology tools should be added to their instructional materials. Technology, generally, was only used to assist instruction and was more than often taken as optional. However, technological innovations have changed our understanding of language learning, and technology is no longer an optional tool for language instruction and learning. "Digital-generation" learners have the power to select a variety of tools for communication and learning, and technology is an indispensible part of their daily life.

过去二十年间，电脑辅助语言教学研究的中心逐渐改变(Chapelle，2009)。在过去，教师有权决定是否在教学材料中使用科技工具。由于教师决定科技的使用与否，科技仅仅被视为可用来辅助教学的工具之一。然而，科技创新改变了我们对语言学习的理解，而科技也不再只是语言教学与学习的众多辅助工具之一。"数码时代"的学习者有权在众多选择中挑选交际与学习的工具，而科技也成为我们日常生活中不可或缺的一部分。

The development of technology has had a huge impact on language acquisition (Chapelle, 2009). First, it has broadened the scope of communicative competence. As technology now allows communication to take place in a variety of venues and mediums — remote, written, oral, and face-to-face, Chapelle (2009) suggested that definitions of communicative competence should include the ability to select and use appropriate L2 technology in communication. Furthermore, as technology has created a variety of possibilities for communication, it has gradually changed the range of contexts, input, and interactions. For example, as written language is used during online chat, the format of linguistic input and how learners access that input have changed in ways that are likely to affect the process of learning L2.

科技的进展对语言习得影响巨大(Chapelle, 2009)。首先,它拓展了交际能力范畴。由于现今科技的发展,交际能通过各种媒介以各种形式发生——远程、书面、口语以及面对面的形式,Chapelle (2009)建议交际能力的定义应该包括在交际中适当地选择与使用二语科技的能力。

由于科技创造了交际的许多可能性,也逐渐改变了二语习得中语境、语言输入以及互动的范畴。例如,当文字成了线上对话的交际媒介,语言输入的形式以及学习者取得语言输入的方式就有了改变,而这些改变自然也就影响了二语习得的过程。

7.2 CALL in Pedagogical Application　电脑辅助语言教学之教学应用

7.2.1. Why Technology? Reasons to Use Technology in a Language Classroom 语言课上使用科技的原因?

As computers have become closely tied to our daily lives, increasing number of students expect instructors to be familiar with and proficient in the use of educational technology (Windham, 2005). Instructors with low technology knowledge or skills are regarded as being outdated (Grabe & Grabe, 2004). This means that a teacher's proficiency with technology directly influences students' impressions and evaluations of their instructors (Arnold & Ducate, 2006). However, most of the teachers are not aware of these expectations.

当电脑与我们的日常生活越来越密不可分时,越来越多的学生期待教师能熟悉且擅长使用教育技术 (Windham, 2005)。电脑知识或技术贫乏的教师被认为是落伍的(Grabe, 2004),这意味着教师的电脑技术能力直接影响学生对老师的印象以及评价(Arnold & Ducate, 2006)。然而,大多数的教师并未察觉到学生的这些期待,他们在教学上的努力也没有满足学生的期待。

Technology can be used to emphasize certain important language features and create supplementary materials for teaching and learning. Technology use enhances the diversity of activities. A variety of tools, which can be used online or offline, can be incorporated into student-centered collaboration or discussion,

teacher-directed drills, in-class activities, after-class assignments, and self-study exercises. Technology provides a new learning environment, which increases learners' exposure to authentic materials in the target language and encourages multi-path progression, critical thinking, and decision making.Technology also facilitates effectiveness in time and class management. Course management systems (CMS), such as WebCT, ICON, and Moodle, allow instructors to create a course material database and share information on the web without specialized computer skills. It also allows various types of interaction among students taking the course as well as between the students and the instructor. In addition, CMS makes grade management more efficient and extends in-class discussion to a virtual environment. Lastly, technology facilitates understanding of learners' individual needs. It allows teachers to set different goals for different students based on their age, proficiency level, and interests.

电脑科技可以用来强调某些重要的语言特征以及为教学或学习提供补充材料。电脑科技的使用提高了活动的多样性。许多工具,无论是连线或是离线,都可以与以学生为中心的协作讨论、教师主导的口语操练、课上的活动、课后的作业以及自修练习相结合。电脑科技提供一个新的学习环境,增加学习者接触真实语料的机会,更鼓励多元轨迹的拓展、批判性思维以及决策判断。

电脑科技同时促进了管理时间及课堂的有效性。WebCT、ICON 和 Moodle 等课堂管理系统(CMS)使教师不需要特别的电脑技巧就可以建立一个课件资料库,并在网络上分享信息。电脑也可以让学生可以通过不同的互动形式与同学或是教师交流。此外,对教师而言,这套系统让成绩管理更加便利,也可把课间的讨论延续到虚拟空间里来进行。

再者,电脑科技更能深入考虑学习者的个人需求。它让教师能根据不同学生的年龄、语言程度、兴趣设定不同的目标。

7.2.2. The Evolution of the Forms of CALL
电脑辅助语言教学 (CALL)形式的演变

According to Luke (2006), CALL has changed a great deal in the last 20 years.

Warschauer (1996, 2000) pointed out that CALL has gone through three stages of development in the last four decades, evolving from structural CALL to communicative CALL and integrative CALL (Table 7.1).

Luke (2006)表示,电脑辅助语言教学(CALL)在过去二十年间有了明显的改变。Warschauer (1996, 2000)指出,在过去的四十年间,CALL 经历了三个不同的发展阶段,从结构性电脑辅助语言教学(Structural CALL)到交际性电脑辅助语言教学(Communicative CALL)再到整合性电脑辅助语言教学(Integrative CALL)。(如表7.1)

Stage	1970s–80s: Structural Call	1970s–1990s: Communicative CALL	21st Century Integrative CALL
Technology	Mainframe	PCs	Multimedia and Internet
Teaching paradigm	Gammar-translation & audio-lingual	Communicate language teaching	Content-based, for special or academic purposes
View of language	Structural (a formal structural system)	Cognitive (a mentally comstructed system)	Socio-cognitive (developed in social interaction)
Principal use of computer	Drill and practice	Communicative exercises	Authentic discourse
Principal objective	Accuracy	Accuracy and fluency	Accuracy, Fluency, and agency

Table 7.1 Warschauer's three phases of CALL

阶段	1970s–80s: 结构性 Call	1970s–1990s: 交际性 CALL	21st Century 整合性 CALL
科技	大型中央处理器	电脑	多媒体与网络
教学范例	语法翻译教学法 听说教学法	交际语言教学法	以内容为主、为了特殊或是学术需求
语言观	结构的 (正式的结构体系)	认知的 (心理建构的体系)	社会认知的 (在社会互动中形成的)
电脑使用的原则	口语操练	交际的练习	真实对话
主要目标	准确度	准确度与流利度	准确、流利与媒介

图7.1 Warschauer 提出的 CALL 三个阶段

Warschauer (2000) explained that these stages did not occur sequentially, but were combined at different times for different purposes. However, as new perspectives about language learning and technological innovations have been incorporated in CALL, there has been a general trend over the years. In Structural CALL, drills and practice courseware are based on the concept of the computer as a tutor. A computer is an ideal vehicle for carrying out repeated drills, presenting the same material with minor modifications over and over again, and providing immediate feedback. As students proceed at their own pace, it frees up class time for other activities (Warschauer, 1996).

　　Warschauer (2000) 阐明这几个阶段并非依序发生，在不同的时间点，任何一个理论方法都可能因为不同的原因而和另一个理论方法结合。然而，随着电脑辅助教学的设计融入与语言习得相关的新想法以及科技的创新，这几年间也产生了一个普遍的潮流。
　　在结构性电脑辅助语言教学(Structural CALL)中，口语操练与其他练习的课件均基于"电脑及助教"的概念。电脑是一个执行反复口语操练、重复呈现相同材料以及提供即时反馈的理想工具。由于学生依他们各自的步调进行电脑上的练习，相对之下，课堂上就可腾出更多时间用来从事其他活动(Warschauer, 1996)。

Proponents of Communicative CALL focus on incorporating more authentic communication tasks into activity design. "The Premises for Communicative CALL," developed by Underwood in 1984 include a focus on language use, implicit grammar instruction, as well as students' utterances and immersion in a target-language-only environment. According to Warschauer (1996, 2000), Communicative CALL is based on a cognitive view of language learning, which emphasizes that learners develop an internal mental system of language through interaction. The input generated by the process of interaction is much more important than the content of the interaction.

With the development of the Internet and multimedia computer, Integrative CALL has become increasingly popular. Multimedia technology allows learners to access a variety of media, such as text, graphics, sound, animation, and video, on a single machine, while the Internet makes cross-time and-place interaction possible.

交际性电脑辅助语言教学(Communicative CALL) 的重心在于把更多真实交际任务融入活动的设计。由Underwood在1984年提出的"交际性电脑辅助语言教学的假说",包括语言使用、内隐式语法教学、学生的口语表达以及只使用目的语的沉浸式环境。Warschauer (1996, 2000)指出,交际性的CALL是根据语言学习的认知角度,强调学习者通过互动形成内部心理的语言系统。在互动过程中产生的语言输入远比互动的内容重要。

In contrast to Communicative CALL, Integrative CALL is based on a sociocognitive view of language learning, which emphasizes that learning a language involves communicating with new discourse communities. The purpose of interaction is to help learners to access new communities and familiarize themselves with new genres and discourses. As a result, the content of the interaction and the nature of the community are extremely important (Warschauer, 2000). When compared with Communicative CALL, Integrative CALL includes agency in its objectives. Agency refers to the authoring power that allows learners to create their own work using various types of media and share it with an international audience. Learners are empowered to post their work on the Internet to enhance their self-confidence, such as oral performance or movie reviews. The purpose of language study is not just to construct a conceptual framework for the target language, but to be able to use it and have an impact on the real world.

随着网络与多媒体电脑的发展,整合性CALL变得越来越受欢迎。多媒体科技让学习者在一部机器上就能接触各种各样的媒介,像文字、图案、声音、动画以及视频。网络则使互动跨越时空的限制。不同于交际性CALL,整合性CALL基于语言学习的社会认知观,强调语言学习涉及与新的对话社群交流。因此,对话的内容以及社群的本质都十分重要(Warschauer, 2000)。与交际性CALL相比,整合性CALL的目标中包含了媒介。媒介可激发一种创作力,让学习者运用各类媒体创作以及与世界各个角落的观众分享。学习者有权把他们的作品,像口语表演或电影影评公

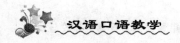

开在网络上。这个与外人分享的过程无疑可以增强他们的自信心。语言学习的目的并不只在于建造一个目的语的理念架构,而是能运用语言影响现实世界。

7.2.3. Tutorial CALL vs. Tool CALL
　　辅导型 CALL vs. 工具型 CALL

In addition to the three stages of development, CALL researchers have identified two primary types of CALL used in language learning. CALL was originally developed as a tutorial. However, recently, an increasing number of researchers have been developing the tool function of CALL.

　　在三个发展阶段以外,CALL 的研究者也指出,运用在语言学习的 CALL 有两种主要的类型。CALL 原先是作为辅导的材料。然而,最近,越来越多的研究者开发出 CALL 的工具性功能。

In earlier forms, CALL primarily worked as a tutorial, using different types of controlled language drills. CALL made it more convenient to organize materials, display items on the screen, and assess learners' performance with multiple-choice questions. Learners could interact with the computer through the pre-programmed feedback, individualized tutorial help, and multimedia representation of terms and concepts. As suggested by Hubbard and Siskin (2004), tutorial forms of CALL continue to be used to help learners develop a conscious understanding of the target language and its linguistic forms, patterns, and rules. Pedagogically, Tutorial CALL can be used to effectively enhance learners' proficiency in receptive skills, such as reading and listening, and is very helpful in pronunciation training (Hubbard & Siskin, 2004). In the next section, we discuss how Computer-Assisted Pronunciation Training (CAPT) has been developed as a tutorial and applied to speaking acquisition, using automatic speech recognition (ASR) software.

　　早期 CALL 主要作为辅导的材料,使用各种操控式的语言操练。

CALL让组织材料、在屏幕上展示条目以及评估学习者在多重选择题的表现更加便利。学习者可以通过程序化的反馈、个人化的辅导协助以及以多媒体呈现的术语概念与电脑互动。Hubbard & Siskin (2004)表示,辅导型的CALL仍用于协助学习者理解目的语及其语言形式、句型和规则。

教学上,辅导型的CALL可以有效提高学习者在阅读以及听力等与接受性技能有关的能力,在听力训练上也是十分有帮助的(Hubbard & Siskin, 2004)。在下一个章节,我们将讨论电脑辅助发音训练(CAPT)如何运用自动语音识别(ASR)软件成为一个口语习得的辅导工具。

Nowadays, an increasing number of CALL materials have emphasized the use of computer technology to provide language instruction with the active involvement of learners in the learning process. With Internet communication tools, such as email, bulletin boards, discussion forums, Skype, and MSN messenger, learners have the opportunity to interact with each other or with people from the target language community. Also, with online co-authoring tools, such as wiki and blogs, learners can work together to co-construct materials in the target language. Pedagogically, these tools can be used in classroom activities and take-home assignments. For example, students can discuss their collaborative project in an online chat room or via Skype or MSN messenger. They can post their work on a blog or a wiki page, which allows readers to comment on it or make further changes. In Section 7.3.2, we talk about the use of CMC tools in speaking acquisition.

时至今日,越来越多的CALL材料强调在语言教学中使用电脑科技,让学习者能更主动投入学习。通过电子邮件、电子布告栏、讨论区、Skype与MSN messenger等网络交际工具,学习者有机会与同学或目的语的使用者互动,并体验文化的相异性。此外,包括维基(wiki)与博客(blog)等线上共同创作工具让学习者可以用目的语共同创作。教学上,这些工具可以用于课堂活动以及课外的作业。举例来说,学生可以在线上聊天室或通过Skype或MSN messenger讨论小组合作的作业。之后,他们可以把作品成果公布在博客或是维基网页上,让读者留言评论甚至进行更改。在7.3.2小节,我们会讨论口语习得与网络互动交际的使用。

7.3 CALL in Speaking Acquisition　CALL 在口语习得上的应用

Computer technology has been widely used in language instruction. In this section, we discuss how CALL is used to facilitate learners' pronunciation and communication skills in speaking acquisition.

电脑科技已经被广泛地应用在语言教学上。在这个章节,我们将把重点放在口语习得,讨论如何运用 CALL 提高学习者的二语发音以及沟通能力。

7.3.1. CAPT
　　　电脑辅助发音训练

Although the majority of the language instructors agree that achieving a target-like pronunciation is essential for effective communication with native speakers, classroom practice does not always allow pronunciation training due to the lack of instructional time and limited interests and motivation among students. O'Brien (2006) suggested that computer technology is ideal for pronunciation training. CAPT allows students to acquire correct pronunciation effectively and efficiently without the assistance of an instructor. According O'Brien (2006), there are three types of CAPT courseware: basic pronunciation training conducted in a language lab, ASR software, and visualization techniques. Currently, most of the ASR software have already incorporated visualization techniques, allowing learners to observe the pitch contours, waveforms, and spectrograms of their utterances.

　　虽然所有的语言教师都同意习得母语般的发音对和母语使用者有效地交际十分重要,由于时间限制以及学生对此缺乏兴致,发音的训练并非每次都能放在课堂上进行。O'Brien (2006)建议,电脑科技十分适用于发音训练。电脑辅助发音训练 (CAPT)使学生在没有老师的协助下也能有效而省时地习得正确的发音。

　　O'Brien (2006)总结出三种电脑辅助发音训练的课件:在语言实验室中进行的基础发音训练、自动语音辨识软件 (ASR) 以及视觉化技术。目前,多数 ASR 软件已经与视觉化技术结合,让学习者能观察他们发音的音高升降曲线、声波以及声谱图。

Nowadays, most of the language learning software programs, such as Tell me More and Rosetta, use cutting-edge automatic speech recognition technology in pronunciation training. The software is able to recognize the four Chinese tones, and learner pronunciation errors can be detected, analyzed, and compared with native speakers. As the computer provides one-on-one individualized practice and allows unlimited attempts, learners can proceed at their own pace, and can get a wide range of assistance from the "help" section, toggling back and forth between the help tools, and the exercise screens. When compared with repeating a teacher's verbalization, interacting with a computer is less stressful and more personalized (Godwin-Jones, 2009). In addition, the software can also be programmed to adapt to an individual learner's progress by customizing exercises to the student's needs. In this situation, learner autonomy is emphasized and individual differences are recognized. With the ASR technology, researchers can collect sufficient data from learners, identify the development of pronunciation skills, and apply the findings to future training.

现在多数的语言学习软件,像 Tell me More 和 Rosetta,在发音训练上使用最尖端的语音识别技术。由于这个软件可以识别汉语的四个声调,学习者的发音错误可以被检测、分析以及用来和母语者进行比较。因为电脑提供一对一个人化的关注,且允许学习者进行无限次数的尝试,学习者可以按他们各自的步调前进。在使用电脑辅助发音训练软件时,学习者可以在"帮助"区寻求各种协助,并在练习的视窗以及协助工具之间快速地来回切换。相较于重复教师的发音,与电脑互动的压力较小,也比较个人化(Godwin-Jones, 2009)。此外,软件也可根据个别学习者的进展来"客制化"练习以满足学生的个人需求。在这个情况下,电脑辅助发音训练软件强调学习者的自主性,也承认学习者个别差异的重要性。藉由自动语音识别(ASR)技术,研究者可以收集充足的学习者的数据、发现发音技巧发展的轨迹以及将这些发现应用在未来的训练中。

The main issue in ASR is finding a balance between reinforcing target-like pronunciation and allowing for variation in learners' pronunciation attempts. If the ASR system does not recognize enough of what a learner is producing, it will become a very frustrating learning experience. On the other hand, if an ASR system is set to tolerate too much of the variety of the target language attempts, the learner will not be able to acquire target-like pronunciation.

　　自动语音识别(ASR)技术的主要问题是在强调标准发音和容许学习者发音变异之间寻找一个平衡点。要是ASR系统对发音的标准太高而无法充分识别学习者的发音,会让学习者感到十分挫折。然而,要是ASR系统设定的标准太过宽松,对发音变异度的容许范围太大,学习者将无法习得标准的发音。

In addition, computer-based speech recognition can be used to interpret the meaning of speakers' utterance. This technology has been widely used in commercial customer services, such as travel reservations, bill payments, stock price quotes, weather reports, and laptop repair status updates. Many people have had the experience of interacting with disembodied voices through phone ASR systems in a variety of helpdesk or customer service environments. When ASR systems are used to recognize language learners' meaning, they tend to have problems with non-grammatical constructions and broken sentences (Godwin-Jones, 2009). As these systems are programmed to give positive responses to pre-defined lexical domains and grammatical structures, they may encounter difficulties with non-standard vocabulary and sentences.

　　此外,电脑语音识别也可以用于理解说话者话语的意思。这个技术已经被广泛地应用在客户服务,像旅游预订、账单缴费、股票报价、天气预报以及笔记本电脑维修进度查询。许多人都有通过电话语音识别系统和各种各样客服机器语音打交道的经验。当ASR系统用于识别语言学习者的语义时,在辨别不符合语法的结构以及断句时常常出现问题(Godwin-Jones, 2009)。由于语音识别系统被设计来检测既定词汇与语法,当遇到标准外的词汇以及句子时,这个系统就会出现问题。

In spite of its limitations in accuracy and range, there is great potential to use computer-based speech recognition technology in language learning. To recognize common grammatical misconstructions, Godwin-Jones (2009) suggested including samples of non-native language verbalization in the language models. However, collecting learners' speech could be a difficult task due to logistical and legal reasons.

即使在准确度与范围有所局限,将电脑语音识别技术应用在语言学习上仍具极大的潜力。为了识别共同的语法错误结构,Godwin-Jones (2009) 建议将非母语的语言表现范例纳入语言模型中。然而,由于技术支持的缺失等问题,收集学习者的口语范例将是一个艰巨的任务。

7.3.2. CMC
网络互动交际研究 (CMC)

As the Internet has become indispensable to daily life, more and more interactions are carried out in virtual environments. Over the past decade, the use of CMC has changed the learning environments and has become a subject of discussion among an increasing number of SLA researchers. According to Thurlow, Lengel, and Tomic (2004), CMC is a dynamic and creative force, which provides more possibilities in language instruction and learning. CMC is presented in a variety of formats, ranging from synchronous online chat to asynchronous email correspondence. It has been extensively used in collaborative language learning, in which learners work together in various kinds of Internet-based activities.

随着网络已经成为日常生活中不可或缺的一部分,越来越多的互动是在虚拟空间发生的。在过去十年间,网络互动交际(CMC)改变了学习的环境,也成为越来越多二语习得研究者的讨论主题。Thurlow, Lengel & Tomic (2004)表示,CMC是一股动态且充满创造性的力量,提供语言教学与学习更多的可能性。

CMC 呈现的形式有许多种,从同步的在线聊天到非同步的电子邮件往来都包括在内。CMC被广泛地使用在协作语言学习上,学习者在各种以网络为基础的活动中互助合作。

Internet-based communication has expanded time and space. According to Warschauer (1996), CMC provides learners with a less stressful learning environment, in which they can communicate with other learners or native speakers of the target language directly, inexpensively, and conveniently. As learners spend more time engaging in online interaction, they have better control of the activities. CMC has shifted the focus of language learning from instructor-orchestrated styles to a student-centered style.

　　以网络为基础的交际突破了时空的局限。Warschauer (1996)表示，CMC 提供学习者一个压力较小的学习环境，学习者在其中可以与同伴或是目的语的母语使用者进行直接、便捷又不昂贵的交流。当学习者花在线上互动的时间越长，他们对活动的掌握也就越好。CMC 让语言学习的中心从教师策划指挥的形式转变为比较以学生为中心的形式。

As Web 2.0 tools and social interaction software are widely used all over the world, it is not surprising that language acquisition occurs on the Internet. Learners are able to interact with language partners, classmates, and instructors in oral or written communication using a variety of social interaction tools, such as Skype, MSN messenger, and GoogleTalk. During synchronous online communications, learners can immediately obtain feedback from their peers, instructors, or native language partners and improve their accuracy, fluency, and complexity in speaking. Web 2.0 tools, such as Wikis, Blogs, Youtube, and GoogleDoc, provide learners with a stage to practice and show their skills. They can videotape speeches or conversations and post clips online to share with friends. This authoring power greatly enhances learners' motivation and self-confidence.

　　随着 Web 2.0 工具与社交互动软件在使用上的普及，我们丝毫不意外语言习得可以通过网络而发生。借由 Skype、MSN messenger 与 GoogleTalk 等各种社交互动工具，学习者可以与语言伙伴、同学以及教师用口语或文字的形式进行交际。在同步的在线交际中，学习者可以马上从同伴、教师或母语语言伙伴那里得到反馈，并从而增进他们口语的准确度、流利度以及复杂度。Web 2.0 的工具，像维基(wiki)、博客(blogs)、Youtube 及

GoogleDoc，提供给学习者一个展现他们技能的舞台。他们可以摄影录下自己的口语或是对话，并将这些片段发布在网络上与朋友共享。这种创作力大大地提升了学习者的动机和自信。

To achieve the highest effectiveness in using CMC-based activities, Chun (2008) suggested that well-designed tasks, monitoring of online collaboration, and a supportive attitude are essential. First, it is crucial to set clear objectives in the CMC task design. Without clear instructional goals and step-by-step procedures, CMC activities devolve into aimless chat. In addition, as pointed out by Meskill & Anthony (2005), CMC does not serve as a replacement for live instruction. Instead, with careful monitoring, CMC can provide an additional forum to enhance learners' communicative competence.

不过，为了在使用CMC活动时达到最大的成效，Chun (2008)指出，设计完善的任务、监督在线的协作以及支持的态度至关重要。首先，在设计CMC的活动时必须建立明确的目标。如果没有教学目标以及明确的连续步骤，CMC活动将沦为漫无目的的闲聊。此外，Meskill & Anthony (2005)主张，CMC并不能取代真正的教学。然而，在支持与监控下，CMC可以为学习者提高口语能力提供另一个练习的平台。

Chapter Eight 第八章
ACTFL Speaking Guidelines and National Foreign Language Standards
全美外语教学委员会口语标准和全美外语教学国家标准

In this chapter, we introduce two nationally recognized foreign language standards in the U.S.A. and their applications to second language (L2) speaking learning and teaching. We start by introducing the *ACTFL Proficiency Guidelines*. In particular, we look at the *Speaking Guidelines* and its major levels. Following that, we then move to the *National Standards for Foreign Language Learning*, whose organizing principles are introduced and its five-C goals are defined in foreign language instruction. These two standards, widely used in the U.S.A., have inspired many empirical research studies in L2 speaking, which provide further implications for L2 speaking acquisition and instruction. Specifically, in our case of Iowa instructional Model of spoken language development, the program has used the ACTFL Proficiency Guidelines as the curriculum organizing principle.

　　我们将在本章重点介绍美国广泛使用的两个全国性的外语评估标准以及它们在二语口语教学中的应用。我们先介绍全美外语教学委员会制定的语言水平纲领，特别是口语水平纲领和其主要的能力水平层次。接下来，介绍全美外语学习国家标准，包括组织原则和为美国外语教育界所熟知的5Cs的外语教育目标。这两个在全美范围内广泛使用的标准带动了许多相关的实践研究，也为二语口语习得与教学提供了诸多启示。具体到爱荷华大学汉语口语教学模式，我们采用了全美外语教学委员会（ACTFL）的语言水平纲领作为我们的课程设置准则。

8.1 Introduction of ACTFL Speaking Guidelines
全美外语教学委员会口语标准介绍

8.1.1. What is ACTFL?
全美外语教学委员会

The American Council on the Teaching of Foreign Languages (ACTFL), is a national membership organization dedicated to promoting the study of languages and cultures as an integral component of American education and society. It was established in 1967 by the Modern Language Association. It was the first national organization representing teachers of all foreign languages at all educational levels.

全美外语教学委员会(以下简称 ACTFL)是一个全国性的会员制组织,致力于推动语言和文化的学习。现代语言协会在1967年创立这个组织,现在已经成为美国教育界的一个重要组织。除此之外,ACTFL 也是首个代表美国各教育体系外语教师的全国性组织。

8.1.2. What are the ACTFL Proficiency Guidelines?
全美外语教学委员会语言水平纲领

Based on the language skill level descriptions for oral proficiency used by the Federal Interagency Language Roundtable (FILR) and the Foreign Service Institute (FSI), the *ACTFL Proficiency Guidelines* (hereafter, the *Guidelines*) were published in 1986 with some revisions in 1999. Unlike the guidelines used by the FILR and FSI, which were developed by agencies of the American government, the *Guidelines* were designed for use in academic environments.

以联邦局际语言圆桌协定和美国国务院外事学院制定的语言口语水平能力标准为蓝本,全美外语教学委员会语言水平纲领(以下简称为水平纲领)于1986年发表,并在1999年做了相应的调整。不同于联邦局际语言圆桌协定和美国国务院外事学院针对美国各个政府机构制定的语言水平准则,ACTFL 的水平纲领主要是针对学术界而制定的。

The *Guidelines* are proficiency based, and are intended for global assessment. It presented and arranged the global characterizations of integrated performance in each of the four major language skills—speaking, listening, reading, and writing—in a hierarchical order. Each description is representative, not exhaustive.

这个水平纲领是以评估语言整体能力为主的综合性评估纲领。它分级详细描述了语言能力的四个方面，以及主要语言技能在不同阶段所呈现的整体表现与普遍特点。这四个方面也就是为大家所熟知的听、说、读、写四种能力。不过，这个纲领对于每个水平阶段的描述仅是罗列了具有代表性的能力表现，而非彻底全面的详述。

8.1.3. The ACTFL Speaking Guidelines
   全美外语教学委员会口语标准

The *Guidelines* has become the foundation for ACTFL Speaking Guidelines (1986), with revisions in 1999. Based on a hierarchy of global tasks, the ACTFL Proficiency Guidelines—Speaking (hereafter, *Speaking Guidelines*) presents four major levels of language performances, which are delineated as follows:

ACTFL水平纲领为其对应的口语标准提供了基础。ACTFL口语标准列举了四个主要水平层次的语言表现，图示如下：

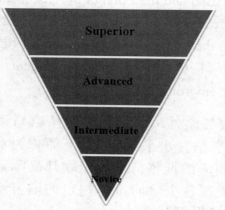

Figure 8.1   Major Levels of ACTEL Rating Scale

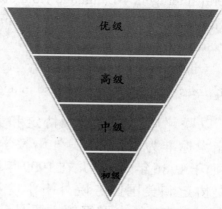

图示8.1   ACTFL主要评判等级

Each of the four levels encompasses a range of performances, which are further defined in terms of the linguistic, pragmatic, and strategic skills, and how well the speaker can accomplish these skills. However, only sustained performance of tasks required at a level qualifies for a rating at that level. A general description of speakers' abilities characterized at each of the four major levels is summarized in Table 8.1:

根据上图，每个水平等级里涵盖了一定范围的语言表现，具体细化到说话者在语言、语用以及策略技能方面所能成就的语言技能。但是，唯有在受试者稳定表现出某个等级所要求的能力时，我们才能将其评定为该语言等级。我们在下表中概述说话者在这四个主要等级所体现出来的具体口语能力表现：

	General Descriptions of the Major Levels ACTFL Proficiency Guidelines—Speaking (Revised 1999)
Superior-level Speakers	·Participate fully and effectively in conversations in formal and informal settings on topics related to practical needs and areas of professional and/or scholarly interests. ·Provide a structured argument to explain and defend opinions, and develop effective hypotheses within extended discourse. ·Discuss topics concretely and abstractly. ·Deal with a linguistically unfamiliar situation. ·Maintain a high degree of linguistic accuracy. ·Satisfy the linguistic demands of professional and/or scholarly life.
Advanced-level Speakers	·Participate actively in conversations in most informal and some formal settings on topics of personal and public interest. ·Narrate and describe in major time frames with good control of aspect. ·Deal effectively with unanticipated complications through a variety of communicative devices. ·Sustain communication by using, with suitable accuracy and confidence, connected discourse of paragraph length and substance. ·Satisfy the demands of work and/or school situations.

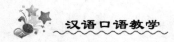

Intermediate-level Speakers	・Participate in simple, direct conversations on generally predictable topics related to daily activities and personal environment. ・Create with the language and communicate personal meaning to sympathetic interlocutors by combining language elements in discrete sentences and strings of sentences. ・Obtain and give information by asking and answering questions. ・Initiate, sustain, and bring to a close a number of basic, uncomplicated communicative exchanges, often in a reactive mode. ・Satisfy simple personal needs and social demands to survive in the target language culture.
Novice-level Speakers	・Respond to simple questions on the most common features of daily life. ・Convey minimal meaning to interlocutors experienced in dealing with foreigners by using isolated words, lists of words, memorized phrases, and some personalized recombinations of words and phrases. ・Satisfy a very limited number of immediate needs.

Table 8.1 The Hierarchy of Global Tasks at Four Major Levels

	主要阶段水平描述 ACTFL 口语标准(1999年修订)
优级者	・充分有效地参与正式和非正式语境中的交谈。话题涉及从满足实际需要到专业和/或者学术方面的交谈； ・能够提供结构性很强的论点来解释和支持某一观点同时在扩展性的语篇交流中发展有效的假设； ・能够对具体和抽象的话题展开讨论； ・能够处理语言不熟悉情况下的相关语用技巧； ・保持语言的高度准确性； ・满足对于一个专业人士和/或者学者所具体的语言水平要求。
高级者	・积极参与大多数非正式和一部分正式场合的交谈。话题涉及个人和公众兴趣的各个方面； ・能够在主要时间框架下进行阐述和描绘，具有对语态的良好把握； ・能够通过多种交流工具有效处理意料之外的复杂情境； ・能够自信应用相对准确的,互相关联的语篇段落长度的语言来保持交流； ・满足工作岗位和/或者学校情景中的语言水平要求。

中级者	• 参与简单直接的交谈。话题通常是可预见性的,与日常活动和个人环境息息相关的; • 能够结合相关语言元素组合而成独立的句子和句子成分,与有同情心的交谈者交流个人所想表达的意思; • 能够通过问答的形式获取和提供信息; • 能够开始,保持和结束一系列的基本日常的交谈对话,但常常是在一个回应性的情景下完成的; • 能够满足简单个人需要以及在目标环境中生存状况下社会要求所需要的语言水平。
初级者	• 能够回应大多数与日常生活息息相关的日常问题; • 能够用个体词汇、系列词组,或者是强记的短语和个人重组后的有关词汇和短语与跟外国人有交流经验的交谈者进行最基本的信息互换; • 能够满足非常有限的一些直接需要的语言要求。

表格 **8.1** 四个主要等级水平表现

As we can see from Table 8.1, the four major levels are delineated according to a hierarchy of global tasks. Other assessment criteria are incorporated in assessing speakers' oral proficiency: 1) The social contexts and specific content areas that the speaker is able to perform; 2) The accuracy with which the tasks are accomplished; and 3) The oral text types that the speaker is capable of producing; that is, discrete words and phrases, sentences, paragraphs, or extended discourse. Each major level subsumes the criteria of the levels below it.

  如上表格所示,四个主要等级主要通过一系列分级任务体现。除此以外,其他的评估细则也融入其中,来综合评估学生的口语水平:1)说话者能够表达社会环境和特殊内容话题;2)说话者所完成的交流任务的准确度;3)说话者能够表达的口语文体类型,即孤立的字词、句子、段落或者延长的语篇。每一个主要水平包括了所有其他低一级水平能力的评判细则。

In addition, among the four major levels (novice, intermediate, and advanced levels), there are three sublevels, namely, low, mid, and high, which are delineated in Figure 8.2.

  除此以外,在四个主要等级水平中的初、中、高级中又各有三个下一级水平分类。具体图示如下:

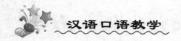

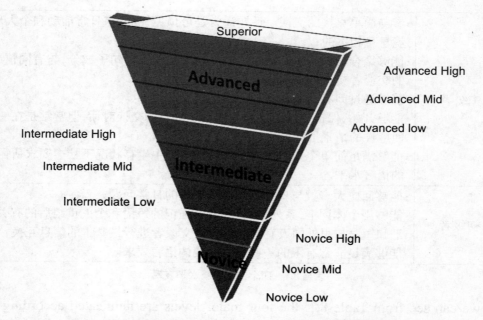

Figure 8.2　ACTFL Rating Scale with Major Ranges and Sublevels

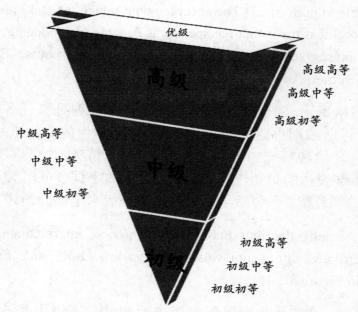

图示 8.2　ACTFL 主要水平及次水平等级分布

From Figure 8.2, we can observe that the LOW sublevel of each major level represents the threshold performance for the level, which is commonly called as the "floor" of the level. The MID sublevel of each level represents the number of speech profiles that the speakers can perform for the level, whose performance is comparatively juicier than the skeletal low sublevel. The HIGH sublevel of each level represents a fall from the next higher level, which is commonly called the "ceiling" of the level. Table 8.2 presents an elaborate description of the major levels and their pertinent sublevels in our case, Chinese.

如图8.2所示，每一个主要水平中的次级初等水平代表了该等级的入门级水平，也常常被称为该等级的"下限"。每个等级的中等水平则代表了说话者在此等级所能表达的大量的口语形式。相对于表达能力较为单薄的初级水平，中等水平的口语表达要丰富得多。每一个等级的高等水平则代表了和更高一个等级相比还略有差距的等级水平，常常也被称为该等级的"上限"。为了更具体地阐述每个等级及其次等级水平，尤其是在中文这个语言板块，请参照下面所附表格：

Novice	Novice-Low	No functional ability to speak Chinese. Oral production is limited to a few common loan words in English (Kungfu, chow mein) and perhaps a few high-frequency phrases (xiexie, nihao).
	Novice-Mid	No functional ability to speak Chinese. Oral production is limited to basic courtesy formulae (Ni/Nin guixing?). Can count from one to ten, name basic colors (hong, lan), common nouns (qishui, che), and food items (fan, mian, rou). Pronunciation and tones may be barely intelligible and strongly influenced by the first language.
	Novice-High	Emerging ability to make short statements utilizing simple formulaic utterances (Wǒ yào hē shuǐ.) and ask simple questions. Often misplaces question words and makes statements with incorrect word order. Vocabulary is limited to basic objects, common measures, numbers, names of immediate family members, and high-frequency place names. Can correctly use common verbs and adjectives in the present timeframe (kàn, mǎi, guì), but often confuses the use of verbs. Pronunciation and tones are often faulty.

Intermediate	**Intermediate-Low**	Can ask and answer simple questions (Nǐ zhù zài nǎr?) and initiate and respond to simple statements in the present time. Can use limited constructions, such as common verb-object phrases (hē píjiǔ) and simple modifications with de (wǒ de dàxué) and le (Wǒ lèi le.), indicating completion/status change. Most utterances contain fractured syntax and other grammatical errors. Misunderstandings frequently arise from poor pronunciation, wrong tones, and limited vocabulary.
	Intermediate-Mid	Can ask and answer simple questions involving areas of immediate need, leisure time activities, and simple transactions at the post office. Quantity of speech is increased and quality of speech is improved. Greater accuracy in word order, basic instructions, and use of high-frequency verbs and auxiliaries (shì, yǒu, yào, xǐhuan) and other time markers to indicate various time relations. Possess basic knowledge of differences among sets of terms, such as huì, néng, yào, zhīdào, but still makes errors.
	Intermediate-High	Possess flexibility in expressing time relationships, actual and a few potential resultative compounds, and simple comparisons. Can describe daily activities, likes and dislikes in detail, and express agreement and disagreement. Emerging ability to state opinions (Nǐ xiǎng zhè liǎng mén kè, wǒ xuǎn nǎ mén hǎo?). Evidence of connected discourse is also increasingly observed. While common word order is established, errors still occur in more complex patterns.

Advanced	**Advanced**	Can mark rather complicated factual comparisons. Has fairly consistent control of shì...de structure, question words used as indefinites, and some cohesive devices(búdàn... érqiě, suīrán...dànshì). Can handle arrangements with Chinese administrators; that is, regarding travel to China. Can talk in general way about topics of public interest. Can explain a point of view in an uncomplicated fashion (Wǒ rènwéi chāojí dàguó bù yīnggāi gānshè biéde guójiā de shìqing.)
	Advanced-Plus	Emerging ability to support opinions, explain in detail, and hypothesize (Yàoshì Zhōng-Měi guānxì èhuà, nà jiù huì yǐng xiǎng dào Měiguó gōngsī zài Zhōngguó de tóuzī.). Can discuss topics of current and personal interest. Has good control of many cohesive devices (yìfāngmiàn... yìfāngmiàn, búshì...jiùshì). Errors still occur in complicated structures.
Superior		Can support opinions and hypothesize on a broad range of concrete and abstract topics. Vocabulary is broad and hesitating or groping for words is rare. Pronunciation may still be foreign. Occasional unpatterned errors are evident, but there are no patterned errors, even though control of some low-frequency structures (Chúfēi...yàobùrán...jiù) may be less consistent. Control of general idiomatic expressions and slang may vary, and confusion may arise over terms, such as jiǎnchá and diàochá. A small proportion of utterances may still be literal translations from the native language.

Table 8.2　Chinese Proficiency Guidelines—Speaking (ACTFL, 1987)

初级	初级初等	不具备用中文进行基本交流的能力。口语表达局限于少量英文中的外来语(功夫、炒面)和一些高频词(谢谢、你好)。
	初级中等	不具备用中文进行基本交流的能力。口语表达局限于基本的礼貌语和套话(你/您贵姓?)。能从一数到十,列举基本的颜色(红、蓝),常见名词(汽水、车)和基本食物(饭、面、肉)。语音语调受母语影响很大,可能难以达到交流目的。
	初级高等	通过在交谈中使用简单的惯用语逐步显示进行简单陈述和提问的能力(我要喝水)。但在表达时常常用错词序和疑问词的位置。词汇量局限于基本物品,常用量词,数字,直属家庭成员称谓和一些高频地名。能够在当前时间范围内正确使用常用动词和形容词(看、买、贵),但常常误用动词用法。语音语调常常不够准确。

中级	中级初等	能够问答简单问题(你住在哪儿?)并能在当前时间范围内表达和回应简单的立场陈述。能够应用有限的结构比如像常用的动宾短语(喝啤酒),包含"的"的简单修饰语(我的大学)和了(我累了。),表示完成或状态变化。大多数表达包含散乱的句法结构和其他语法错误。因为蹩脚的发音,错误的音调以及有限的词汇而造成的交流误解时有发生。
	中级中等	能够问答简单的问题,包括满足直接需要的,闲暇时间活动的和诸如在邮局的简单交涉。口语表达无论从量上和质上都有提高。在词序、基本结构、高频动词和助动词(是、有、要、喜欢)、以及其他表示各种时间关系的时间标志语的使用上表现出很高的准确性。对一些常用词的区别有基本了解,比如像会,能,要,知道,但仍常犯错误。
	中级高等	能够灵活表达时间关系,实际的和一些表示可能性的结果复合词,能进行简单比较。能够描述日常活动,善恶喜好细节和表达相同和不同意见。逐步体现表达观点的能力(你想这两门课,我选哪门好?)。关联性语篇结构也逐步发展起来。尽管已经掌握基本语序,在表达更复杂的形式上还是会有错误出现。
高级	高级	能够进行比较复杂的事实性的比较。基本掌握是……的结构,非限定性疑问词和连词结构(不但……而且,虽然……但是)。能够处理与中方行政人员之间的交涉,即关于到中国旅行的相关事宜。能够就公众话题进行阐述和讨论。能够以不复杂的方式阐述一项观点(我认为超级大国不应该干涉别的国家的事情。)。
	高级优等	具有一定支持论点,详尽解释,和假设的语言表达能力(要是中美关系恶化,那就会影响到美国公司在中国的投资。)。能够就当前的和个人兴趣方面的多种话题展开讨论。对连词地掌握趋于成熟(一方面……一方面,不是……就是)。在复杂结构的表述上仍会出现错误。
优级		能够支持各项观点并能够就广泛范围内的具体和抽象话题提出假设。词汇量丰富,用词时犹疑和搜索的情况并不多见。发音听起来可能仍然洋腔洋调。偶尔会出现非固定化的语误,但是不会有固定化的语误,即便是在一些低频结构的把握上(除非……要不然……就)仍有所偏差。对常用习惯搭配和俚语的掌握可能各有差异,对一些近义词之间的辨析可能还有疑惑,比如检查和调查。仍然会有极少部分的表达是直接从母语翻译过来的。

Table 8.2 汉语水平评估纲领——口语 (ACTFL,1987)

Similar to the generic ACTFL proficiency guidelines, the above-mentioned Chinese guidelines identify different stages of learners' speaking proficiency in Chinese, as opposed to their achievement. It allows assessment of a learner's

Chinese speaking abilities, rather than measuring their achievement through specific language instruction.

正如 ACTFL 语言水平纲领所列举的，上述汉语口语水平评估纲领描述汉语学习者在不同阶段的汉语口语综合能力，而非他们在不同阶段的学习成果。它为评估学习者的汉语口语能力提供了参照标准，而不是直接用于测试学习者通过特定语言教学所取得的成绩。

8.1.4. The ACTFL Oral Proficiency Interview
全美外语教学委员会口语能力面试评估

The ACTFL Oral Proficiency Interview (hereafter, OPI), is a global assessment instrument measuring a language speaker's spoken language abilities. It is not an achievement test. Rather, it is an integrative testing model measuring speakers' oral proficiency. The purpose of the OPI is to find a ratable speaking sample to prove the "floor" and the "ceiling" of the major level described earlier in the ACTFL rating scale.

全美外语教学委员会口语能力面试评估(以下简称 OPI) 是一项综合评估口语能力的测试工具。OPI 并非一项成果测试，而是一项综合评估说话者口语能力的评估模式。OPI 的目标是根据上述的 ACTFL 等级水平评估，获取一个可评估的口语样本以定位受试者口语水平的下限和上限。

Taking the form of a live interview, the OPI is a 10-30-minute tape-recorded natural conversation between a trained interviewer and the person whose speaking proficiency is being assessed. The structure of the OPI is standardized following the ACTFL protocol of four phases, namely, warm-up, repeated level checks, probes, and wind-down. During the interview, there are no fixed series of questions, although the questions formulated by the trained interviewer do follow the standardized question types and tasks relative to each proficiency level. In this sense, the OPI is very different from a traditional standardized test in that neither the tester (the interviewer) nor the testee (the speaker) can truly prepare for the OPI. It is more of an interactive, adaptive, and learner-centered assessment.

Because of these characteristics of the OPI, one of the biggest challenges that educational professionals and language teachers face is that it is very difficult to quantify the sample data collected from the OPI. Still, the ratable speech sample elicited from the active negotiation of meaning between the interviewer and the interviewee makes the OPI an effective, valid, and reliable test to assess speakers' speaking proficiency.

OPI采用现场面谈的形式,由一个受过专业训练的采访者和受访者展开一段约十到三十分钟不等的自然交谈。整个面谈过程被收录下来。OPI的评估程序是依据ACTFL四个评估阶段所生成的标准化评估,即开始时的热身闲聊,反复性的考察并定位说话者的水平下限,探测说话者的水平上限,以及最后的收场结语。在整个面谈过程中并没有固定的问题,尽管这些训练有素的采访者所询问的问题是依据每个能力水平所包含的相关标准化问题类型和所能处理的相关任务提出的。从这个角度上看,OPI与传统的标准化测试在根本上就有所不同。也就是说在测试过程中测试者(采访者)和受试者(说话者)都不能像传统标准化测试那样进行事前的准备。整个面谈评估过程体现出了互动性、灵活调整性和以学习者为中心的特点。由于OPI的这些特点,语言教育专业人士和语言教师所面临的其中一个巨大挑战就是量化OPI收集的口语样本。尽管如此,从采访者和受试者之间积极的意义协商交流而提取的可评估的口语样本,使得OPI成为近年来评估口语能力的一个有效而兼具效度和信度的测试工具。

8.2 Introduction of National Standards 全美外语学习国家标准

8.2.1. What are the National Standards for Foreign Language Learning? 什么是全美外语学习国家标准?

Resulting from the collaborative efforts of ACTFL and many foreign language associations and organizations in the U.S.A., the National Standards in Foreign Language Education Project developed the document called the *Standards for Foreign Language Learning: Preparing for the 21st Century* in 1996, or the *National Standards*, as it is often called.

在 ACTFL 和美国多家外语协会和组织的共同努力下,全美外语教育国家标准方案在 1999 年制定了被命名为《外语学习标准:迎接 21 世纪》的文件,也就是后来大家称之为《国家标准》的文件。

8.2.2. Organizing Principles and Organization
组织原则和组织结构

Rather than separating languages skills into listening, speaking, reading, and writing, as proposed by the *ACTFL Proficiency Guidelines*, the Standards for Foreign Language Learning (the *National Standards*) are organized to describe language use in terms of three modes of communication: interpersonal, interpretive, and presentational. The interpersonal mode is defined as the direct oral and written communication among individuals. It is characterized as a process of active negotiation of meaning among people, which emphasizes the productive abilities. The interpretive mode is defined as the receptive or mediated communication of different types of messages or materials. It is characterized as a process of appropriate cultural interpretation of meanings occurring in written and spoken form, which emphasizes receptive abilities, such as listening and reading. The presentational mode is defined as productive communication using oral or written language. It is characterized as a process of creating messages that facilitates interpretation by people of the other culture, which also mainly emphasizes productive abilities, such as speaking and writing.

有别于 ACTFL 语言水平纲领把语言能力分成听、说、读、写方面的能力,全美外语学习标准(以下简称为国家标准)主要是从交际的三种模式来组织实际的语用形式:人际性、解释性和演示性。人际性的模式主要是指个人之间直接地通过口语或书面的形式交流。它强调人与人之间积极主动的意义协商过程以及语言的创造性。而解释性的模式主要诠释不同类型的信息和资料的能力。它呈现在书面和口语表现中合理化诠释意义的过程,强调了像听和读等语言接收能力。演示性的模式主要是指协助其他文化交流者理解而创造新信息的过程,它同时也强调口语与写作等语言创造能力。

The *National Standards* are organized within the five goal areas for foreign language education, which are commonly called "five Cs." The main organization of the Standards is as follows. Each of the five goal area contains a rationale for its inclusion as a part of foreign language education. Following that, each goal are a contains two or three content standards, which describe the knowledge and abilities that all students should acquire by the end of their high-school education, Kindergarten to 12th grade (K-12). Each standard is then followed by a brief discussion of the standard and the definition of its place within the goal area. Under each standard are sample progress indicators for grades K-4, K-8, and K-12, which define students' progress in meeting the standards, but are not standards themselves. Again, these sample progress indicators are representative, but neither prescriptive nor exhaustive.

国家标准的形成始自外语教育中的五个外语教育目标。这五个目标因各自开头的英文字母均为C,而被称5C目标。在具体介绍5C之前,我们将先简单介绍国家标准的主要组织原则:五个教育目标皆可体现部分的外语教育原则。根据这个基础,每一个目标都包括了两到三个具体内容标准。

这些标准指出学生在完成高中教育或者说从幼稚园到12年级(K-12)教育结束后应该具有的语言知识和能力。以汉语标准为例,在每一个标准下列举了学生在K-4,K-8和K-12几个阶段的语言进步样本,这些样本并非评判标准,而仅仅是提供学生语言水平进步的一些水平样本。我们需要再次强调的是,这些样本只具有代表性,而不具有标准性或者全面性。

8.2.3. Five "Cs"
五个 "Cs"

The *National Standards* have identified five-goal areas that make up foreign language education: communication, cultures, connections, comparisons, and communities. While the communication goal is central, other goal areas also need to be experienced to have content-based understanding. Therefore, these five-goal areas are interconnected content standards, which cannot be viewed in isolation. In the *National Standards*, each goal area has two or three standards. Table 8.3 presents the National Standards for Foreign Language Learning.

国家标准指出了外语教育界的五项主要目标:沟通、文化、贯通、比较和社区。尽管沟通在这五项教育目标中处于主导地位,我们仍需具体深刻地理解其他各项教育目标。因此,我们在看国家标准时,绝对不能将这五项相互贯通的内容标准孤立讨论。如前所述,在国家标准中,每项目标下面包括两到三个对应标准。以下表格将各项目标及下属标准一一列出:

COMMUNICATION 沟通
Communicate in Languages Other Than English
Standard 1.1(语言沟通): Students engage in conversations, provide and obtain information, express feelings and emotions, and exchange opinions
Standard 1.2(理解诠释): Students understand and interpret written and spoken language on a variety of topics
Standard 1.3(表达演示): Students present information, concepts, and ideas to an audience of listeners or readers on a variety of topics.
CULTURES 文化
Gain Knowledge and Understanding of Other Cultures
Standard 2.1(文化习俗): Students demonstrate an understanding of the relationship between the practices and perspectives of the culture studied
Standard 2.2(文化产物): Students demonstrate an understanding of the relationship between the products and perspectives of the culture studied
CONNECTIONS 贯通
Connect with Other Disciplines and Acquire Information
Standard 3.1(触类旁通): Students reinforce and further their knowledge of other disciplines through the foreign language
Standard 3.2(博闻广见): Students acquire information and recognize the distinctive viewpoints that are only available through the foreign language and its cultures
COMPARISONS 比较
Develop Insight into the Nature of Language and Culture
Standard 4.1(比较语文): Students demonstrate understanding of the nature of language through comparisons of the language studied and their own
Standard 4.2(比较文化): Students demonstrate understanding of the concept of culture through comparisons of the cultures studied and their own.

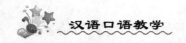

COMMUNITIES 社区
Participate in Multilingual Communities at Home & Around the World
Standard 5.1（学以致用）: Students use the language both within and beyond the school setting
Standard 5.2（学无止境）: Students show evidence of becoming life-long learners by using the language for personal enjoyment and enrichment.

Table 8.3　National Standards for Foreign Language Learning, 1999

COMMUNICATION 沟通
运用英文以外的其他语言沟通
Standard 1.1(语言沟通):学生参与交谈,提供和获取信息,表达情感和感受,交换意见
Standard 1.2(理解诠释):学生理解和诠释书面语和口语所涵盖的各种话题
Standard 1.3(表达演示):学生向听众或读者表达和演示涵盖各种话题的信息,概念和想法
CULTURES 文化
体认其他文化
Standard 2.1（文化习俗):学生显示出对所学文化的文化实践和观点之间联系的了解
Standard 2.2（文化产物):学生显示出对所学文化的文化产物和观点之间联系的了解
CONNECTIONS 贯通
贯通其他学科
Standard 3.1（触类旁通):学生通过外语强化和拓展其他学科的知识
Standard 3.2（博闻广见):学生通过外语和其他文化获取新信息,体认具有文化特殊性的相关视点
COMPARISONS 比较
比较语言文化之特性
Standard 4.1（比较语文):学生通过所学语言和其母语的比较体认语言的本质
Standard 4.2（比较文化):学生通过对所学文化和其自身文化的比较体认文化的概念
COMMUNITIES 社区
应用与国内与国际多元社区
Standard 5.1（学以致用):学生在校内外广泛使用所学语言
Standard 5.2（学无止境):学生使用语言充实自我,成为一个终身学习者

表格8.3　外语学习国家标准,1999

第八章 全美外语教学委员会口语标准和全美外语教学国家标准

Following the *National Standards* from a general perspective that applies to all languages, there are standards dedicated to learning specific languages, such as Chinese, Classical Languages, French, German, Italian, Japanese, Portuguese, Russian, and Spanish. By representing the consensus of the foreign language education field with respect to the overall objectives of L2 study, the language-specific standards provide more fluid sample progress indicators in their standards. For example, with regard to Chinese, when compared with students who are learning other Indo-European languages, those learning Chinese whose first languages are Romance languages may need more time to reach some of the progress indicators for learners of those languages closely related to English (please refer to *Standards for Chinese Language Learning*: *A Project of the Chinese Language Association of Secondary-Elementary Schools (CLASS)* for more details).

  国家标准从宏观角度对语言的教育提出教育的目标，并以此为基础形成不同语言的语言学习标准，包括汉语、拉丁语、法语、德语、意大利语、日语、葡萄牙语、俄语和西班牙语。在与外语教育界和二语学习的总体目标一致的前提下，具体语言标准提供了此种语言在其各个发展进步阶段更为具体动态的语言发展样本。以汉语为例，与其他印欧语系语言的学习者相比，母语为罗马语体的汉语学习者可能需要更长的时间才能达到相对应的水平。(具体样本范例请参照《全美中小学中文学习目标》)

The *National Standards*, including its language-specific sections of standards, is proposed for a wide audience. It does not represent or describe the current state of foreign language education in the U.S.A. It is also not a curriculum guide, because it only suggests the types of content and curricular experiences needed to enable the students to reach the standards, and does not describes specific course content. Moreover, in real-life situations, it is not a stand-alone document. It has to be used in conjunction with other state and local language frameworks and standards.

  国家标准是因应广大读者群的需要而提出的。它并不能代表或描述

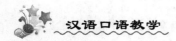

当前美国外语教育的实际状况。它也不能作为一个课程设置的指导纲领。因为它仅仅阐述为协助学生达到相关标准所需要的课程需要,而非具体化课程的教学内容。除此以外,在实际情境中,它也不是一个独立存在的文件,而是必须搭配其他州际或当地的语言框架和标准一起操作。

8.3 Applications to L2 Speaking Teaching and Learning
在二语口语教学中的应用

Both the *ACTFL Proficiency Guidelines* and the *National Standards* have been nationally recognized and well-documented in the literature. Many empirical research studies are conducted based on the two standards. In this section, we only present a couple of studies from the field of teaching Chinese as a foreign language (TCFL). Subsequently, we briefly discuss further pedagogical and curriculum implications of the two standards.

　　ACTFL语言水平纲领和国家标准受到了广泛的认可,同时有大量丰富的文献支持。到目前为止,已经有很多以这两大标准为基础的实践研究。在这一小节中,我们仅选择对外汉语教学界的一些相关研究以及关于口语教学和课程设置的一些启示。

Looking specifically at the performance assessment research in TCFL, Ke (1993) conducted a study on the correlation of Simulated Oral Proficiency Interview (SOPI) (Chinese Speaking Test) and the OPI, both of which have been developed and scored based on the ACTFL Proficiency Guidelines. Unlike the OPI, the SOPI is a semi-direct, tape-based, alternative approach to interview-based speaking proficiency test. It was first developed by the staff at the Center of Applied Linguistics (CAL). It elicits speaking data by means of tape recordings and printed test booklets, rather than face-to-face interaction. One of the direct advantages of using the SOPI is that it could be administered simultaneously in a language lab. The recorded tapes can then be sent to any trained raters. Ke found that the SOPI and OPI are highly correlated. Yet, he concluded that the OPI is a better choice whenever it permits and that the SOPI should be the second choice.

着眼于对外汉语中对能力表现的评估研究,Ke(1993)比较OPI和模拟OPI(中文口语测试,以下简称SOPI)两种评估测试。这两项评估测试均以ACTFL口语标准为基础。不同于OPI,SOPI是一种半直接的,利用录音卡带进行口语能力评估的替代测试。SOPI最初由美国应用语言学中心设计研发。相较于OPI采用面对面交流的形式,SOPI通过录音和打印的考试手册收集口语数据。SOPI测试的一个优势在于可以在语言实验室里同步执行,在短时间内收集大量口语数据。所收集的数据随后分发到受训的评估者手中。这项研究发现,这两种测试有很高的相关性,但在可以选择的前提下,OPI仍然是更佳的选择。

More recently, Ke (2006) presented a model of formative task-based language assessment in the task-based curriculum in the Chinese Language Program at the University of Iowa. Three summative tests modeled on the ACTFL Proficiency Guidelines were administered at the end of each Chinese course: the Chinese Speaking Test (the SOPI by Center for Applied Linguistics, 1992), the Computer-Adaptive Test for Reading Chinese (Yao, 1994), and the Chinese Compute-Adaptive Listening Comprehension Test (Ke & Zhang, 2002). Formative testing is used to assess the developmental achievement of the language learners. Assessment for this purpose is a part of teaching, which is different from summative assessment whose main purpose is to describe learning achieved at a certain time in summative form to other interested parties. Summative assessment has an important role in the overall educational progress of pupils, but not in day-to-day teaching as formative assessment. The task-based instruction emphasizes on the negotiation of meaning in a meaningful context. In this case, the tasks, which are carefully designed by language teachers to be somewhat comparable with real-world activities, are used to assess the performance of learners.

在另外一项研究中,Ke(2006)阐述了爱荷华大学中文部任务教学课程设置中的形成性任务语言评估模式。在每门中文课结束时,学生参与三项根据ACTFL语言水平纲领所制定的总结性评估测试:中文口语测试(SOPI)、网上自适中文阅读测试(Yao,1994)以及网上自适中文听力水平测

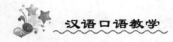

试(Ke & Zhang,2002)。与总结性评估相比,形成性评估主要用于测试语言学习者阶段性的发展成果。评估的目的是教学的一部分。至于总结性评估,主要的目的在于向相关利益群体描述学习者在特定时期所取得的学习成果。不同于形成性评估关注日常教学的进步,总结性评估对掌握学生的总体学习进展十分重要。建立在形成性评估基础上,任务型教学强调在有意义语境中的意义协商。由教师精心设计的模拟现实生活的相关任务被用来评估学生实际的口语表现。

When it comes to curriculum design, the National Standards and the Chinese-specific standards in particular, have provided great guidance in standards-based Chinese curricula development. The sample progress indicators in the Chinese-specific standards not only describe what the students should do to meet the standards at different grade levels, but also take into consideration the fast-increasing Chinese heritage learner population and their special pedagogical needs. There is one section marked by asterisks under the Grade 12 sections in the sample progress indicators focusing specifically on keeping these Chinese heritage learners and more advanced level students challenged and making them perform to their full potential. The *National Standards*, therefore, provides language teachers as well as curriculum designers concrete examples of how the standards could be applied in classroom and how pertinent curricula could be designed based on these foundations and, subsequently, expanded ormodifiedaccordingly at various levels.

在课程设置上,国家标准和具体的中文学习目标为标准化中文课程的发展提供指导的作用。中文学习目标中的语言发展参照范例不仅描述了学生在不同年级段应该表达的语言活动,同时也考虑到不断增加的华裔学习者的特殊需求。在12年级的语言发展参照范例中,有一个有星号标出的小节专门表述这些华裔中文学习者和更高级水平学习者在此年级段可能表达的相关语言活动。国家标准因此为语言教师和课程设置者提供将标准应用到课堂的具体实例,并且由此设计、拓展和修订语言课程。

Chapter Nine 第九章
Common European Framework of Reference for Languages
欧洲共同语言参考框架

In contrast to the American Council on the Teaching of Foreign Languages (*ACTFL*) *Speaking Guidelines* and *National Foreign Language Standards* used in the U.S.A., the Common European Framework (CEF) is a guideline used to describe learners' foreign language achievement across Europe. An increasing number of countries have adopted CEF in the past few years. CEF provides a common basis for developing curriculum guidelines, language syllabi, instructional materials and various types of examinations. In CEF, the knowledge and skills that learners need to acquire to communicate effectively in a second language (L2) is comprehensively described. In addition to linguistic factors, CEF also addresses cultural contexts for appropriate language use.

不同于全美外语教学委员会(ACTFL)语言水平纲领与全美外语学习国家标准 (ACTFL Speaking Guidelines and National Foreign Language Standards),欧洲共同语言参考框架是全欧洲用来描述学习者外语能力表现的指标。在过去几年间,越来越多的国家采用欧洲共同语言参考框架(CEF)。CEF提供课程规划、教学大纲、教材编写以及各类测验一个共同的标准。CEF中详细介绍了外语学习者实现交际所必须掌握的知识和能力。除了讨论语言因素,CEF也特别提出支撑语言使用所必要的文化因素。

The CEF defines six proficiency levels that measure language learning progress systematically over the course of a lifetime. In this chapter, we first discuss the objectives, functions, and political and educational contexts of the CEF. Subsequently, we introduce the six levels of proficiency and its illustrative descriptors. Finally, several qualitative aspects of spoken language use based on CEF descriptors are described. This chapter not only allows readers to better

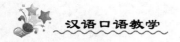

understand the development and content of CEF, it also provides readers with sufficient information regarding how CEF influences the curriculum development of speaking instruction and the design of classroom activities.

　　欧洲共同语言参考框架定出了六个等级,便于有系统地评估学习者在每一个学习阶段和终身检测自己的外语水平以及学习进展。本章我们将先讨论欧洲共同语言参考框架的目标、功能以及出台时的政治与教育背景。之后,我们将简短介绍六个能力等级及其描述性参数。最后,我们将描述基于CEF参数的口语测试的定性的几个方面。借由本章的介绍,读者除了就欧洲共同语言参考框架的发展以及内容有广泛的了解,更可从中认识这套欧洲通行的标准对口语教学课程设置以及课堂活动设计的影响。

9.1 Background　背景

With a rich heritage of diverse cultures and languages, the European Union has realized the importance of protecting and developing its resources, as well as the need to ensure that its diversity is not a barrier to communication, but a source for mutual enrichment and understanding.

　　拥有丰富多样的语言和文化,欧洲理事会开始正视保护与发展资源的重要性,确保多元化不会成为交流的障碍,而是互相理解和互相补充的源泉。

Over the past decade, the concept of plurilingualism has gradually dominated language teaching and learning approaches in Europe. In contrast to multilingualism, which addresses the knowledge of a number of languages in separate mental compartments, plurilingualism emphasizes on the integration of all language knowledge, personal linguistic experiences, and overall communicative competence. An individual does not need to achieve native-like proficiency in a target language; he/she can take advantage of different parts of his/her knowledge to effectively communicate with different interlocutors in various situations. From this perspective, the objectives of language instruction are no longer to master a language and achieve native-like language proficiency, but to develop a linguistic repertoire and encourage life-long learning.

在过去十年，"多元化"的理念逐渐在欧洲成为语言教学与学习方法的主流。"语言多元化"与"多语言化"并不相同。"多语言化"指一个人会说一定数量的外语，而与这几个外语相关的知识储存在不同的内在部分，不相联系；"语言多元化"则强调结合所有的语言知识与个人的语言经验，并建构一种交际能力。从"语言多元化"的角度出发，个人并不需要以达到"如母语者一样的语言能力"为目标，而是要灵活利用交际能力的不同方面，实现与不同对话者在不同情境下的交际。"语言多元化"的目标并非培养学习者如母语者般精通一个语言的能力，而是建构一个语言的资料库，能让学会的各种语言建立联系，并鼓励语言学习者终身学习。

The CEF was developed by the Council of Europe for the project "Language Learning for European Citizenship" between 1989 and 1996. According to Recommendations R(82)18 and R(98)6, which were created by the European Committee of Ministers, the overall aim of CEF is to achieve greater unity among the European countries and pursue this aim by adopting common action in cultural fields. As modern languages are the foundation of mutual understanding, communication, and international cooperation, the European Committee of Ministers called upon member governments to develop an effective European system of language proficiency assessment and language learning, teaching, and research.

欧洲共同语言参考框架是欧洲理事会在1989到1996年为"欧洲公民之语言学习"项目所制定的。根据欧洲理事会部长委员会在1982年通过的《建议》的第十八项以及1998年通过的《建议》的第六项，CEF的总体目标是促进成员国的团结以及在文化领域采取统一的行动。由于语言是相互理解、交流以及跨国合作的基础，欧洲理事会部长委员会呼吁会员国政府制定一套欧洲的标准，用以评估语言能力、学习、教学以及研究。

Consequently, the Committee for Education and the Modern Languages Section, which are subordinate to the Council for Cultural Cooperation, has coordinated the efforts of the member countries to improve language learning. In November

2001, European Union Council Resolution recommended using the CEF to establish a system for validating language ability. Six reference levels have been widely accepted as the European standard for assessing an individual's language proficiency.

因此,文化合作理事会下属的教育委员会和现代语言小组负责协调会员国的共识与,致力促进语言学习。2001年11月,欧盟理事会决议建议用CEF建立一套鉴定语言能力的系统。三级六等的共同语言量表开始成为欧盟会员国用来评估个人语言能力的标准。

9.2 Common Reference Levels 共同语言能力量表

According to the CEF, six Common Reference Levels are used to indicate different stages of language proficiency (Figure 9.1). These are breakthrough, waystage, threshold, vantage, effective operational proficiency, and mastery. These six levels can be categorized into three broad divisions — A (Basic User), B (Independent User), and C (Proficient User).

根据欧洲共同语言参考框架,六个共同语言能力等级被用来标示语言能力的不同阶段。这六个等级包含了入门级、初级、中级、中高级、高级以及精通级。这六个等级又可被划分为三个组:A(初学阶段)、B(独立阶段)和C(精通阶段)。

A general description about each reference level is provided in Table 9.1. Based

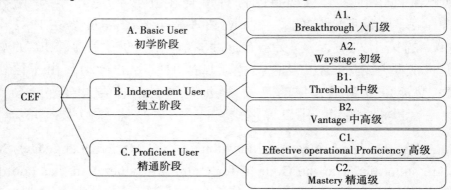

Figure 9.1　Common Reference Levels: three categories and levels

on the information provided in Table 9.1, a language development path could be derived from the language features of proficient user, independent user, and basic user.

六个语言等级的概括性叙述请见表9.1。根据表9.1的信息,我们可从精通阶段学习者、独立阶段学习者以及初学阶段学习者的语言特征发现语言发展的轨迹。

First, language users start from producing high-frequency words and simple sentences to create passages. Second, as language users' proficiency levels become more advanced, they can handle both concrete and abstract topics. Third, as language users become more proficient, they are capable of using the target language for a variety of purposes.

首先,语言学习者先学会使用频率高的词汇以及简单的句子组成段落。其次,随着学习者语言程度的提高,无论是具体和抽象的主题,他们都能游刃有余。第三,当学习者的语言能力越来越高,他们可以用目的语完成不同目的的任务。

Basic User	A1	·Users can understand and use familiar everyday expressions and very basic phrases aimed at the satisfaction of needs of a concrete type. ·Users can introduce themselves and others and can ask and answer questions about personal details, such as where they live, people they know, and things they have. ·Users can interact in a simple way, provided the other person talks slowly and clearly and is prepared to help.
	A2	·Users can understand sentences and frequently use expressions related to area of most immediate relevance (e.g., very basic personal and family information, shopping, local geography, employment). ·Users can communicate in simple and routine tasks requiring a simple and direct exchange of information on familiar and routine matters. ·Users can describe in simple terms aspects of his/her background, immediate environment, and matters in areas of immediate need.

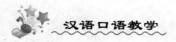

Independent User	B1	· Users can understand the main points of clear standard input on familiar matters regularly encountered in work, school, leisure, etc. · Users can deal with most of the situations likely to arise while traveling in an area where the language is spoken. · Users can produce simple connected text on topics that are familiar or of personal interest. · Users can describe experiences and events, dreams, hopes, and ambitions, and briefly give reasons and explanations for options and plans.
	B2	· Users can understand the main idea of complex text on both concrete and abstract topics, including technical discussions in their field of specialization. · Users can interact with a degree of fluency and spontaneity that makes regular interaction with native speakers quite possible without strain for either party. · Users can produce clear, detailed text on a wide range of subjects and explain a viewpoint on a topical issue, giving the advantages and disadvantages of various options.
Proficient User	C1	· Users can understand a wide range of demanding, longer texts, and recognize implicit meaning. · Users can express themselves fluently and spontaneously without much obvious searching for expressions. · Users can use language flexibly and effectively for social, academic, and professional purposes. · Users can produce clear, well-structured, detailed text on complex subjects, showing controlled use of organizational patterns, connectors, and cohesive devices.
	C2	· Users can understand with ease virtually everything heard or read. · Users can summarize information from different spoken and written sources, restructuring argument and accounts in a coherent presentation. · Users can express themselves spontaneously, very fluently and precisely, differentiating finer shades of meaning even in more complex situations.

Table 9.1　Common Reference Levels: Global scale

独立阶段	B1	・使用者能理解他人在工作中、学校里和休闲时以清楚且标准语言讲话的内容要点。 ・使用者在目的语国家和地区旅游时，能用所学语言应付遇到的大多数情况。 ・使用者能就熟悉或个人感兴趣的主题发表简单而连贯的意见。 ・使用者能叙述经历、事件、梦、与个人理想，并能简单解释说明计划与想法。
	B2	・使用者能理解一篇复杂文章中具体或抽象主题的内容，包括使用者专业领域的技术性讨论。 ・使用者能流利且自如地和母语者进行交际，双方都不感到紧张。 ・使用者能清楚、详细地就广泛的话题进行交谈，能就时事发表自己的观点，并对各种可能性分析其利弊得失。
精通阶段	X1	・使用者能理解管饭领域的高难度长篇文章，并能领会文中隐含的意思。 ・使用者表达自如流畅，不须费心遣词造句。 ・使用者在有效灵活地使用语言因应社交、职业以及学术方面的目的。 ・使用者能对复杂主题发表清楚且结构合理的论述，展现对篇章组织、衔接词和逻辑用词方面的掌握能力。
	X2	・使用者能轻松理解所有听力和阅读的内容。 ・使用者能连贯地总结、重整各类口语和书面的信息，不漏内容及其重要论据。 ・使用者表达自如、精确且流畅，并能掌握复杂主题中细微的含义的差别。

Table 9.1. 共同语言能力量表：测评总表

The above-mentioned description is provided for non-specialist users. A self-assessment grid is created to illustrate major categories of language use at each of the six levels. With detailed descriptors of each level, learners are more likely to profile their language skills and self-assess their language proficiency.

　　上表中的描述是提供给非专业人士的，借此增进他们对这个评估体系的了解。"自我评估表"则是为了阐述六个等级中语言使用的主要种类。通过每一个等级中详细的能力标准描述，学习者更能认识自己的语言能力并进行自我的测评。

As this book is focused on speaking acquisition, the speaking self-assessment

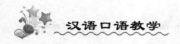

grid is provided in Table 9.2. With regard to speaking ability, two subcategories are presented. Spoken interaction refers to learners' communicative competence on a variety of topics and tasks, while spoken production primarily describes learners' oral ability in terms of accuracy, fluency, and coherence.

由于本书的重点是口语习得，口语的自我评量表请参照下表(表9.2)。关于口语能力的自我评量，可分为两个子项目。"口语互动"是学习者在不同主题与任务上的交际能力。"口语表达"主要描述学习者在准确度、流利度以及连贯性的口语能力。

Level	Speaking	
	Spoken Interaction	Spoken Production
A1	I can interact in a simple way, provided the other person is prepared to repeat or rephrase things at a slower rate of speech and help me formulate what I am trying to say. I can ask and answer simple questions in areas of very familiar topics.	I can use simple phrases and sentences to describe where I live and people I know.
A2	I can communicate in simple and routine tasks requiring a simple and direct exchange of information on familiar topics and activities. I can handle very short social exchanges, even though I cannot usually understand enough to keep the conversation going myself.	I can connect phrases in a simple way to describe experiences and events, my dreams, hopes, and ambitions. I can briefly give reasons and explanations for opinions and plans. I can narrate a story or relate the plot of a book or films and describe my reactions.
B1	I can deal with most of the situations likely to arise while traveling in an area where the language is spoken. I can enter unprepared into conversation on topics that are familiar, of personal interest, or pertinent to everyday life (e.g., family, hobbies, work, travel, and current event).	I can use a series of phrases and sentences to describe in simple terms my family and other people, living conditions, my educational background, and my present or most recent job.

B2	I can interact with a degree of fluency and spontaneity that makes regular interaction with native speakers quite possible. I can take an active part in discussion in familiar contexts, accounting for and sustaining my views.	I can present clear, detailed descriptions on a wide range of subjects related to my field of interest. I can explain a viewpoint on a topical issue giving the advantages and disadvantages of various options.
C1	I can express myself fluently and spontaneously without much obvious searching for expressions. I can use language flexibly and effectively for social and professional purposes. I can formulate ideas and opinions with precision and relate my contribution skillfully to those of other speakers.	I can present clear, detailed descriptions of complex subjects integrating sub-themes, developing particular points, and rounding off with an appropriate conclusion.
C2	I can take part effortlessly in any conversation or discussion and have a good familiarity with idiomatic expressions and colloquialisms. I can express myself fluently and convey finer shades of meaning precisely. If I do have a problem, I can backtrack and restructure around the difficulty so smoothly that other people are hardly aware of it.	I can present a clear, smoothly flowing description or argument in a style appropriate to the context and with an effective logical structure, which helps the recipient to notice and remember significant points.

Table 9.2 Speaking self-assessment grid

Level	口语	
	口语互动	口语表达
A1	要是对话者愿意重复或以较慢的语速改述，或是对话者愿意帮我确切地阐述我想表达的意思，我就能用目的语进行简单的互动。我能就熟悉的主题进行问答。	我能用简单的短语和句子描自己居住的地方以及认识的人。

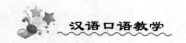

A2	在只需简单和直接交换信息的任务中,我能就熟悉的主题与惯常的活动进行交际。即使在不能完全理解对话内容,甚至对话难以持续的情况下,我可以用非常简短的句子进行社交对话。	我能用一连串的短语或句子简单描述我的家庭、他人情况、自己的生活状况、教育背景和自己目前或是最近的工作。
B1	我能在目的语国家和地区旅游时,用所学语言应付遇到的绝大部分情况。我也能在无准备的状况下谈论熟悉的、自己感兴趣的或是日常生活的话题(例如:家庭、爱好、工作、旅游以及时事等)。	我能简单地讲述经历、时间、自己的梦想、希望和目标。我可以简单叙述自己的观点和个人计划,并提供解释与说明。我也能讲述一本书或一部电影的内容,并对此发表个人的心得。
B2	我的口语流利、自如地和母语者进行正常的互动。我能在熟悉的情境下发表和捍卫自己的观点。	对自己感兴趣的话题,我能作清楚、详细描述。我能阐明自己的观点并就各种可能性陈述其利弊。
C1	我能流利自如地进行对话,而不需刻意的寻找表达的词语。我能为了社交与职业的目的灵活有效地应用语言。我也能精确地表达自己的思想和阐述观点,并有技巧地在对话中与其他谈话者做连结。	我可以清楚、详细地阐述复杂的话题,融入与之相关联的主题,说明自己的观点,并能适当地结束发言。
C2	我能轻松地参与任何会话与讨论,并非常熟悉各种口语和惯用语。我能流利地表达自我并精确地传达语义的细微差别。要是我有任何交际的问题,我会灵活地补救而不让他人发现。	我能以适当的语气清晰、流畅地描述或发表论述,我讲话有逻辑,并能帮助听众注意和记住重点。

Table 9.2　自我评量表

9.3 Common Reference Levels: Qualitative Aspects of Spoken Language Use
共同语言量表：口语使用的定性特征

In the following paragraphs, CEF's qualitative aspects of spoken language use are illustrated in terms of range, accuracy, fluency, interaction, and coherence.

在下面几个小节，我们将在广度、准确度、互动性以及连贯性等方面一一阐明CEF的口语定性特征。

9.3.1. Range
广度

Basic users at Breakthrough (A1) level know a limited number of words and simple phrases related to personal information and specific concrete situations. When they advance to Waystage (A2) level, they can use basic sentence patterns with memorized phrases and groups of a few words to exchange information in daily conversations.

入门级(A1)的初学者知道数量有限的词汇与简单短语，这些词汇与短语和个人信息以及特定的具体情境有关。当学习者的能力进展到初级阶段(A2)，他们能运用基本句型、背诵的短语及成组的词在简单的日常情境中交换信息。

Independent users at Threshold (B1) level have enough language command to express themselves with some hesitation and circumlocutions on topics related to personal information, such as family, hobbies, work, and travel. Vantage level (B2) users have a sufficient range of language to give clear descriptions and express viewpoints on most of the general topics, without searching for words or using some complex sentence forms.

在独立阶段，中级(B1)的语言使用者掌握足够的语言能力，能够表达自己对家庭、休闲、兴趣爱好、工作和旅游等与个人信息相关话题的看法。但表达时会有迟疑、停顿或使用迂回的方式。中高级(B2)的使用者的语言能力足以就一般的主题清楚地描述表达自己的观点，而不需费心遣词造句

或使用复杂的句型。

Proficient users at Effective Operational Proficiency (C1) level have sufficient vocabulary knowledge, which allows them to express themselves clearly and appropriately over a wide range of general, academic, professional, or leisure topics. Mastery (C2) level users have great flexibility in reformulating ideas in differing linguistic forms to convey finer shades of meaning precisely, give emphasis, differentiate, and eliminate ambiguity. They also have a good command of idiomatic expressions and colloquialisms.

　　精通阶段的高级(C1)语言使用者能运用丰富的词汇清楚且适当地表达自己对一般性、学术、职业或休闲等话题的看法。精通级(C2)的使用者能十分灵活地运用不同的语言形式重述自己的想法、精确表达细微的语义、强调重点以及辨别与消除歧义。他们能掌握各种惯用法以及通俗表达法。

9.3.2. Accuracy
　　准确度

Basic users at Breakthrough (A1) level can only control few simple grammatical structures and sentence patterns in a memorized repertoire. Waystage (A2) users use simple structures correctly, but still systematically make basic mistakes.

　　入门级 (A1)的初学者仅能掌握记忆范围的简单语法结构和句型。初级(A2)使用者能正确运用简单的语法结构,但仍会经常地犯基础性的错误。

Independent users at Threshold (B1) level can accurately use high-frequency words and patterns related to more predictable situations, while Vantage (B2) users show a relatively high degree of grammatical control. They do not make errors that cause misunderstanding. They are also capable of self-correcting most of their mistakes.

　　在独立阶段,中级(B1)使用者在较能预知的情境中,能准确地使用较常出现的词汇或使句型进行交际。中高级(B2)的使用者对语法有较高程度的掌握。他们所犯的错误不会引起误解,并通常能自行纠错。

Proficient users at Effective Operational Proficiency (C1) level maintain a high degree of grammatical accuracy consistently. Mastery (C2) level users maintain consistent grammatical control of complex language, even while attention is otherwise engaged in forward planning or monitoring others' reactions.

  精通阶段的高级 (C1)使用者能保持相当程度的语法准确度。精通级(C2)使用者即使当注意力分散在做预先计划或观察他人反应时,也能准确地掌握复杂的语法。

9.3.3. Fluency
  流利度

Basic users at Breakthrough (A1) level can manage very short, isolated, and mainly pre-packaged utterance with much pausing to search for expressions, articulate less familiar words, and repair communication. Waystage (A2) users can make themselves understood in very short sentences, even though pauses, false starts, and reformulation are very obvious.

  入门级 (A1)的初学者能用简短、单独的以及成套的话语应对交际,但说话时常因需要寻找措辞、拼读不熟悉的单词以及补救交流障碍而出现停顿。即使有明显的停顿、句首错误或是重述,初级 (A2) 使用者也能使用十分简短的句子让他人理解自己的话语。

Independent users at Threshold (B1) level can converse comprehensibly, even though they may need to pause for grammatical or lexical planning and self-repair in a longer oral production. Vantage (B2) users can produce stretches of language with a fairly even tempo, although they may feel hesitant as they search for patterns and expressions. Their oral utterance may have few noticeably long pauses.

  独立阶段的中级(B1) 使用者能让他人理解自己的话语,但在较长的自由发言时,他们可能需要停下来思索语法或选择适当的词汇,自我纠错的情况也很明显。中高级(B2)的使用者能用较正常的语速发表较长的言论,即使他们可能在选择表达法和句型上略有迟疑,他们的口语中也较少出现明显的长的停顿。

Proficient users at Effective Operational Proficiency (C1) level can express themselves fluently and spontaneously. Only a conceptually difficult subject may make them to talk with some pauses and hesitation. Mastery (C2) level users can express themselves spontaneously at length with a natural colloquial flow, avoiding or backtracking around any difficulty so smoothly that the interlocutor is hardly aware of it.

精通阶段的高级 (C1)使用者能流利且自然地表达自我。唯有在概念较难表达的主题时,他们的口语才会出现停顿或迟疑。精通级 (C2)使用者能流利自然地发表长篇的演说,并在不让对话者察觉的情况下,回避或灵活补救表达的难点。

9.3.4. Interaction
互动性

Basic users at Breakthrough (A1) level can ask and answer questions in relation to exchanging personal information. They can interact in a simple way, but communication is totally dependent on repetition, rephrasing, and repair. Waystage (A2) users can respond to simple questions and follow the conversation. However, they are rarely able to understand the whole conversation and lead communication.

入门级 (A1)的初学者能就个人情况简单进行问答。他们能进行简单的交流,但交流的有效程度完全依赖于重复、重述以及纠错。初级 (A2) 使用者能回答简单的问题并在对话中做简短的回应。不过,他们很难全面理解谈话内容或主导对话。

Independent users at Threshold (B1) level can make a simple face-to-face conversation on familiar topics or areas related to their personal interests. Vantage (B2) users are able to interact with people in an appropriate way, although they may not always do this elegantly. They can move the discussion along on familiar topics by showing confirming comprehension and inviting others to talk.

独立阶段的中级(B1)使用者能就个人感兴趣的话题进行面对面的简单交谈。中高级(B2)的使用者能适当地与人交流，即使对话可能不够优美。对于自己熟悉的话题，他们能通过理解确认以及邀请他人发言等方法来延续讨论。

Proficient users at Effective Operational Proficiency (C1) level select a suitable phrase from their readily available discourse to preface their remarks to get or maintain the flow of conversation and relate their own contributions skillfully to those of other speakers. Mastery (C2) level users interact with ease and skill, picking up and using non-verbal and intonational cues effortlessly. They can interweave their contribution into the joint discourse with fully natural turn-taking, referencing, allusion making, etc.

精通阶段的高级(C1)使用者会在他们的对话中选用适当的话语发表开场白、要求发言或有技巧地在对话中与其他谈话者做连结。精通级(C2)使用者能轻松地发现、使用非语言的提示与对话人进行自然而灵活的互动交流。他们在交谈中能自如地进行问答，会旁征博引，或使用间接暗示。

9.3.5. Coherence
连贯性

Basic users at Breakthrough (A1) level can link words or groups of words with very basic linear connectors, such as "and" or "then". Waystage (A2) users can link groups of words with simple connectors, such as "and," "but," and "because".

入门级(A1)的初学者能使用"和"、"然后"等非常基础的连词衔接单词和词组。初级(A2)的使用者能用"和"、"但是"、"因为"等简单的连词衔接词组。

Independent users at Threshold (B1) level can link a series of shorter, discrete simple elements into a connected, linear sequence of points. Vantage (B2) users are able to use few cohesive devices to link their utterances into clear, coherent discourse. However, there may be some "jumpiness" in a long utterance.

独立阶段的中级(B1)使用者能将一系列简短、独立的词语串联成连贯的线性要点。中高级(B2)的使用者能运用少数衔接词连接句子,使他们的口语清晰连贯。但在发表长篇谈语时,他们的发言可能有"短路"的情况。

Proficient users at Effective Operational Proficiency (C1) level produce clear, smooth, and well-structured speech, which shows their controlled use of organizational patterns, connectors, and cohesive devices. Mastery (C2) level users create coherent and cohesive discourse, which shows their full and appropriate control of a variety of organizational patterns and a wide range of connectors and other cohesive devices.

精通阶段的高级(C1)使用者谈话清晰、流畅且结构完整,显示出他们对句型、连词、衔接词的精确掌控能力。精通级(C2)使用者的谈话连贯,遣词造句丰富多样、完整得体,并能善用许多关联词语和连词。

9.4 Application: How to Use Scales of Descriptors of Language Proficiency
应用:如何使用语言能力量表

Developed by a group of linguists, foreign language educators, and policy makers, CEF presents a researcher perspective, depicting what language users at different levels can do. However, it attempts to make the scales of Common Reference Levels available for language users, instructors, assessors, and curriculum developers. It provides global scales and self-assessed grids for language users, and gives more detailed descriptors for assessment and curriculum design.

在一组语言学家、外语教育者和政策制定者的共同研究下,欧洲共同语言参考框架呈现出研究者的观点,描绘不同阶段的语言使用者能完成的任务。然而,欧洲共同语言参考框架力图使语言能力量表对语言使用者、教师、考官以及课程规划者皆可适用。它提供测评总表和自我评量表给语言使用者,并为测量评估和课程设计提供了更详细的分级叙述。

9.4.1. User-oriented
以学习者为中心

User-oriented scales simply reflect typical behaviors of learners at different levels. The scales aim to discuss what the learner can do with positive phrases, even describing low-proficiency levels. User-oriented scales are often holistic, offering one descriptor per level. The global scale of Common Reference Levels, shown in Table 9.1, offers users a general summary of typical proficiency at each level.

以学习者为中心的量表反映出不同等级的学习者所具有的典型语言行为。量表的目标在于用肯定、正面的语气探讨学习者能做的事情，即使是描述低语言程度的学习者。以学习者为中心的量表一般为概括性的，为每个等级提供一个描述性指标。表9.1的测评总表就根据每个能力等级概括性地描述了这个等级所具有代表性的能力。

9.4.2. Assessor-oriented
以考官为中心

Assessor-oriented scales aim to guide the grading process. The scales focus on how well the learner performs. Statements are typically expressed in terms of aspects of the quality of the expected performance. Some assessor-oriented scales are general, offering one descriptor per level. Others are analytic scales, focusing on different aspects of the performance, such as Range, Accuracy, Fluency, and Coherence. The qualitative aspects of spoken language use, presented in the previous section, provide a good example of diagnosing what the learners need to work on.

以考官为中心的语言能力量表旨在知道评分的过程。评估的标准着重在学习者所能达到的最佳表现。评估报告通常为定性的应用语言的预期能力。某些以考官为中心的能力量表是概括性的，提供一个等级总体的描述。有的能力量表是分析性的，侧重语言表现的不同面向，像广度、准确

度、流利度和连贯性。在上个章节,这些定性的口语评估指标可以帮学习者定位,判断出他们应该继续改进的方向。

9.5 Application: Language Instruction and Learning
应用:语言教学与学习

When the concepts of the CEF are applied to language instruction and language learning, we can better understand how a language curriculum is developed and what a language learner is expected to learn in Europe. In the following paragraphs, we discuss the learning objectives and teaching methods within the CEF.

当CEF的理念被体现在语言教学和语言学习上,我们能更了解欧洲语言课程的设置以及学习者的学习目标。在下面几个小节,我们将讨论以CEF为基础所发展的语言学习目标以及教学法。

9.5.1. Learning Objectives
学习目标

According to CEF, the objectives of language learning and teaching should be based on an appreciation of the needs of learners and society, and on the tasks, activities, and processes that the learners must carry out to satisfy those needs. They should also take into consideration the competences and strategies that students need to develop to do so. In addition, it is important to consider the developmental path of language learners who are acquiring plurilingual and pluricultural competencies, and make necessary adjustments for different contexts.

根据CEF,语言学习与教学的目标必须基于对学习者和社会需求的理解、学习者为了满足这些需求而执行的任务、活动与过程,以及他们为了满足需求而培养的能力与策略。此外,学习目标必须考虑语言学习者的发展轨迹、习得多元化语言和多元化文化的重要性以及根据不同的情况作适度的调整。

9.5.1.1. Following the Language Learning Evolutionary Process
　　　　依循语言学习的演进发展

To better understand the progress of language learners, it is useful to examine their abilities at a series of levels. CEF allows learners to profile their own language skills according to the descriptors provided for each level and identify problems or unevenly developed skills.

　　为了更了解语言学习者的进展,我们能通过语言能力量表对照检测他们的表现。CEF 也让学习者能根据各个等级的描述性指标检验自己的语言能力,并从中找出问题或发现发展不均衡的语言能力。

9.5.1.2. Developing Plurilingual Competence and Pluricultural Competence
　　　　发展多元化的语言能力和多元文化能力

According to CEF, it is of particular importance to develop plurilingual and pluricultural competencies when acquiring a new language. However, plurilingual and pluricultural competencies are, in general, unevenly developed in one or more ways. Learners generally attain greater proficiency in one language. It is also commonly noted that competence profiles may be different from one language to another. For example, a learner may have excellent speaking competence in two languages, but high writing competence in only one language. In addition, a learner's pluricultural profile may differ from his/her plurilingual profile. He/she may have extensive knowledge of one culture, but a poor linguistic ability in its language, or have poor cultural knowledge, but good language skills.

　　根据 CEF,在习得一个新语言时,培养多元化的语言能力和多元文化能力格外重要。然而,多元化的语言能力和多元文化能力通常以许多形式呈现不均衡地发展。学习者一般只精通一门语言。我们也常看到一种语言在听说读写某一方面的能力有别于另一种语言。例如,某人可能两门外语的口语能力都很不错,但只有其中一门的写作能力较佳。此外,学习者的多元文化和多元化语言的特征也可能不一致。学习者有可能非常了解某个语言社群的文化,却对其语言不太了解;或者相反,不了解某一社群的文化却能熟练地使用其语言。

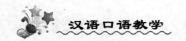

These imbalances are entirely normal. A language learner draws upon both general language skills and cultural knowledge during communication. In other words, the strategies used to carry out language tasks involve the appropriate use of both linguistic and cultural knowledge. For example, when interacting with a native speaker, a learner must compensate for any linguistic deficiency by using gestures, facial expressions, and open and friendly attitudes. Plurilingual and pluricultural competencies are not simply additions of monolingual skills, but combinations and alternations that permit a variety of strategies. It is possible to code switch during conversations and resort to bilingual forms of speech. A single, richer repertoire of this kind thus allows a choice of strategies for task accomplishment, drawing on interlinguistic skills and language switching abilities, wherever appropriate.

  这个不均衡的现象是一种常态。语言学习者在交际的过程中运用自己已有的一般语言能力和文化知识。换而言之,学习者用以完成语言任务的策略涉及适当地使用语言和文化的知识。比如,当与母语者互动交流时,学习者必须使用手势、面部表情以及开放友好的态度来弥补语言方面的不足。多元化语言能力和多元文化能力并非简单地将几种语言能力加起来,而是多种语言和文化能力多角度、多层面的综合体现与策略性地灵活应用。在会话中,语言的相互切换以及双语的使用都有可能出现。拥有较强的多元化语言能力和多元文化能力的人会根据情况选择适当的策略,运用跨语言的技巧和语言切换能力完成任务。

Plurilingual and pluricultural competencies promote the development of linguistic and communication awareness, and even metacognitive strategies, which enable an individual to become more aware of and in control of problem-solving methods to accomplish tasks. As a result, plurilingual and pluricultural competencies during language learning are highly emphasized as a learning objective in the European countries.

  多元化语言和多元文化能力促进语言和交际意识的发展,更包括了元认知学习策略的发展。元认知学习策略让我们能提高自我意识,有助于有效解决问题、完成任务。因此,欧洲国家特别重视语言学习过程中多元化语言和多元化能力的培养。

9.5.1.3. Types of Objectives in Relation to the CEF Framework
根据《共同参考框架》划分的语言教学目标类型

According to the CEF framework, five types of objectives for language instruction and learning have been identified.

(1) Development of learners' general competencies: Declarative knowledge, skill and know-how, personality traits, attitudes, etc.

(2) Extension and diversification of communicative language competence: Linguistic, pragmatic, and sociolinguistic knowledge.

(3) Pursuing better performance in one or more specific language activities: Reception, production, interaction, or mediation.

(4) Pursuing optimal functional operation in a given domain: The public, occupational, educational, or personal domain.

(5) Enrichment or diversification of strategies and the fulfillment of tasks: The management of actions linked to the learning and use of one or more languages, and the discovery or experience of other cultures.

根据欧洲共同语言参考框架，有五个语言教学目标：

(1) 培养和发展学习者的一般综合能力：技能、知识、个性、态度等。

(2) 拓展和丰富学习者的语言交际能力：语言学、语用学和社会语言学知识。

(3) 培养技能，以求在一个或多个特定语言活动有更好的表现：听说读写、互动与中介翻译能力。

(4) 培养和发展最大限度地功能性融入某个领域的能力：公共领域、职场、教育领域和个人生活领域。

(5) 丰富和扩展学习策略以及完成交际任务的能力：应用一门或多门语言的行为能力以及发现和体验他国文化的能力。

9.5.2. Methods for Language Instruction and Learning
语言教学和学习的方法

According to the Council of Europe, the fundamental principle of language instruction and learning methods is to consider the needs of the individual learners in their social context. There are many ways in which modern languages are currently learned and taught. For many years, the Council of Europe has promoted a communicative approach and the use of materials for communicative language teaching. However, it is not the function of the CEF to promote one particular methodology in language instruction. Instead, CEF wants to present a variety of options. Therefore, an extensive discussion and exchange of information on these options are necessary.

对于语言教学与学习的方法，欧洲理事会奉行的根本原则是根据特定社会环境中学习者的具体情况，因时、因地、因人制宜。目前教授和学习语言的方法很多，在过去几年，欧洲理事会曾鼓励教师采用交际为主的教学法以及使用为交际语言教学设计的课件与教材。然而，欧洲共同语言参考框架的目的并非在刻意推动某一个特定的教学法，而是希望能引介各种不同的教学法以供选择。因此，广泛的讨论与多种信息的交换是必要的。

Chapter Ten 第十章
Task-Based Language Instruction:
Chinese Speaking Class Sample Lessons
任务型语言教学：汉语口语课堂教学方案

Based on our in-depth discussion on Iowa Instructional Model developed in the Chinese Program at the University of Iowa, we provide two concrete examples in this chapter. The contents and the teaching guidelines present the justifications and the step-by-step instructional procedures of two graduate teaching assistants at the University as they implement the model in two classes at different instructional levels. The two lesson plans are not meant to serve as model lessons to be emulated, but are presented here as the basis for further discussion.

　　通过前面章节对爱荷华大学中文部汉语口语教学模式进行的深入讨论，本章提供了两个具体的教学方案实例。两个方案的内容、教学理论指导以及具体的教学步骤，是该校两位助教在各自任教的班级，将爱荷华的任务教学模式融入具体课堂的教学实践。这两个课堂教学方案并非作为标准的教学示范，随书附上仅供各位读者进一步探讨，希望对汉语教学界各位同仁有所启发。

中文口语课堂教学方案（一）

年级：一年级
授课内容（课本、课文）：《中文听说读写》(*Integrated Chinese*)第十一课交通
授课教师：朱嘉
教学目标：通过有目的、有意义、循序渐进的口语练习引导学生逐步表达相关场景，强调学生的理解与应用。
话题：交通
语法重点：1. 或者 vs. 还是
　　　　　2. 先……再……

教学步骤	理论依据	语言能力训练目标	教学材料	课堂活动/教学环节
生词复习 （6分钟）	1. 认知重构：新知识与原有知识、经验间的相互作用和建构。	词：生词的单项强化练习和在语境中的练习和拓展相结合，巩固所学生词。	PowerPoint 词卡	活动：春假计划 （一）教师以本文主题"交通"为出发点，结合实际让学生分享即将到来的春假计划。鼓励学生积极思考，列举相关交通工具生词及词汇。 （二）教师通过具体情境将所学生词有机结合，真实自然的串起相关生词，帮助学生进一步巩固所学生词，完成由词到句的过渡。
句型练习 （14分钟）	1. 辨识新信息(Noticing)帮助学生在输入信息中辨识关键句型。 2. 信息加工(Input Processing: From Input to Intake)通过系统和循序渐进的信息加工训练，深化输入的表象信息，进行自主的信息加工和重组。 3. 双编码理论（Dual Coding Theory)通过信息的语言与非语言机制的联结和转换，在实际语境中深化语言的学习和运用。	句型：培养学生信息加工的综合能力和语言的规范使用能力。	PowerPoint	1.或者 vs. 还是 2.先……再…… 　　教师通过图片提供具体情景，引导学生辨别、理解和练习使用相关句型。 活动一：困难的选择 　　教师提供一个虚拟的情景，学生根据虚拟情境中人物所遇到的实际问题用所学句型完成相关任务。在接下来教师与学生一问一答的过程中，通过学生的任务完成情况检测学生对所练习句型的情景把握和应用。 活动二：中文班的旅行 　　教师通过句子接龙的形式让学生积极动脑使用介绍的句型造句。句句相扣的形式既抓住了学生的注意力，又鼓励学生多回顾所学生词，以此全面检验学生对介绍句型的实际掌握情况。

课堂讨论(10分钟)	1. 可理解输出假设（Comprehensible Output Hypothesis） 2. 适当迁移加工理论（Transfer Appropriate Processing）	社会交际能力:通过与人在实际情景中的交流,培养社会交际能力。 批判思维能力 口语表达能力	PowerPoint Picture cards	课堂讨论:好与不好 　　学生两人一组讨论具体某项交通工具的利与弊,并向全班汇报,完成信息共享和交流。 　　教师在学生小组汇报的同时以板书形式记录学生的讨论结果并鼓励其他学生参与讨论,加入可能的新信息。
综合活动(20分钟)	1. 学习动机理论（Motivation） 2. 社会文化理论（Sociocultural Theory）	情景认知能力 解决实际问题能力 口语表达能力	Traveler's map (handout) PowerPoint	综合活动:暑期旅行计划DIY 　　教师提供基本信息和具体要求,学生两人一组讨论并制作一份相关旅行计划并列举具体细节,然后在全班分享并简要说明选择理由。

中文口语课堂教学方案（二）

年级:二年级

授课内容（课本、课文）:《中文听说读写》(Integrated Chinese) Level II 第六课 租房子

授课教师:黄懿慈

总目标:通过目的性、多样化的综合任务帮助学生熟悉、掌握所学话题的内容,有效提高口语表达与沟通的能力。

话题:租房子

句型重点:1.（要是）……的话,……
　　　　 2. 最……不过了……

教学步骤	理论依据	语言能力训练目标	教学材料	课堂活动/教学环节
复习生词 (5分钟)	互动模式/认知重构 激活相关知识(activating appropriate schemata) 教师运用故事情节帮助激活学生对词汇的提取。	训练学生分辨重点生词的发音、词义和用法的能力。 技能训练： 1. 快速链接词义与发音 2. 训练学生用生词造句的能力	PowerPoint 字卡	活动：搬家：生词网络 1. 脑力激荡：教师先以"搬家"为主题，让学生动动脑，想出和搬家相关的词汇，写在白板上。 2. 故事接龙：教师再以课文情节为背景，将本课生词串成一个故事，通过生词间的联系与应用，帮助学生巩固生词。
练习句型 (10分钟)	辨认新信息(Noticing) 帮助学生在输入信息中辨识出关键的句型，找出所需要的语言成分，准备进一步的信息加工。 信息加工(Input Processing: From Input to Intake) 提高学生对本课主要句型的敏感度，以及使用句法加工的能力。	培养学生信息加工的综合能力和语言的规范使用能力。 技能训练： 1. 单句层次的口语反应 2. 识别句型的语义功能 3. 识别句型的语法结构 4. 应用句型解决问题	PowerPoint	句型一：(要是)……的话，…… 句型二：最……不过了 1. 教师佐以插图，通过具体情景，通过提问的方式引导学生从短句问答中理解句型用法。 2. 层层递进，减少提供的信息量，训练学生运用句型，凭借个人经验回答各种真实情况中的问题。

中文地址 (5分钟)	图示理论 (Schema theory) 语言输入与输出之间的关联性:学生将教师输入信息转换成意义表征,再以语音输出表达他们对输入信息的理解。	训练学生正确叙述中文地址,理解中文与英文在描述日期、地址观念上的不同。	PowerPoint 图片活动单	活动:怎么写中文地址? 教师先复习日期的描述方式,帮助学生回想中文与英文针对日期、时间叙述方式的不同,再带入本课重点,让学生分组练习叙述中文地址。 活动操作: 1. 教师将四个地点的中文地址裁剪成数片。 2. 学生两到三人一组,每一组分到一叠与某地一点地址相关的纸片。 3. 学生须协力合作,正确拼凑出该地点的中文地址。
课堂辩论 (13分钟)	社会文化理论 (Sociocultural Theory) 最近发展区理论 (Zone of Proximal Development) 通过小组任务的形式,学生在协力完成任务的过程中,培养沟通协调与表达意见的能力,进而达成语言学习的目的。	训练学生针对话题分析比较、成段表达的能力。 技能训练: 1. 掌握主题、分析比较的能力 2. 成段表达的连贯能力 3. 诘问、说服的能力	PowerPoint 活动单	活动:住校内还是住校外? 全班学生分成两组,一组代表赞成住在校内宿舍的张天明的父母,另一组代表希望能够在校外租屋的张天明。 活动操作: 1. 学生分为两大组,每组用五分钟讨论各自的立场与可陈述的论点。 2. 两组各利用一分钟陈述立场,说明住校内与校外的主要好处。 3. 之后两组有两分钟时间,针对对方所提论点提出疑问或巩固己方论点。

课堂任务 (15分钟)	社会文化理论 (Sociocultural Theory) 最近发展区理论 (Zone of Proximal Development) 通过小组任务，学生在协力完成任务的过程中，培养沟通协调与表达意见的能力，进而达成语言学习的目的。	训练学生认知情境、沟通协调、解决问题的能力。 技能训练： 1. 通过沟通排除理解障碍的能力。 2. 解决实际问题能力。 成段表达的能力	PowerPoint 活动单	活动一：公寓出租 学生两人一组协力完成信息沟的任务。学生必须合作、分享各自公寓出租名单上的部分信息，拼凑出完整的公寓名单。 活动操作： 1. 学生两人一组，每个学生都拿到一份不完整的公寓名单。 2. 学生必须协力找出公寓名单上的六套公寓的资讯。 活动二：最佳选择 在完成信息沟任务之后，学生继续以两人小组的形式，根据拿到的"客户信息"，从完整的公寓名单中挑选出最适合客户的公寓，并上台报告选择的理由。

References

ACTFL. (1987). ACTFL Chinese Proficiency Guidelines. *Foreign Language Annals, 20*, 471-487.

ACTFL. (1997). *ACTFL Oral Proficiency Interview Tester Training Manual*. ACTFL, Inc.

ACTFL. (1999). *ACTFL Proficiency Guidelines-Speaking*. Yonkers, NY: ACTFL, Inc.

Al-Humaidi, M. (2007). Communicative Language Teaching Retrieved 03/07, 2011, from http://faculty.ksu.edu.sa/alhumaidi/Publications/Communicative% 20 Language% 20 Teaching. pdf

Anderson, J. (1983). *The architecture of cognition*. Cambridge, MA: Harvard University.

Anderson, J. (1985). *Cognitive psychology and its implications* (2 ed.). New York, NY: Freeman.

Archibald, J. (1998). *Second Language Phonology*. Amsterdam: John Benjamins.

Arnold, N., & Ducate, L. (2006). *Calling on CALL: From Theory and Research to New Directions in Foreign Language Teaching*. San Marcos, TX: CALICO.

Asher, J. (1977). *Learning Another Language through Actions: The Complete Teacher's Guide Book* (2nd edition ed.). Los Gatos, California: Sky Oaks Productions.

Atkinson, D. (2002). Toward a Sociocognitive Approach to Second Language Acquisition. *The Modern Language Journal, 86*(4), 525-545.

Baddeley, A. D. (1966). Short-term memory for word sequences as a function of acoustic, semantic and formal similarity. Quarterly Journal of Experimental Psychology, 18, 362-365.

Baddeley, A. D. (2000). The episodic buffer: a new component of working memory? Trends in Cognitive Science 4, 417-423.

Baddeley, A. D., Gathercole, S. E., & Papagno, C. (1998). The phonological loop as a language learning device. Psychological Review, 105(1), 158-173.

Baddeley, A. D. (1986). *Working memory*. New York: Oxford University Press.

Baddeley, A. D. (2001). Is working memory still working? *American psychologist, 56*, 849-864.

Bandura, A. (1986). *Social foundations of thought and action : a social cognitive theory*.

Englewood Cliffs, NJ: Prentice-Hall

Bandura, A. (1994). Self-efficacy. In V. S. Ramachaudran (Ed.), *Encyclopedia of human behavior* (Vol. 4, pp. 71-81). New York: Academic Press.

Bateman, B. (2002). Promoting openness toward culture learning: Ethnographic interviews for students of Spanish. *Modern Language Journal, 86*, 318-331.

Barcroft, J. (2002). Semantic and structural elaboration in L2 lexical acquisition. *Language Learning, 52*, 323-363.

Barcroft, J. (2004). Theoretical and methodological issues in research on semantic and structural elaboration in lexical acquisition. In B. VanPatten, J. Williams, S. Rott & M. Overstreet (Eds.), *Form-Meaning Connection in Second Language ACquisition* (pp. 219-234). Mahwah, NJ: Lawrence Erlbaum.

Bialystok, E. (1979). Explicit and implicit judgments of L2 grammaticality. *Language Learning, 29*, 81-103.

Bjork, R. A. (1994). Memory and metamemory considerations in the training of human beings. In J. Metcalfe & A. Shimamura (Eds.), *Metacognition: Knowing about knowing*. CAmbridge, MA: MIT Press.

Block, D. (2003). *The social turn in second language acquisition*. Washington, D.C: Georgetown University Press.

Block, D. (2007). The rise of identity in SLA research: post Firth and Wagner (1997). *Modern Language Journal, 91*, 863-876.

Brinton, D. M., Snow, M. A., & Wesche, M. B. (1989). *Content-Based Second Language Instruction*. New York: Newbury House.

Brook, N. (1964). *Language and Language Learning: Theory and Practice* (2nd edition ed.). New York: Harcourt Brace.

Brooks, F., & Donato, R. (1994). Vygotskian approaches to understanding foreign language learner discourse. *Hispania, 77*(2), 262-274.

Brown, H. D. (2007). *Principles of language learning and teaching*. New York: Pearson Education, Inc.

Bygate, M. (2009). Teaching and testing speaking. In M. H. Long & C. Doughty (Eds.), *The handbook of language teaching* (pp. 412-440). Oxford. : Blackwell.

Bygate, M., Skehan, P., & Swain, M. (2001). *Researching Pedagogical Tasks: Second Language Learning, Teaching and Testing*. New York: Pearson Education Limited.

Canale, M., & Swain, M. (1980). Theoretical bases of communicative approaches to second language teaching and testing. *Applied Linguistics, 1*(1), 1-47.

Cao, J. (2003). *The Rhythm of Language*. Beijing, China.: Institute of Linguistics, CASS.

Canale, M. (1983). From communicative competence to communicative language pedagogy. In J. Richards & R. Schmidt (Eds.), *Language and communication* (pp. 2-27). London: Longman Group, Ltd.

Carroll, J. (1981). Twenty-five years of research on foreign language aptitude. In K. Diller (Ed.), *Individual differences and universals in language learning aptitude* (pp. 83-118). Rowley, MA: Newbury House.

Carroll, S. E. (2007). Autonomous Induction Theory. In B. VanPatten & J. Williams (Eds.), *Theories in Second Language Acquisition* (pp. 155-174). Mahwah, NJ: Erlbaum.

Chao, Y.-R. (1969). *A Grammar of Spoken Chinese*. Berkeley and Los Angeles: University of California Press.

Chapelle, C. A. (2004). *Computer applications in second language acquisition: Foundations for teaching, testing, and research*. Cambridge, UK: Cambridge University Press.

Chapelle, C. A. (2009). The Relationship Between SLA Theory and Computer-Assisted Language Learning. *The Modern Language Journal, 93*, 741-753.

Chomsky, N. (1965). *Aspects of the Theory of Syntax*. Cambridge: MIT Press.

Chun, D. M., & Payne, J. S. (2004). What makes students click: working memory and looking up behavior. *System, 32*, 481-503.

Chun, D. M. (2008). Computer-mediated discourse in instructed environments. In S. Magnan (Ed.), *Mediating discourse online.* (pp. 15-45). Amsterdam: Benjamins.

Conrad, R. (1964). Information, acoustic confusion and memory span. British Journal of Psychology, 55, 429.

DeKeyser, R. (1998). Beyond focus on form: Cognitive perspectives on learning and practicing second language grammar. In C. Doughty & J. Williams (Eds.), *Focus on form in classroom second language acquisition* (pp. 42-63). New York: Cambridge University Press.

DeKeyser, R. (2003). Implicit and explicit learning. In C. Doughty & M. H. Long (Eds.), *The handbook of second language acquisition* (pp. 313-348). Malden, MA: Blackwell.

DeKeyser, R. (2007a). Introduction: Situating the concept of practice. In R. DeKeyser (Ed.), *Practice in a second language* (pp. 1-18). Cambridge: Cambridge University Press.

DeKeyser, R. (2007b). Skill acquisition theory. In B. VanPatten & J. Williams (Eds.), *Theories in Second Language Acquisition* (pp. 97-114). Mahwah, NJ: Erlbaum.

Donato, R. (1994). Collective scaffolding in second language learning. In J. Lantolf & G. Appel (Eds.), *Vygotskian approaches to second language research* (pp. 33-56). Norwood, NJ: Ablex.

Donato, R. (2004). Aspects of collaboration in pedagogical discourse. *Annual Review of*

Applied Linguistics, 24, 284-302.

Dörnyei, Z. (2001). *Motivational strategies in the language classroom.* New York: Cambridge University Press.

Dörnyei, Z. (2009). *The Psychology of Second Language Acquisition.* Oxford: Oxford University Press.

Dörnyei, Z., Csizer, K., & Nemeth, N. (2006). *Motivational dynamics, language attitudes and language globalisation: A Hungarian perspective.* Clevedon, UK: Multilingual Matters.

Dörnyei, Z., & Ottó, I. (1998). Motivation in action: A process model of L2 motivation. *Working Papers in Applied Linguistics, 4*, 43-69.

Doughty, C. (1987). Relating second-language acquisition theory to CALL research and application. In B. VanPattern & J. Williams (Eds.), *Theories in second language acquisition* (pp. 97-114). Mahwah, NJ: Erlbaum.

Doughty, C., & Long, M. H. (2003). *The handbook of second language acquisition.* Malden, MA: Blackwell.

Doughty, C., & Williams, J. (1998). Pedagogical choices in focus on form. In C. Doughty & J. Williams (Eds.), *Focus on Form in Classroom Second Language Acquisition* (pp. 197-262). Cambridge: Cambridge University Press.

Duanmu, S. (2000). *The Phonology of Standard Chinese.* Oxford: Oxford University Press.

Duff, P. A. (2002). The discursive co-construction of knowledge, identity, and difference: An ethnography of communication in the high school mainstream. *Applied Linguistics, 23*(3), 289-322.

Duff, P. A., & Li, D. (2009). Indigenous, Minority, and Heritage Language Education in Canada: Policies, Contexts, and Issues. *The Canadian Modern Language Review, 66*(1), 1-8.

Ellis, N. (1994). Implicit and explicit language learning — an overview. . In N. Ellis (Ed.), *Implicit and Explicit Learning of Languages* (pp. 1-31). London: Academic Press.

Ellis, N. (2002). Frequency effects in language acquisition: A review with implications for theories of implicit and explicit language acquisition. *Studies in Second Language Acquisition, 24*, 143-188.

Ellis, N. (2003). Constructions, chunking, and connectionism: the emergence of second language structure. In C. Doughty & M. H. Long (Eds.), *The handbook of second language acquisition* (pp. 63-103). Oxford: Blackwell Publishing.

Ellis, N. (2005). At the interface: dynamic interactions of explicit and implicit language knowledge. *Studies in Second Language Acquisition, 24*, 297-339.

Ellis, N. (2006). Language acquisition as rational contingency learning. *Applied Linguistics, 27*, 1-24.

Ellis, N. (2007). The associative-cognitive CREED. In B. VanPatten & J. Williams (Eds.), *Theories in Second Language Acquisition* (pp. 77-96). Mahwah, NJ: Erlbaum.

Ellis, N. (2008). Implicit and Explicit Knowledge about Language. In J. Cenoz & N. H. Hornberger (Eds.), *Encyclopedia of Language and Education* (2 ed., Vol. 6, pp. 1-13). New York, NY: Springer Science & Business Media.

Ellis, N., & Larsen-Freeman, D. (2006). Language emergence: Implications for applied linguistics — Introduction to the Special Issue. *Applied Linguistics, 27*(4), 558-589.

Ellis, N., & Schmidt, R. (1997). Morphology and longer distance dependencies: laboratory research illuminating the A in SLA. *Studies in Second Language Acquisition, 19*, 145-171.

Ellis, N., & Schmidt, R. (1998). Rules or associations in the acquisition of morphology? The frequency by regularity interaction in human and PDF learning of morphosyntax. *Language and Cognitive Processes, 13*, 307-336.

Ellis, R. (1997). *Second language acquisition*. Oxford: Oxford University Press.

Firth, A., & Wagner, J. (1997). On discourse, communication and some fundamental concepts in SLA research. *The Modern Language Journal, 81*, 285-300.

Firth, A., & Wagner, J. (2007). Second/foreign language learning as a social accomplishment: Elaborations on a reconceptualized SLA. *The Modern Language Journal*, 91, Focus Issue, 800-819.

Ford, C., & Thompson, S. (1996). Interactional Units in Conversation: Syntactic, Intonational and Pragmatic Resources for the management of turns. In E. Ochs, E. Schegloff & S. Thompson. (Eds.), *Interaction and Grammar* (pp. 134-184). Cambridge: Cambridge University Press.

Gardner, R. C. (1985). *Social psychology and second language learning: the role of attitudes and motivation*. London: Edward Arnold.

Gardner, R. C. (2001). Integrative motivation and second language acquisition. In Z. Dörnyei & R. Schmidt (Eds.), *Motivation and second language acquisition* (pp. 1-19). Honolulu, HI: National Foreign Language Resource Center.

Gardner, R. C., & Lambert, W. E. (1972). *Attitudes and motivation in second-language learning*. Rowley, MA: Newbury House.

Gass, S. (1997). *Input, interaction, and the second language learner*. Mahwah, NJ: Erlbaum.

Gass, S., & Mackey, A. (2006). Input, interaction and output: an overview. In k. Bardovi-Harlig & Z. Dornyei (Eds.), *AILA Review* (pp. 3-17). Amsterdam: John

Benjamins.

Gass, S. (1998). Apples and oranges: Or, why apples are not orange and don't need to be a response to Firth and Wagner. The Modern Language Journal, 82(1), 83-90.

Gass, S. M., & Selinker, L. (2008). *Second Language Acquisition: An Introductory Course* (3 ed.). New York, NY: Routledge.

Grabe, W. (2004). Perspectives in applied linguistics: A North American view. . *AILA Review, 17*, 105-132.

Gatbonton, E., & Segalowitz, N. (1988). Creative automatization: Principles for promoting fluency within a communicative framework. TESOL Quarterly, 22, 473-492.

Gatbonton, E., & Segalowitz, N. (2003). Rethinking communicative language teaching: A focus on ACCESS to fluency. Canadian Modern Language Review, 61(325-353).

Gathercole, S. E. & Baddeley, A. D. (1993). Working Memory and Language. Hove, England: Lawrence Erlbaum Associates Ltd.

Godwin-Jones, R. (2009). Emerging technologies: Speech tools and technologies. Language Learning and Technology, 13(3), 4-11.

Grabe, M., & Grabe, C. (2004). *Integrating Technology for Meaningful Learning.* Boston: Houghton-Mifflin.

Haliday, M. A. K. (1970). Language structure and language function. In J. Lyons (Ed.), *New Horizons in Linguistics.* (pp. 140-465). Harmondsworth: Penguin.

Haliday, M. A. K. (1975). *Learning How to Mean: Explorations in the Development of Language.* London: Edward Arnold.

Harrington, M., & Sawyer, M. (1992). L2 working memory capacity and L2 reading skill. *Studies in Second Language Acquisition, 14*, 112-121.

Hatch, E. (Ed.). (1978). *Second language acquisition: A book of readings.* Rowley, MA: Newbury House.

Hatch, E., & Long, M. H. (1980). Discourse analysis, what's that? In D. Larsen-Freeman (eds), Discourse analysis in second language research (pp. 1-40). Rowley, MA: Newbury House Publishers.

He, A. W. (2000). The grammatical and interactional organization of teachers' directives: Implications for socialization of Chinese American children. *Linguistics & Education*, 11, 119-140.

Higgs, T., & Clifford, R. (1982). The Rush toward Communication. In T. Higgs (Ed.), *Curriculum, Competence, and the Foreign Language Teacher* (pp. 57-59). Lincolnwood: National Textbook. Hinkel, E. (2005). *Handbook on research in second language teaching and learning.* Mahwah, NJ: Lawrence Erlbaum.

Hubbard, P., & Siskin, C. (2004). Another look at tutorial CALL. *ReCALL, 16*(2), 448-461.

Hudson, R. (2008). Word grammar, cognitive linguistics, and second language learning and teaching. In P. Robinson & E. Ellis (Eds.), *Handbook of cognitive linguistics and second language acquisition* (pp. 89-113). New York: Routledge.

Hulstijn, J. H. (1995). Not all grammar rules are equal: Giving grammar instruction its proper place in foreign language teaching. In R. Schmidt (Ed.), *Attention and awareness in foreign language learning* (pp. 359-386). Honolulu: University of Hawaii Press.

Hulstijn, J. H. (2002). Towards a unified account of the representation, processing and acquisition of second language knowledge. *Second Language Research, 18*(3), 193-223.

Hymes, D. (1972a). Models of the interaction of language and social life. In J. J. Gumperz & D. Hymes (Eds.), *Directions in sociolinguistics: The ethnography of communication* (pp. 35-71). New York: Holt, Rinehart & Winston.

Hymes, D. (1972b). On communicative competence. In J. B. Pride. & J. Holmes. (Eds.), *Sociolinguistics* (pp. 269-293). Harmondsworth: Penguin.

Hymes, D. (1974). *Foundations in sociolinguistics: An ethnographic approach.* Philadelphia: University of Pennsylvania Press.

Ke, C. (1992). Dichotic Listening with Chinese and English Tasks. *Journal of Psycholinguistic Research., 21*, 463-471.

Ke, C. (1993). An empirical investigation of the relationship between a simulated oral proficiency interview and the ACTFL oral proficiency interview. SELECTA, 14, 6-10.

Ke, C. (2005). Acquisition Patterns of Chinese Linguistic Features for CFL Learners. *Journal of the Chinese Language Teachers Association, 40*, 1-24.

Ke, C. (2006). A Model of Formative Task-based Language Assessment for Chinese as a Foreign Language. *Language Assessment Quarterly, 3*(2), 207-227.

Ke, C., & Li, A. (2011). Chinese as a foreign language in the US. *Journal of Chinese Linguistics, in press.*

Ke, C., & Reed, D. (1995). An analysis of results from the ACTFL Oral Proficiency Interview and the Chinese Proficiency Test before and after intensive instruction in Chinese as a foreign language. *Foreign Language Annals, 28*, 208-222.

Ke, C., & Zhang, Z. (2002). *Chinese computerized adaptive listening comprehension test.* Columbus: The Ohio State University Foreign Language Publications.

Kellogg, R. T. (2007). *Fundamentals of Cognitive Psychology.* Thousand Oaks, CA: Sage Publications.

Kempe, V., & MacWhinney, B. (1998). The acquisition of case-marking by adult learners of Russian and German. *Studies in Second Language Acquisition, 20*, 543-587.

Kinginger, C. (2004). Alice doesn't live here anymore: Foreign language learning and identity construction. In A. Pavlenko & A. Blackledge (Eds.), *Negotiation of identities in multilingual contexts* (pp. 219-242). Clevedon, UK: Multilingual Matters.

Kramsch, C., & Whiteside, A. (2007). Three fundamental concepts in second language acquisition and their relevance in multilingual contexts. *The Modern Language Journal, 91,* 907-922.

Kramsch, C. J. (1993). *Context and culture in language teaching.* Oxford: Oxford University Press.

Krashen, S. D. (1981). *Principles and Practice in Second Language Acquisition.* London: Prentice-Hall International (UK) Ltd.

Krashen, S. D. (1982). *Principles and Practice in SEcond Language Acquisition.* Pergamon: Oxford.

Krashen, S. D. (1985). *The input hypothesis.* London and New York: Longman.

Krashen, S. D. (1994). The input hypothesis and its rivals. In N. Ellis (Ed.), *Implicit and explicit learning of languages* (pp. 45-77). London: Academic Press.

Krashen, S. D. (1999). Seeking a role for grammar: A review of some recent studies. *Foreign Language Annals, 32*, 245-257.

Lafford, B. (2007). Second language acquisition reconceptualized? The impact of Firth and Wagner (1997). *Modern Language Journal Focus Issue, 91*, 735-942.

Lantolf, J. (2000). *Sociocultural Theory and Second Language Learning.* Oxford: Oxford University Press.

Lantolf, J. (2006). Language emergence: Implications for applied linguistics—A sociocultural perspective. *Applied Linguistics,* 27/4: 717-728.

Lantolf, J., & Genung, P. (2003). "I'd rather switch than fight": An activity theoretic study of power, success, and failure in a foreign language classroom. . In C. Kramsch (Ed.), *Language acquisition and language socialization* (pp. 175-196). London: Continuum.

Lantolf, J., & Appel, G. (Eds.). (1994). *Vygotskian approaches to second language research.* Norwood, NJ: Ablex.

Lantolf, J., & Thorne, S. L. (2006). *Sociocultural theory and the genesis of second language development.* Oxford: Oxford University Press.

Lantolf, J. P., & Johnson, K. (2007). Extending Firth and Wagner's (1997) ontological perspective to L2 classroom praxis and teacher education. *The Modern Language*

Journal Focus Issue, 91, 877-892.

Lardire, D. (2007). *Ultimate attainment in second language acquisition: a case study.* Mahwah, NJ: LAwrence Erlbaum.

Larsen-Freeman, D. (1997). Chos/complexity science and second language acquisition. *Applied Linguistics, 18*, 141-165.

Larsen-Freeman, D. (2002). Language acquisition and language use from a chaos/complexity theory perspective. In C. Kramsch (Ed.), *Language acquisition and language socialization* (pp. 33-46). London: Continuum.

Larsen-Freeman, D. (2006). The Emergence of Complexity, Fluency, and Accuracy in the Oral and Written Production of Five Chinese Learners of English. *Applied Linguistics, 27* (4), 590-619.

Larsen-Freeman, D. (2007). Reflecting on the cognitive-social debate in second language acquisition. *The Modern Language Journal Focus Issue, 91*, 773-787.

Larsen-Freeman, D., & Cameron, L. (2008). *Complex Systems and Applied Linguistics.* Oxford University Press.

Larsen-Freeman, D., & Long, M. H. (1991). *An introduction to second language acquisition research.* London: Longman.

Levelt, W. J. M. (1989). *Speaking: From Intention to Articulation.* Cambridge: MA: MIT Press.

Liberman, M., & Pierrehumbert, J. (1984). Intonational Invariance under Chinese in Pitch Range and Length. In M. Aronoff & O. Richard (Eds.), *Language Sound Structure,* Cambridge: MA: MIT Press.

Lightbown, P. M. (2008). Transfer Appropriate Processing as a Model for Classroom Second Language Acquisition. In Z.-H. Han (Ed.), *Understanding Second Language Process* (pp. 27-44). Clevedon, UK: Multilingual MAtters Ltd.

Lightbown, P. M., & Spada, N. (2006). *How Languages are Learned* (3 ed.). Oxford: Oxford University Press.

Littlewood, W. (1981). *Communicative Language Teaching.* Cambridge: Cambridge University Press.

Long, M. H. (1996). The role of the linguistic environment in second language acquisition. In W. C. Ritchie & T. K. Bahtia (Eds.), *Handbook of second language acquisition* (Vol. 413-468). New York: Academic Press.

Long, M. H. (2009). Methodological principles for language teaching. In M. H. Long & C. Doughty (Eds.), *The handbook of language teaching* (pp. 373-394). Oxford: Blackwell.

Long, M. H., & Doughty, C. (2009). *The Handbook of Language Teaching*. Oxford: Blackwell.

Luke, C. L. (2006). Situating CALL in the Broader Methodological Context of Foreign Language Teaching and Learning: Promises and Possibilities. In L. Ducate & N. Arnold (Eds.), *Calling on CALL: From Theory and Research to New Directions in Foreign Language Teaching*. San MArcos, TX: CALICO.

Mackey, A. (1999). Input, interaction and second language development. *Studies in Second Language Acquisition, 21*, 557-587.

MacWhinney, B. (1999). *The emergence of language*. Mahwah, NJ: Lawrence Erlbaum.

Masoura, E. V., & Gathercole, S. E. (2005). Contrasting contributions of phonological short-term memory and long — term knowledge to vocabulary learning in a foreign language. *Memory, 13*, 422-429.

Meskill, C., & Anthony, N. (2005). Foreign language learning with CMC: Forms of online instructional discourse in a hybrid Russian Class. System. 33(1), 89-105.

McCarthy, M. (1991). *Discourse analysis for language teachers*. New York: Cambridge University Press.

McGinnis, S. (1997). Tonal Spelling versus Diacritics for Teaching Pronunciation of Mandarin Chinese. *Modern Language Journal, 81*(2), 222-236.

McLaughlin, B. (1978). The monitor model: Some methodological considerations. *Language Learning, 28*, 309-332.

McLaughlin, B. (1987). *Theories of second language learning*. London: Edward Arnold.

McLaughlin, B. (1990). Restructuring. *Applied Linguistics, 11*, 113-128.

Mitchell, R., & Myles, F. (2004). *Second Language Learning Theories* (2 ed.). London, UK: Hodder Arnold.

National Standards in Foreign Language Education Project. (1999). *Standards for Foreign Language Learning in the 21st Century. Including Chinese, Classical Languages, French, German, Italian, Japanese, Portuguese, Russian, and Spanish*. Lawrence, KS: Allen Press.

National Standards in Foreign Language Education Project. (1999). Standards for Chinese Language Learning: A Project of the Chinese Language Association of Secondary-Elementary Schools (CLASS). In *Standards for Foreign Language Learning in the 21st Century. Including Chinese, Classical Languages, French, German, Italian, Japanese, Portuguese, Russian, and Spanish*, pp.111-152. Lawrence, KS: Allen Press.

Neisser, U. (1967). *Cognitive Psychology*. New York: Appleton.

Norman, J. (1998). *Chinese*. Cambridge: Cambridge University Press.

Norris, J. M., & Ortega, L. (2000). Effectiveness of L2 instruction: A research synthesis and quantitative meta-analysis. *Language Learning, 50*, 417-528.

Norton, B. (2000). *Identity and language learning*. London: Longman.

Norton Pierce, B. (1995). Social identity, investment, and language learning. *TESOL Quarterly* 29, 9-31.

Nunan, D. (2004). *Task-based language teaching: A comprehensively revised edition of designing tasks for the communicative classroom*. Cambridge: Cambridge University Press

O'Brien, I., Segalowitz, N., Collentine, J., & Freed, B. (2006). Phonological memory and lexical, narrative, and grammatical skills in second language oral production by adult learners. *Applied psycholinguistics*, 27, 377-402.

Ortega, L. (2007). Meaningful L2 practice in foreign language classroom: A cognitive-interactionist SLA perspective. In R. DeKeyser (Ed.), *Practice in a second language* (pp. 180-207). New York: Cambridge University Press.

Ortega, L. (2009). *Understanding Second Language acquisition*. London, UK: Hodder Education.

Pavlenko, A., & Blackledge, A. (Eds.). (2004). *Negotiation of identities in multilingual settings*. Clevedon, UK: Multilingual Matters.

Peng, S.-h., Chan, M., Tseng, C.-y., Huang, T., Lee, O., & Beckman, M. (2005). Towards a Pan-Mandarin System for Prosodic Transcription. In S. Jun (Ed.), *Prosodic Typology: The Phonology of Intonation and Phrasing* (pp. 230-270). Oxford: Oxford University Press.

Pica, T., Young, R., & Doughty, C. (1987). The impact of interaction on comprehension. *TESOL Quarterly*, 21, 737-758.

Pica, T. (1994). Research on negotiation:What does it reveal about second language learning, conditions, processes, outcomes? *Language Learning, 44*, 493-527.

Pienemann, M. (1998). *Language processing and second language acquisition: processability theory*. Amsterdam: John Benjamins.

Pienemann, M. (2003). Language processing capacity. In C. J. Doughty & M. H. Long (Eds.), *The handbook of second language acquisition* (pp. 679-714). Oxford: Blackwell Publishing.

Pienemann, M. (2007). Processability theory. In B. VanPatten & J. Williams. (Eds.), *Theories in second language acquisition* (pp. 137-154). Mahwah, NJ: Erlbaum.

Pinker, S. (1991). Rules of language. *Science, 253*, 530-535.

Richards, J. C., & Rodgers, T. S. (2001). *Approaches and Methods in language Teaching*. Cambridge, UK: Cambridge University Press.

Robinson, P. (2001). Task complexity, cognitive resources, and syllabus design: A triadic theory of task influences of SLA. In P. Robinson (Ed.), *Cognition and second language instruction* (pp. 287-318). New York: Cambridge University Press.

Robinson, P. (2002). Learning conditions, aptitude complexes, and SLA: a framework for research and pedagogy. In P. Robinson (Ed.), *Individual differences and instructed language learning* (pp. 113-133). Amsterdam: John Benjamins.

Robinson, P., & Ellis, N. (2008). Conclusion: Cognitive linguistics, second language acquisition and L2 instruction-issues for research. In P. Robinson, N. Ellis & (Eds.), *Handbook of cognitive linguistics and second language acquisition* (pp. 489-545). New York: Routledge.

Robinson, P., & Ellis, N. (2008). *Handbook of Cognitive Linguistics and Second Language Acquisition*. New York: New York.

Savignon, S. (2005). Communicative language teaching: Strategies and goals. In E. Hinkel (Ed.), *Handbook of research in second language teaching and learning* (pp. 635-651). Mahwah, NJ: Lawrence Erlbaum Associates.

Schmidt, R. (1990). The role of consciousness in second language learning. *Applied Linguistics, 11*, 129-158.

Schmidt, R. (1995). Consciousness and foreign language learning: A tutorial on the role of attention and awareness in learning. In R. Schmidt (Ed.), *Attention and awareness in foreign language learning,* pp. 1-63. Honolulu: University of Hawaii Press.

Seabrook, R., BRown, G. D. A., & Solity, J. E. (2005). Distributed and massed practice: from laboratory to classroom. *Applied Cognitive Psychology,* 19, 107-122.

Segalowitz, N., & Lightbown, P. M. (1999). Psycholinguistic approaches to SLA. *Annual Review of Applied Linguistics,* 19, 23-43.

Service, E. (1992). Phonology, working memory and foreign-language learning. *Quarterly Journal of Experimental Psychology,* 45A(1), 21-50.

Service, E., & Kohonen, V. (1995). Is the relation between phonological memory and foreign language learning accounted for by acquisition? *Applied psycholinguistics,* 16 (155-172).

Shen, X. (1990). *The Prosody of Mandarin Chinese*. Berkeley, CA: University of California Press.

Shiffrin, R. M., & Schneider, W. (1977). Controlled and automatic human information processing. II: perceptual learning, automatic, attending, and a general theory. *Psychological*

Review, 84, 127-190.

Siegal, M. (1995). The role of learner subjectivity in second language sociolinguistic competency: Western women learning Japanese. *Applied Linguistics,* 17, 356-382.

Sinclair, J.M., & Coulthard, R. M. (1975). *Towards an analysis of discourse: The English used by teachers and pupils.* Oxford: Oxford University Press.

Skehan, P. (1998). *A cognitive approach to language learning.* Oxford: Oxford University Press.

Skehan, P. (2002). Theorizing and updating aptitude. In P. Robinson (Ed.), *Individual differences and instructed language learning* (pp. 69-93). Amsterdam: John Benjamins.

Skehan, P., & Foster, P. (2001). Cognition and tasks. In P. Robinson (Ed.), *Cognition and second language instruction,* pp. 183-205, Cambridge: Cambridge University Press.

Sokolik, M. E. (1990). Learning without rules: PDP and a resolution of the adult language learning paradox. *TESOL Quarterly,* 24, 685-696.

Sokolik, M. E., & Smith, M. (1992). Assignment of gender to French nouns in primary and second langauge: a connectionist model. *Second Language Research,* 8, 39-58.

Spada, N., & Lightbown, P. M. (1993). Instruction and the development of questions in the L2 classroom. *Studies in Second Language Acquisition,* 15, 205-221.

Sprling, G. (1960). The information available in brief visual presentation. *Psychological Monographs* (Vol. 74).

Stern, H. H. (1992). *Issues and options in language teaching.* Oxford Oxford University Press.

Stroller, F. (1997). Project work: a means to promote language and content. *English Teaching Forum,* 35(4), 2-9, 37.

Swain, M. (1985). Communicative competence: some roles of comprehensible input and comprehensible output in its development. In S. Gass & C. G. Madden (Eds.), *Input in second language acquisition,* pp.235-253, Rowley, MA: Newbury House.

Swain, M. (2000). The output hypothesis and beyond: Mediating acquisition through collaborative dialogue. In J. Lantolf (Ed.), *Sociocultural theory and second language learning,* pp. 97-114, Oxford Oxford University Press.

Swain, M. (2005). The output hypothesis: Theory and research. In E. Hinkel (Ed.), *Handbook on research in second language teaching and learning,* pp. 471-484, Mahwah, NJ: Lawrence Erlbaum.

Swain, M., & Lapkin, S. (1995). Problems in output and the cognitive processes they generate: A step towards second language learning. *Applied Linguistics,* 16, 371-391.

Swain, M., & Lapkin, S. (1998). Interaction and second language learning: two adolescent French immersion students working together. *Modern Language Journal,* 82, 320-337.

Swain, M., & Lapkin, S. (2003). Talking it through: Two French immersion learners' response to reformulation. *International Journal of Educational Research,* 37, 285-304.

Tarone, E., & Liu, G. (1995). Situational context, variation, and second language acquisition theory. In G. Cook & B. Seidlhofer (Eds.), *Principle and practice in applied linguistics: Studies in honor of H. G. Widdowson* (pp. 107-124). Oxford: Oxford University Press.

Thurlow, C., Lengel, L. & Tomic, A. (2004). Computer Mediated Communication: Social Interaction and the Internet. London: Sage.

Towell, R., & Dewaele, J.-M. (2005). The role of psycholinguistic factors in the development of fluency amongst advanced learners of French. In J.-M. Dewaele (Ed.), *Focus on French as a foreign language: multidisciplinary approaches,* pp. 210-239, Clevedon, UK: Multilingual Matters.

Tulving, E. (2002). Episodic memory: from mind to brain. *Annual Review of Psychology,* 53, 1-25.

Ushioda, E. (1997). The role of motivational thinking: A cognitive theoretical approach to the study of language learning motivation. In D. Little & B. Voss (Eds.), *Language centres: Planning for the new millennium,* pp. 39-50, Plymouth.: CERCLES, Centre for Modern Languages, University of Plymouth.

Van Den Branden, K. (2006). *Task-Based Language Education: From Theory to Practice.* Cambridge, UK: Cambridge University Press.

VanPatten, B. (1996). *Input processing and grammar instruction: Theory and research.* Norwood, NJ: Ablex.

VanPatten, B. (2004). *Processing Instruction.* Mahwah, NJ: Lawrence Erlbaum.

VanPatten, B. (2007). Input processing in adult second language acquisition. In B. VanPatten & J. Williams (Eds.), *Theories in second language acquisition,* pp. 115-135, Mahwah, NJ: Erlbaum.

Vygotsky, L. (1978). *Mind in society.* Cambridge, MA: Harvard University Press.

Vygotsky, L. (1987). Thinking and speech. In R. Rieber & A. Carton (Eds.), *L. S. Vygotsky, collected works,* Vol. 1, pp. 39-285, New York: Plenum.

Waldrop, M. M. (1993). *Complexity: The Emerging Science at the Edge of Order and Chaos.* New York: Touchstone.

Warschauer, M. (1996). *Virtual connections: online activities and projects for networking language learners.* Honolulu, HI: University of Hawaii Second Language Teaching and Curriculum Center.

Warschauer, M. (2000). The changing global economy and the future of English teaching. *TESOL Quarterly,* 34, 511-535.

Walsh, S. (2006). *Investigating classroom discourse.* New York: Routledge.

Watson-Gegeo, K. A. (1992). Thick explanation in the ethnographic study of child socialization and development: A longitudinal study of the problem of schooling for Kwara'ae (Solomon Islands) children. In W. A. Corsaro & P. J. Miller (Eds.), *New directions for child development: Vol. 58. The production and reproduction of children's worlds: Interpretive methodologies for the study of childhood socialization* (Vol. 58, pp. 51-66). San Francisco: Jossey-Bass.

Watson-Gegeo, K. A. (2004). Mind, language, and epistemology: toward a language socialization paradigm for SLA. *Modern Language Journal,* 88, 331-350.

Wesche, M. B. (1981). Language aptitude measures in streaming, matching students with methods, and dialgnosis of learning problems. In K. Diller (Ed.), Individual differences and universals in language learning aptitude (pp. 119-139). Rowley, MA: Newbury House.

Wills, J. (1996). A framework for task-based learning. Harlow: Longman.

Windham, C. (2005). The student's perspective. In D. Oblinger & J. Oblinger (Eds.), Educating the Net Generation (pp. 5.1-5.16). Boulder, CO.

Windham, C. (2005). The Student's Perspective. In D. E. Oblinger& J. L. Oblinger (Eds.), *Educating the Net Generation.* Boulder, CO: EDUCAUSE Center for Applied Research.

Yao,T. (1994).*Computer-adaptive test for reading Chinese.* Honolulu: University of Hawaii at Manoa.

Yao, T. (1994). Reading Chinese for Proficiency: An Introduction to Signs. New Haven, CT: Yale University Press.

Young, R. F. (2009). *Discursive practice in language learning and teaching.* Malden, MA: Wiley-Blackwell.

Young, R. F., & Miller, E. R. (2004). Learning as changing participation: Discourse roles in ESL writing conferences. *Modern Language Journal,* 88, 519-535.

冯胜利 (1997)《汉语的韵律、词法与句法》,北京大学出版社。

沈炯 (1985)《北京话声调的音域和语调》,北京大学出版社。

王洪君 (2008)《汉语非线性语音学》,北京大学出版社。

王瑞烽 (2007) 小组活动的任务形式和设计方式及其在对外汉语教学中的应用,《语言教学与研究》,第1期,82-88。